The Use and Need of the Life of Carry A. Nation

Carry Amelia Nation

Alpha Editions

This edition published in 2024

ISBN : 9789362090171

Design and Setting By
Alpha Editions
www.alphaedis.com
Email - info@alphaedis.com

Contents

CHAPTER I.

MY OLD KENTUCKY HOME AND WHAT I REMEMBER OF MY LIFE UP TO THE TENTH YEAR.

I was born in Garrard County, Kentucky. My father's farm was on Dick's River, where the cliffs rose to hundreds of feet, with great ledges of rocks, where under which I used to sit. There were many large rocks scattered around, some as much as fifteen feet across, with holes that held water, where my father salted his stock, and I, a little toddler, used to follow him. On the side of the house next to the cliffs was what we called the "Long House," where the negro women would spin and weave. There were wheels, little and big, and a loom or two, and swifts and reels, and winders, and everything for making linen for the summer, and woolen cloth for the winter, both linsey and jeans. The flax was raised on the place, and so were the sheep. When a child 5 years old, I used to bother the other spinners. I was so anxious to learn to spin. My father had a small wheel made for me by a wright in the neighborhood. I was very jealous of my wheel, and would spin on it for hours. The colored women were always indulgent to me, and made the proper sized rolls, so I could spin them. I would double the yarn, and then twist it, and knit it into suspenders, which was a great source of pride to my father, who would display my work to visitors on every occasion.

The dwelling house had ten rooms, all on the ground floor, except one. I have heard my father say that it was a hewed-log house, weather-boarded and plastered as I remember it. The room that possessed the most attraction for me was the parlor, because I was very seldom allowed to go in it. I remember the large gold-leaf paper on the walls, its bright brass dogirons, as tall as myself, and the furniture of red plush, some of which is in a good state of preservation, and the property of my half-brother, Tom Moore, who lives on "Camp Dick Robinson" in Garrard County, this Dick Robinson was a cousin of my father's. There were two sets of negro cabins; one in which Betsey and Henry lived, who were man and wife, Betsey being the nurse of all the children. Then there was aunt Mary and her large family, aunt Judy and her family and aunt Eliza and her's. There was a water mill behind and almost a quarter of a mile from the house, where the corn was ground, and near that was the overseer's house.

Standing on the front porch, we looked through a row of althea bushes, white and purple, and there were on each side cedar trees that were quite large in my day. There was an old-fashioned stile, instead of a gate, and a long avenue, as wide as Kansas Avenue, in Topeka, with forest trees on either side, that led down to the big road, across which uncle Isaac Dunn lived, who was a widower with two children, Dave and Sallie, and I remember that Sallie had all kinds of dolls; it was a great delight of mine to play with these.

To the left of our house was the garden. I have read of the old- fashioned garden; the gardens written about and the gardens sung about, but I have never seen a garden that could surpass the garden of my old home. Just inside the pickets were bunches of bear grass. Then, there was the purple flag, that bordered the walks; the thyme, coriander, calamus and sweet Mary; the jasmine climbing over the picket fence; the syringa and bridal wreath; roses black, red, yellow and pink; and many other kinds of roses and shrubs. There, too, were strawberries, raspberries, gooseberries and currants; damson and greengages, and apricots, that grew on vines. I could take some time in describing this beautiful spot.

At the side of the garden was the family burying ground, where the gravestones were laid flat on masonry, bringing them about three feet from the ground. These stones were large, flat slabs of marble, and I used to climb up on top and sit or lie down, and trace the letters or figures with my fingers. I visited this graveyard in 1903. The eight graves were there in a good state of preservation, with not a slab broken, although my grandfather was buried there, ninety years ago. My father had a stone wall built around these graves for protection, when he left Kentucky. I am glad that family graveyards have given place to public cemeteries, for this place has changed hands many times and this graveyard is not pleasant for the strangers who live there. We who are interested in these sacred mounds, feel like we intrude, to have the homes of our dead with strangers.

{illust. caption =
MY OLD HOME WHERE I WAS BORN IN GARRARD COUNTY, KENTUCKY.
THE OLD GRAVE YARD NEAR BY, AND MY GRANDFATHER's GRAVE.}

The memories of this Kentucky home date from the time I was three years old. This seems remarkable, but my mother said this incident occurred when I was three years old, and I remember it distinctly. I was standing in the back yard, near the porch. Mr. Brown, the overseer, was in the door of my half-brother Richard's room, with my brother's gun in his hands. At the end of the porch was a small room, called the "saddle room." A pane of glass was out of the window and a hen flew out, cackling. Aunt Judy, the colored woman, went in to get the egg, and walked in front of Mr. Brown, who raised the gun and said: "Judy, I am going to shoot you," not thinking the gun was loaded. It went off, and aunt Judy fell. Mr. Brown began to wring his hands and cry in great agony. I screamed and kept running around a small tree near by. This was Sunday morning. Runners were sent for the doctor, and for my parents, who were at church. Aunt Judy got well, but had one eye out; we could always feel the shot in her forehead. She was one of the best servants, and a dear good friend to me. She used to bring two of her children and come up to my room on Sundays and sit with me, saying, she did not want to be in the cabin when "strange niggers were there." This misfortune had disfigured her face and she always avoided meeting people. I can see her now, with one child at the breast, and another at her knee, with her hand on its head, feeling for "buggars." I was very much attached to this woman and wanted to take care of her in her old age. I went to Southern Texas to get her in 1873. I found some of her children in Sherman, Texas, but aunt Judy had been dead six months. She always said she wanted to live with me.

My mother always left her small children in the care of the servants. I was quite a little girl before I was allowed to eat at "white folk's table." Once my mother had been away several days and came home bringing a lot of company with her. I ran out when I saw the carriages driving up, and cried: "Oh, ma, I am so glad to see you. I don't mind sleeping with aunt Eliza, but I do hate to sleep with uncle Josh," think I was quite dirty, and some of the colored servants snatched me out of sight. Aunt Eliza was aunt Judy's half-sister, her father was a white man. She was given to my father by my grandmother, was very bright and handsome, and the mother of seventeen children. My grandmother remembered aunt Eliza in her will, giving her some linen sheets, furniture, and other things.

One of aunt Eliza's sons was named Newton. My father had a mill and store up in Lincoln County, near Hustonville. Newton used to do the hauling for my father with a large wagon and six-mule team. He would often do the buying for the store and take measurements of grain, and my father trusted him implicitly. Once a friend of my father said to him, as Newton was passing along the street with his team: "George, I'll give you seventeen hundred dollars for that negro." My father said: "If you would fill that wagon-bed full of gold, you could not get him." A few weeks after that Newton died. I remember seeing my father in the room weeping, and remember the chorus of the song the negroes sang on that occasion: "Let us sit down and chat with the angels."

The husband of aunt Eliza was "uncle Josh," a small Guinea negro, as black as coal and very peculiar. I always stood in awe of him, as all the children did. I remember one expression of his was: "Get out of the way, or I'll knock you into a cocked hat." The reason I had to sleep with aunt Eliza, Betsy, my nurse, was only ten years older than I was. Betsy was a girl given by my grandfather Campbell to my mother when my father and mother were married. My mother was a widow when she married my father. She had married Will Caldwell, a son of Capt. Caldwell, who died in Sangamon County, Ill., he had freed his negroes and moved there from Kentucky. Will Caldwell died after three years, leaving my mother with two children. Both of them died at my grandfather Campbell's in Mercer county, Kentucky, before she married my father.

I was about four years old when my grandmother Moore died. She lived on a farm in Garrard County, about two miles from my father. She used to ride a mare called "Kit." Whenever we would see grandma coming up the avenue, the whole lot of children, white and black, ran to meet her. She always carried on the horn of her saddle a handbag, then called a "reticule," and in that she always brought us some little treat, most generally a cut off of a loaf of sugar, that used to be sold in the shape of a long loaf of bread. We would follow her down to the stile, where she would get off, and delight us all by taking something good to eat out of the "reticule." We would tie old Kit, and then take our turn in petting the colt. The first grief I remember to have had was when I heard of the death of my grandmother. I wanted to see her so badly and go to the funeral, and for weeks I would go off by myself and cry about her death. I used to love to lie and sit on her grave at the back of the garden. Older people often forget the sorrows of childhood, but I felt keenly the injustice of not being allowed to see her dead face and do to this day.

We left that home, when I was about five years old, for a place about two miles from Danville, Kentucky. The house had a flat roof, the first one built in that county; it had an observatory on top. Our nearest neighbors were Mr. Banford's family, Mr. Caldwell, and Mr. Spears. Dr. Jackson and Dr. Smith were both our physicians, and my father used to hire his physicians by the year. Dr. Jackson was a bachelor and said he was going to wait for me, and I believed him. I remember visiting Dr. Smith in Danville and seeing a human skeleton for the first time. I also saw leeches he used in bleeding. I remember when one of my little brothers was born, they told me Dr. Smith found him in a hollow stump. After that I spent hours out in the woods looking in hollow stumps for babies.

My mother's father was James Campbell, born in King and Queens County, Virginia. His parents were from Scotland. He was married twice. By his first wife he had two sons, William and Whitaker. William married and died young, and I heard, left one child, a daughter. Uncle "Whitt" lived to be an old man. The second time my grandfather married a Miss Bradshaw. He had four sons and six daughters. I used to stay at grandma's with my aunt Sue. When my mother would take long trips or visits, she would send the younger children, with my nurse Betsy, over there to stay until she returned. The only thing I construe into a cross word, that my grandfather ever spoke to me, was when I was running upstairs and stumbled and he said: "Jump up, and try it again, my daughter." I was so humiliated by the rebuke that I hid from him for several days. He was a Baptist deacon for years. When gentlemen called on my aunts, lie would go in the parlor at 10 o'clock in the evening and wind the big clock. He would then ask the young men if he should have their horses put up. This was the signal to either retire or leave. He never went to bed until everyone else had retired. My grandfather lived in Mercer County, not far from Harrodsburg. My grandmother was an invalid for years, and kept her room. My aunt Sue was housekeeper. In the dining room was a large fireplace. The teakettle was brought in at breakfast, water was boiled by being set on a "trivet," over some coals of fire.

Every morning my grandfather would put in a glass some sugar, butter and brandy, then pour hot water over it, and, while the family were sitting around the room, waiting for breakfast, he would go to each, and give to those who wished, a spoonful of this toddy, saying: "Will you have a taste, my daughter, or my son?" He never gave but one spoonful, and then he drank what was left himself. This custom was never omitted. I remember the closet where the barrel of spirits was kept. He used to give it out to the colored people in a pint cup on Saturdays. Persons have often said to me: "Our grandfathers used it, and they did not get drunk." Truly, we are reaping what they have strewn. They sowed to the wind and we are reaping the whirlwind.

After breakfast, the colored man, Patrick, who waited on my grandfather, would bring out a horse and grandfather would ride around the place. He was very fond of hunting, and always kept hounds. My father would tell this joke on him. When "Daddy" Rice was baptising him in Dick's River grandpa said: "Hold on, Father Rice, I hear Sounder barking on the cliffs." Sounder was his favorite hound. There was a Mr. Britt who was a great fox hunter, who lived near my grandfather, and whose wife was opposed to his hunting. One morning my grandfather went by Mr. Britt's house winding his hunter's horn. Mr. Britt jumped for his trousers and so did Mrs. Britt, who got them first and threw them into the fire. Another time, quite a party of ladies and gentlemen had gathered at my grandfather's place, to go on a fox hunt. Grandfather went upstairs hurriedly to put on his buckskin suit. He jumped across the banisters to facilitate matters, lost his balance and tumbled down into the hall, where the company was waiting. He did not get hurt, it was a great joke on him. When he was a young man he learned carpentering in company with Buckner Miller, who was of the same trade. These two young men came to Kentucky from Virginia, on horseback, seeking their fortunes. They had many experiences, always endeavoring to stop at houses for the night where there were young ladies. One house where there were quite a number of girls, Buckner Miller played off this joke on my grandfather. The girls occupied the room below where the men were sleeping. The men heard a commotion in the girls' room. My grandfather tipped softly, down and Buckner after him, to find out what was going on. They opened the door sufficiently to see the girls in their gowns, circling around the candle, playing "poison." Mr. Miller, to pay my grandfather for some pranks he had played off on him, gave him a push, and grandfather rushed into the middle of the room in his night clothes. The girls flew under the beds and the men ran upstairs and climbed out at the window.

{illust. caption = MY FATHER, GEORGE MOORE.}

My father's name was George Moore, and his father's name was Martin Moore. He was of Irish descent. He had two brothers who died when the cholera raged in Kentucky, about 1842. One of them, William Moore, married a Miss Blackburn of Versailles, Ky. He had several sisters, some of them died young.

Mark Antony, in his memorial address over the body of Caesar, said that Brutus was Caesar's angel. If I ever had an angel on earth, it was my father. I have met many men who had lovable characters, but none equaled him in my estimation. He was not a saint, but a man—one of the noblest works of God. He was impetuous, quick, impatient, but never nervous, could collect himself in a moment and was always master of the situation. I have seen him in many trying places but never remember to have seen him in a condition of being afraid. When he lived in Cass County, Mo., during the war, we saw Quantrell's men coming up to the house. These men were dressed in slouch hats, gray suits, and had their guns and haversacks roped to their saddles. My father was a union man, but a southern sympathizer. He cried like a child when he heard the south had seceded and taken another flag. He did not know to what extent he was disliked by this gang of bushwhackers, and we were very much alarmed; fully expected some harm was meant. Men on both sides were frequently taken out and shot down. When the Bushwhackers would kill a union man then the Jayhawkers would kill "a secesh."

My father said to us: "You stay in the house and keep quiet. I will meet them." I watched him through a window. He was tall and straight as an Indian. He walked up to them, taking off his hat and called "Good morning" to them in a friendly tone. Asked them to get off their horses, for he had a treat for them. In the corner of the yard was the carriage house and under that was a rock spring house, through which a living stream of water ran around the pans of milk. He took them to the door, gave them seats, then went in this milkhouse and brought out a jar of buttermilk. I have heard it said that buttermilk is one of the greatest treats to a soldier. He talked with these men as if they had been friends; brought out fruit; loaded them with bread, butter and milk; and they left without even taking a horse from us. I fully believe it was their intention to do some harm, but by the tact of my father they were disarmed. "A soft answer turneth away wrath, but grievous words stir up strife." He was a thorough business man, but his social qualities exceeded all others. He often had to pay security debts, one for Mr. Key, his brother-in-law, of five thousand dollars. Just before the election of Lincoln, he took a large drove of mules to Natchez, Miss., twenty-two of these mules were of his own raising. While there Lincoln was elected, which threw the south into war. He sold the mules on time and never got a dollar for them. To the honor of my father be it said, he gave up all his property to pay his debts, never withholding, where he could have done so. A short while before he died there was one debt of a few hundred dollars he could not pay. He wept and told me of this. A year ago I settled up with Mr. Wills' heirs and paid this debt to his children, who live near Peculiar in Cass county, Mo. It would be such a joy to my father to know that I did this to save his honor. When I see him, in our heavenly home, he will bless me for this. "Love knows no sacrifice."

I can not call to mind when the thought of self, governed any of my father's actions. It was his delight to provide for the comfort of others. Devoted to his family and friends, and such a friend to the poor; I have heard my mother say that he made every one rich who worked for him. When I first remember him he was a "Trader" and left his farm to an overseer. My father drove hogs to Cincinnati before there were any railways. I was always at his heels, when I could be. He was standing on the stile one day giving directions to have a drove of hogs meet him at a certain place on Sunday. I said: "Pa, you will lose on those hogs. You ought not to do that on Sunday." He gave me a quick, light, playful slap, saying: "Stop that, every time you say that, I do lose."

I can see that a responsibility to God was the fundamental principle in my father's life. After the negroes were freed, and we lived on the farm, there was so much to do, especially for him, but there was always a conveyance prepared to take his family to church and Sunday School—I took the "New York Ledger". Mrs. Southworth wrote for it then. 'Capitola', The Wrecker's Son, with other thrilling stories, were so fascinating to me—The paper came late Saturday and I would rather read it Sunday morning than go anywhere. One morning I took my paper and went to the back of the orchard, thinking to get out of the sound of my father's voice when he would call me to get ready for church. I could just hear him but did not move. After reading my paper, I returned to the house, Pa was just coming back with the rest of the family from church. He looked at me with grief and anger in his glance and said, "Never mind, you ungrateful girl, you cannot say at the judgment Day, that your father did not provide a way for you to go to church." I never did this again and never was free from remorse for this ingratitude. I know how Dr. Johnson felt when he was seen standing on a corner of the street with the sun beaming down upon his bare head, when asked why he did that he said, "My father had a book stand on this corner, when I was a boy once he asked me to stand here in his place as he was sick. I would not, now I would expiate that by blistering my bare head in the sun if I could. To this day I weep to think of grieving so noble a parent.

My mother was a very handsome woman. My father was what you might call good looking. I was very anxious to look like him; used to try to wear off my teeth on the right side, because his were worn off. About two years before he died, he came to Texas to visit me. I was then in the hotel business. During the first meal he ate at the hotel, he looked up and seeing me waiting on the table, he got up and began waiting on the table himself. I had to work very hard then and it was a grief to him to have no means to give me. One morning he came into my room while I was dressing and said: "Daughter, I have not slept all night for thinking of you. The last thing last night was you in the kitchen and the first thing this morning. I have always hoped to have something to leave you, and it is such a grief to me that I can not help you. Carry, it seems the Lord has been so hard on you." I said: "No, Pa; I thank God for all my sorrows. They have been the best for me, and don't you worry about not leaving me money, for you have left me something far better." He looked up surprised and said: "What is it?" I answered: "The memory of a father who never did a dishonorable act." My father's eyes filled with tears, and after that he seemed to be happier than I had ever seen him; everything seemed to go right.

My father was a very indulgent master to his colored servants, who loved him like a father. They always called him "Mars George." The negro women would threaten to get "Mars George" to whip their bad children, and when he whipped them, I have heard them say: "Served you right. Did not give you a lick amiss." This was proving their great confidence, they being willing for some one else to whip their children. They were very sensitive in this matter and were not willing for my mother to do this. My father would lay in a supply, while in Cincinnati, of boxes of boots and shoes, arid get combs, head handkerchiefs, and Sunday dresses, which would greatly delight his colored people. Happy, indeed, would the negroes have been if all their masters had been as my father was.

When we moved to Mercer County from Garrard, we had a sale. It was customary then at such a time to have a barbecue and a great dinner. The tables were set in the yard. I remember Mr. Jones Adams, a neighbor and great friend of my father, brought over a two bushel sack of turnip greens and a ham. I remember seeing him shake them out of the bag. At this sale for the first, and only time, I saw a negro put on a block and sold to the highest bidder. I can't understand how my father could have allowed this. His name was "Big Bill," to distinguish him from another "Bill". He was a widower or a batchelor and had no family. There was one colored man my father valued highly, and wanted to take with him, but this man, Tom, had a wife, who belonged to a near neighbor. After we got in the carriage to go to our new home, Tom followed us crying: "Oh, Mars George, don't take me from my wife." My father said: "Go and get some one to buy you." This Tom did, the buyer being a Mr. Dunn. Oh! What a sad sight! It makes the tears fill my eyes to write it.

But a worse slavery is now on us. I would rather have my son sold to a slave-driver than to be a victim of a saloon. I could, in the first case, hope to see him in heaven; but no drunkard can inherit eternal life. The people of the south said no power could take from them their slaves, but 'tis a thing of the past. People now say, you can't shut up saloons. But our children will know them as a thing of the past. My father was glad when the slaves were free. He felt the responsibility of owning them. Have heard him say, after having some-trouble with them: "Those negroes will send me to hell yet." He would gather them in the dining- room Sunday evenings and read the Bible to them and have prayer. He would first call aunt Liza and ask her to have them come in. The negroes would sing, and it is a sweet memory to me.

{illust. caption =
THIS IS A PICTURE OF MYSELF AND SISTER EDNA, SITTING ON EACH SIDE OF OUR
MOTHER.I AM ON THE LEFT AND WAS ABOUT SIX YEARS OLD.}

CHAPTER II.

MY EXPERIENCE WITH THE NEGROES AS SLAVES.—THEIR SUPERSTITIONS.— A BEAUTIFUL FAIRY TALE.

The colored race, as I knew them, were generally kind to the white children of their masters. Their sympathy was great in childish troubles. They were our nurses around our sick beds. Their lullabyes soothed us to sleep. Very frequently my nurse would hold me in her arms until both of us would fall asleep, but she would still hold me secure. When any of my misdoings came to the ears of my parents, and I was punished their testimony would, as far as possible, shield me, and not until I would try their patience out of all bounds would they tell my mother on me. I never heard an infidel negro express his views, even if very wicked. They had firm belief in God and a devil. I always liked their meetings, their songs and shoutings. They always told me that no one could help shouting. The first time I ever heard a white woman shout was in Northern Texas, during the war. I did not wish the spirit to cause me to jump up and clap my hands that way, for these impulses were not in my carnal heart, so, for fear I should be compelled to do so, I held my dress down tight to the seat on each side, to prevent such action. The negroes are great readers of character; despise stingy people or those who were afraid of them. These colored friends taught me the fear of God. The first time I ever attended church, I rode behind on horseback, and sat with them in the gallery. I imbibed some of their superstitions. They consider it bad to allow a sharp tool, as a spade, hoe or ax, to be taken through the house; to throw salt in the fire, for you would have to pick it out after death. They would kill a hen if she crowed; looked for a death, if a dog howled; or, if one broke a looking-glass, it meant trouble of some kind for seven years. They believed that persons had power to put a "spell" on others, would, if taken sick, frequently speak of having "stepped on something" put in their way or buried in their dooryard.

There is no dialect in the world that has the original characteristics so pleasing to the ear as the negro. There is a softness and music in the voice of a negro not to be found in any other race on earth. No one can sing a child to sleep so soothingly as a negro nurse. After I left Texas and went to Medicine Lodge, Kansas, when I had a headache or was otherwise sick, I would wish for the attendance around my bed of one of the old-fashioned colored women, who would rub me with their rough plump hands and call me "Honey Chile," would bathe my feet and tuck the cover around me and sit by me, holding my hand, waiting until I fell asleep. I owe much to the colored people and never want to live where there are none of the negro race. I would feel lonesome without them. After I came to Medicine Lodge, I did not see any for some time. One day, while looking out, I saw one walking up the street toward the house. I ran to the kitchen, cut an apple pie, and ran out and said: "Here, Uncle, is a piece of pie." He was gray-headed, one of the old slaves. He seemed so glad to see my friendly face and took the pie with a happy courtesy. I watched for his return, as he came in on the train, and was going out. At last he came. I asked him in the kitchen, fixed a meal for him, and waited on him myself. Before eating, he folded his hands, closed his eyes, with his face toward heaven, thanked God for the meal, as I had often seen them do in slave time. As a race, the negroes have not the characteristics of treachery. They are faithful and grateful.

In my hotel experience, I would often ask Fannie, my cook: "What kind of a man is that?" Fannie would say: "Don't trust him too far Mrs. Nation, he steps too light." When a child my playmates were a lot of colored children. Betsy came to the table with the children and ate with us. But the sweetest food was that left in the skillets, both black and white children would go around the house, sit down and "sop" the gravy with the biscuits the cooks would give us. I was fond of hearing ghost stories and would, without the knowledge of my mother, stay in the cabin late at night listening to the men and women telling their "experiences." The men would be making ax handles and beating the husk off of the corn in a large wooden hopper with a maul. The women would be spinning with the little wheel, sewing, knitting and combing their children's heads. I would listen until my teeth would chatter with fright, and would shiver more and more, as they would tell of the sights in grave-yards, and the spirits of tyrannical masters, walking at night, with their chains clanking and the, sights of hell, where some would be on gridirons, some hung up to baste and the devil with his pitchfork would toss the poor creatures hither and thither. They would say: "Carry, you must go to the house," and I would not go with one, but have two, one on each side of me. I remember seeing the negro men laugh at me, but the women would shake their heads and say: "You better quit skeering that chile." But there was one pleasure above all the rest, it was to hear any one tell "tales." When my mother would have a visitor, very frequently the lady would bring a nurse to care for one child or children, she might bring with her. Oh, how pleased the black and white children would be to see such visitors. We would gather around and in every way made our pleasure known. Would give them doll-rags, nuts, or apples, and in many ways express our delight at having them come. As soon as they were made comfortable, the next thing was: "Tell us a tale." And seating ourselves around on the floor, or in a close group, we would be all attention. Of course there would be some raw heads and bloody bones, but not so much as the stories told at night in the cabins.

One of the prettiest stories I ever heard, and never tired of hearing, that taught me a great moral, was about two girls the children of a couple who were hard working people. One of the girls was named Sarah, the other Mary.

Sarah was a very pretty girl with curls. Mary was rather ugly and had straight hair. Curls in my childhood days were something very much sought for. Although Sarah was pretty in the face she had very rude ways; she would not speak kindly and politely; would not help her hard working mother; but was idle and quarrelsome, always wanted some one to wait on her; while Mary was the reverse; would pick up chips to make a fire, would sweep the yard and bring water, and was kind to all, especially to her mother. One day the well went dry and there was no water to make the tea for supper. Mary saw her mother crying and said: "Don't cry, mother; I will go and get some at the Haunted Spring."

Her mother said: "Oh, no, dear sweet child, those goblins will kill you."

"No, mother," replied Mary. "I will beg them to let me have some water for dear father, and I am not afraid."

So her mother got a light bucket for her, and went to the top of the hill with her, and said: "God bless you, my dear child, and bring you back to me."

Then Mary went on until she came to the high iron gate. She said: "Please gate open and let me through. I mind my father and mother and love everybody."

And the gate opened and she passed into the "haunted" grounds— She saw a funny, little, short man come running with a stick and said: "Please, nice man, don't hit me. I have come down to get some good water to make tea for my father's supper. He has been working all day, and our well has gone dry. May I please have some of your spring water?"

"Well, little girl, as you talk so nice, you can have some. Tell the little folks to open the briars for you."

So she went on and came to a briar patch and saw down at the roots little people, not much longer than your finger. Mary spoke so kindly to them; said she would be so glad if they would open a path for her to walk in, she would thank them so much; so they began to pull the briars back until there was a good path. Mary thanked them and went on until she came to the spring and there was a rabbit jumping up and down in it. Mary said: "Please Mr. Rabbit, don't muddy the water for I would like to get a bucket of nice clean water to take home to make tea for supper." The rabbit ran off and she dipped her bucket full of pure water.

Then she looked down the branch, and there was a little lamb that had fallen in and was lying down, and could not get up. The lamb said: "Little girl, please pick me up and lay me on the grass to dry." Mary stepped on some rocks till she got to the lamb and lifted him up and laid him on the bank to dry. The lamb said: "When you go home, spit in your mother's hand." Mary thought that would not be right, but she said nothing. She went back through the briar patch and the little folks held them from scratching her, and the little old man spoke nicely to her and the gate opened for her. Her mother was watching for her and helped her home with the water, kissed her, and prepared them a good supper.

While they were sitting at the table Mary said: "Mother, the little lamb told me to do something I do not like to do."

"What was it?"

"He told me spit in your hand."

"Well, you can my child; come on;" and the mother held out her hand and Mary spat in it, a diamond and a pearl. This made the family happy and rich; they had men come the next day and dig a new well.

Now Sarah wished to try her fortune, her mother did not want her to go, because she knew what a bad girl she was, to talk saucy; but Sarah said she would do as well as Mary. Her sister told her how she must do; she got angry at her, and said: "You mind your own business; I reckon I know what I am about."

So she took her bucket and went on until she came to the gate; she gave that a kick and said: "Open gate!" and the gate opened and slammed on her. The little old man came running with his stick. Sarah said: "Don't you hit me, old man; I'll tell my father." And the old man beat her and the little folks pushed up the briar bushes so she tore her clothes and scratched herself badly. The little rabbit was in the spring and he jumped up and down and she threw at him, telling him she would knock his head off; but the rabbit jumped up and down 'till the spring was a lob-lolly of mud, so she had to take muddy water in her bucket. The little lamb had gotten back into the branch and said: "Please, little girl, pick me up and put me on the bank to dry."

But Sarah said: "I won't do it."

The lamb replied: "Spit in your mother's hand when you go home."

So Sarah had to go through the briars, that scratched her, and the old man beat her, and the gate slammed on her, and when her mother met her she was a "sight." Her face was dirty, her dress torn, her legs and arms were scratched and bleeding, and her curly hair was in a mass of tangles. Her mother washed the dirt off and scolded her for being so naughty. Mary helped to wash and dress her for supper. Then they all sat down to eat, and every one was happy but Sarah.

Sarah said: "Mother, the lamb told me to spit in your hand."

"Very well, come on," answered the mother. So Sarah spat in her mother's hand and out jumped a lizard and a frog.

A child ever so small will see the moral, and that, I never forgot. Of course the pearls and the diamonds are the politeness and kindness, which is so beautiful in children; and the lizard and the frog are rudeness and impudence. Very often the nurse would say: "Look here, you Sarah, you."

I remember how shocked I would be to think I would ever be like that naughty Sarah.

A positive indication of a corrupt age is the lack of respect children have for parents. This is largely owing to the neglect of teachers. I am heartily thankful I was taught to say 'Yes Ma'am, and 'No, ma'am,' 'Yes, Sir, and No, Sir.' Now it is—'Yah! Yes, No, What, etc. Nothing is a greater letter of credit than politeness and it costs nothing. T'is not the child's fault but the parents and teachers.

I was, when a child, always doing something; was very fond of climbing; seemed to have a mania for it. I never saw a tall tree that I did not try to climb, or wish I could. I used to run bareheaded over the fields and woods with the other children, lifting up rocks and logs to look at the bugs and worms. When we found a dead chicken, bird, rat or mouse, we would have a funeral. I would usually be the preacher and we would kneel down and while one prayed, the rest would look through their fingers, to see what the others were doing. We would sing and clap our hands and shake hands, then we would play: "Come and see."

I never had but one doll, bought out of a store, it was given to me by Dr. Jackson for taking my medicine, when I was sick. We made rag dolls out of dresses. My delight was to have one of the colored women's babies. We would go visiting and take our dolls, and would tell of the dreadful times we had and of how mean our husbands were to the children; sometimes one would tell of how good instead. And then we would catch bees in the althea blooms. One of the delightful pastimes was to make mud cakes and put them on boards to dry. We had some clay that we could mould anything out of— all kind of animals, and, indeed, there were shapes worked out by little fingers never seen before.

The race question is a serious one. The kindly feeling between black and white is giving place to bitterness with the rising generations. One reason of this seems to be a jealousy of the whites for fear the negroes will presume to be socially equal with them. The negro race should avoid this, should not desire it, it would be of no real value to them. They are a distinct race with characteristics which they need not wish to exchange. When a negro tries to imitate white folks, he is a mongrel. I will say to my colored brothers and sisters in Christ Jesus; Never depart from your race lines and bearings, keep true to your nature, your simplicity, and happy disposition—and above all come back to the 'Oldtime' religion, you will never strand on that rock.

CHAPTER III.

MOVED TO WOODFORD COUNTY, KENTUCKY.—ALSO MOVED TO MISSOURI.—SAVED FROM BEING A THIEF.— MY CONVERSION—GOING SOUTH AT OPENING OF THE CIVIL WAR.—AN INCIDENT OF MY GIRLHOOD SCHOOL DAYS.—WHY I HAD TO BELIEVE IN REVELATION.— SPIRITUALISM OR WITCHCRAFT.

In 1854, we moved to Woodford County, Kentucky, and bought a farm from Mr. Hibler, on the pike, between Midway and Versailles. Mr. Warren Viley was our nearest neighbor. My father was one of the trustees in building the Orphans' Home at Midway. Here in Midway I attended Sunday school and I had a very faithful teacher who taught me the Word of God. I have forgotten her name but I can see her sweet face now, as she planted seed in my heart that are still bringing forth fruit.

A minister came to our house one day and gave me a book to read, which made a very deep impression on me. As well as I can remember it was called: "The Children of the Heavenly King." This story represented three brothers, one, the youngest, was named Ezra, the other Ulrich, the third I forget. These three were intrusted with watching certain passes in the mountains during the warfare between a great, good king, and a bad one, and in proportion as these boys were faithful, the good king was victorious in battle, but when they neglected their duty, he would suffer loss. The character of little Ezra was a sweet, unselfish one. He tried so hard to help, and have his brothers do right. He would run from his post to wake them up, and tried to make up for their neglect; would do without rest and food for himself, and plead with them to do their duty. At last, when the king came, little Ezra was richly rewarded; Ulrich barely passed, and the unfaithful one was taken out amidst weeping, wailing and gnashing of teeth, and the door was shut. The minister did not know what good he had done.

> "Only a thought, but the work it wrought,
> Could never by tongue or pen be taught;
> For it ran thro' a life, like a thread of gold,
> And the life bore fruit, an hundred fold.
> Only a word, but it was spoken in love,
> With a whispered prayer to the Lord above;
> And the angels in heaven rejoiced once more
> For a new-born soul entered in, at the door."

I resolved to be like little Ezra as near as I could. When I was a child I fought against my selfish nature. I would often give away my doll clothes and other things that I wanted to keep myself. Some of the strongest characteristics of my life were awakened in my childhood. I would often blush with shame, when committing sins, and I had a great fear of the judgement day; it would terrify me when hearing of Jesus coming to the earth. I would often ask myself: "Where can I hide?" If the public knew of the smashing God gave me the strength to do in my heart, they would not wonder at my courage in smashing the murder- shops of our land. "He that ruleth his own spirit, is greater than he that taketh a city."

In 1855, we moved to Missouri, just a year before the trouble broke out between Kansas and Missouri. Missouri determined to make Kansas a slave state; but Kansas said she would not have a slave upon her soil. Squads of men in Missouri would often go into Kansas and commit depredations. At one time they burned Lawrence, Kansas, and killed many people. This trouble continued to grow worse until it brought on the great Civil War.

When we moved from Kentucky to Missouri, I took a severe cold on the boat, which made me an invalid for years. I was not a truthful child, neither was I honest. My mother was very strict with me in many ways and I would often tell her lies to avoid restraint or punishment. If there was anything I wanted about the house, especially something to eat, I would steal it, if I could. The colored servants would often ask me to steal things for them. My nurse Betsy, would say: "Carry get me a cup of sugar, butter, thread or needles," and many other things. This would make me sly and dishonest. I used to go and see my aunts and stay for months. I would open their boxes and bureau drawers and steal ribbons and laces and make doll clothes out of them. I would steal perfumery and would run out of the room to prevent them from smelling it. I am telling this for a purpose. Many little children may be doing what I did, not thinking of what a serious thing it is, and I write this to show them how I was cured of dishonesty: I got a little book at Sunday school and it told the way people became thieves, by beginning to take little things naming them, and some of these were the very things I had been taking. I was greatly shocked to see myself a thief; it had never occurred to me that I was as bad as that. I thought one had to steal something of great value to be a thief. My repentance was sincere, and I was made honest by this blessed book, so much so that even after I became grown, if any article was left in my house I would give it away, unless I could find the owner. I was perfectly delighted when I was entirely free. I asked for everything I wanted, even a pin. After that, I could show my doll clothes, and it was not necessary for me to be sly or tell stories any more. It was about this time I was converted. There was a protracted meeting at a place called Hickman's Mill, Jackson County, Missouri. The minister was gray haired and belonged to the Christian or Disciples church, the one my father belonged to. I was at this time ten years old and went with my father to church on Lord's Day morning. At the close of the sermon, and during the invitation, my father stepped to the pulpit and spoke to the minister and he looked over in my direction. At this I began to weep bitterly, seemed to be taken up, and sat down on the front bench. I could not have told any one what I wept for, except it was a longing to be better. I had often thought before this that I was in danger of going to the "Bad place," especially I would be afraid to think of the time that I should see Jesus come. I wanted to hide from Him. My father had a cousin living at Hickman's Mill, Ben Robertson. His wife, cousin Jennie, came up to me at the close of the service, and said: "Carry, I believe you know what you are doing." But I did not. Oh, how I wanted some one to explain to me. The next day I was taken to a running stream about two miles away, and, although it was quite cold and some ice in the water, I felt no fear. It seemed like a dream. I know God will bless the ordinance of baptism, for the little Carry that walked into the water was different from the one who walked out. I said no word. I felt that I could not speak, for fear of disturbing the peace that is past understanding. Kind hands wrapped me up and I felt no chill. I felt the responsibility of my new relation and tried hard to do right.

A few days after this I was at my aunt Kate Doneghy's. Uncle James, or "Jim," we called him, her husband, was not a Christian. He shocked me one day by saying: "So those Campbellites took you to the creek, and soused you, did they 'Cal'?" (A nick name.) What a blow! My aunt seemed also shocked to have him speak thus to me. I left the room and avoided meeting him again. How he crushed me! It had the effect to make me feel like a criminal.

The Protestant Church here makes a fatal error which the Catholics avoid. The ministers of the latter have all young converts come so often to them for instruction. A child may be born, but not being nursed and fed, it will die. God has command them to be fed in the sincere milk of the word. My greatest hindrance has been from the lack of proper Christian teaching. I love the memory of my father, he used to have me read the bible to him, and while I did not enjoy it then, it is a blessed memory. The family altar is essential to the welfare of every home, no other form of discipline is equal to it. The liberty, chivalry, and life of a nation live or die in proportion as the Altar fires live or die.

"And these words which I command thee this day shall be in thine heart and thou shalt teach them diligently unto thy children and shalt talk of them when thou sittest in thine house and when thou walkest by the way and when thou liest down and when thou risest up."

When I was fifteen, the war broke out between the north and the south. My father saw that Missouri would be the battle ground and he, with many others, took their families and negroes and went south, taking what they could in wagons, for there were no railroads then in that section. There was quite a train with the droves of cattle, mules and horses. One wagon had six yoke of oxen to it; had to get into it by a ladder, the kind that was used to freight across the plains. The family went in the family carriage that my father brought from Kentucky. I remember the time when this carriage was purchased, with the two dapple gray horses, and silver mounted harness, and when my mother would drive out she had a driver in broadcloth, with a high silk hat, and a boy rode on a seat behind, to open the gates. This was one of the ways of traveling in Kentucky in those days. My mother was an aristocrat in her ideas, but my father was not. He liked no display. He was wise enough to see the sin and folly of it.

{illust. caption =
THIS IS THE PICTURE OF MY GIRLHOOD HOME IN CASS
COUNTY, MO.
UNDER THE TREES OF THIS DEAR OLD PLACE I LISTENED
TO THE SWEET STORY OF MY LOVE OF A MAN MURDERED BY
DRINK.
"WHEN THOU HAST LOVED ONE LIVING MAN, THEN MAYEST
THOU LOOK
UPON THE DEAD."}

After being on the road six weeks, we stopped in Grayson County, Texas, and bought a farm. As we started from Missouri one of the colored women took sick with typhoid fever. This spread so that ten of the family, white, and black, were down at one time. As soon as we could travel, my father left the colored people south, and took his family back to Missouri. That winter south was a great blessing to me, for I recovered from a disease that had made me an invalid for five years— consumption of the bowels. Poor health had keep me out of school a great deal. My father at one time sent me to Mrs. Tillery's boarding school in Independence, Mo., but I was not in the recitation room more than half of the time.

After I recovered my health in Texas, it was my delight to ride on horseback with a girl friend. The southern boys were preparing to go to war. Many a sewing did we attend, where the mothers had spun and woven the gray cloth that they were now working up so sorrowfully for their sons to be buried in, far away from home. They thought their cause was right. There were many good masters. And again there were bad ones. Whiskey is always a cruel tyrant and is a worse evil than chattel slavery. We were often stopped on our trip by southern troops, in the Territory and Texas, and then again by northerners. We passed over the Pea Ridge battle ground shortly after the battle. Oh! the horrors of war. We often stopped at houses where the wounded were. We let them have our pillows and every bit of bedding we could spare. We went to our home in Cass County, Missouri.

Shortly after this we, with all families living in that country, were commanded by an order from Jim Lane, to move into an army post. This reached several counties in Missouri. It was done to depopulate the country, so that the "Bushwhackers" would be forced to leave, because of not being able to get food from the citizens. This caused much suffering. But such is war. We moved to Kansas City. I was in Independence, Mo., during the battle, when Price came through. I went with a good woman to the hospital to help with the wounded. My duty was to comb the heads of the wounded. I had a pan of scalding water near and would use the comb and shake off the animated nature into the hot water. The southern and northern wounded were in the same rooms. In health they were enemies, but I only saw kindly feeling and sympathy.

Mothers ought to give their daughters the experience of sitting with the sick; of preparing food for them; of binding up wounds. It is a pitiful sight to see a helpless woman in the sick room, ignorant through lack of experience and education, of ways to be useful at the time and place where these characteristics of woman adorn her the most of all others.

After we returned from Texas, being the oldest child and the servants all gone, my mother sick, and the younger children going to school, I had the house work, cooking and most of the washing to do. It was a new experience for me, and it was twice as hard as it ought to have been. I exposed my health; would slop up myself when I washed, and almost ruined my health, because I had not been properly educated. Herein was the curse of slavery. My father saw this, and I don't believe he had a regret when the slaves were free. Mother, it matters not what else you teach your daughters, if they have not an experience in doing the work themselves about a home, they are sadly deficient. It is not the soft, palefaced, painted, fashionable lady we want, for the world would be better without her; but the woman capable of knowing how, and willing to take a place in the home affairs of life. It is an ambition of mine to establish a Preparatory College in Topeka, Kansas, where girls may be taught, as women should be, that they in turn may teach others, how to wash, cook, scrub, dress and talk, to counteract the idea that woman is a toy, pretty doll, with no will power of her own, only a parrot, a parasite of a man. To be womanly, means strength of character, virtue and a power for good. Let your women be teachers of good things, says the Holy Spirit.

The last school I attended was at Liberty, Missouri, taught by Mr. and Mrs. Love. Only went there a year, but it was of untold value to me. I was so eager to get an education. On account of ill health and the war, I knew but little. I wanted a thorough education. I had read a good many books, and would write sketches; kept a diary part of the time.

I will here relate an incident that will give my readers a little insight into my impulses. At Liberty School we had a class in Smellie's "Natural Philosophy." There was an argument among the girls. Some said animals had reasoning faculties. Others said not. Miss Jennie Johnson, our teacher, said: "Have that for a question to debate on in your society." So it was ordered. I was given the affirmative. The Friday came. I was taken by surprise and was in confusion, when I saw the room crowded. The two other societies of the Seminary, "The Mary Lyons" and "Rising Star," also all the teachers, were present. Our Society was the "Eunomian". I had made no preparations. When I was called I know I looked ridiculously blank. The president tried to keep her face straight. I got no farther than, "Miss President". All burst out in uncontrollable laughter. I went to my seat put my face in my arms and turned my back to the audience. I wept with tears of humiliation. I felt disgraced. I thought of what a shame this would be to my parents. How ever after this I must be considered a "Silly" by my schoolmates. These things nerved me. I dried my tears, turned around in my seat, looked up, and the moral force it required to do this was almost equal to that which smashed a saloon. I arose and said: "Miss President, I am ready to state my case." I began in this style: "I know animals have the power to reason for my brothers cured a dog from sucking eggs by having him take a hot one in his mouth, and it was the last egg we ever knew him to pick up. Why? Because he remembered the hot one and reasoned that he might get burned. Why is it that a horse will like one person more than another? Because he is capable of reasoning and knows who is the best to him." I went on in this homely style and spoke with a vehemence which said: "I will make my point," which I did amidst the cheers of the school. I was eighteen at this time and you would say: "You must have been rather green." So I was in some things.

I believe I have always failed in everything I undertook to do the first time, but I learned only by experience, paid dearly for it, and valued it afterwards. My failures have been my best teachers. I see no one more awkward than I once was, but I had determined to conquer. My defects were the great incentives to perseverance, when I felt I was right.

I shall not in this book speak much of my love affairs, but they were, nevertheless, an important part of my life. I was a great lover. I used to think a person never could love but once in this life, but I often now say, I would not want a heart that could hold but one love. It was not the beauty of face or form that was the most attractive to me in young gentlemen, or ladies, but that of the mind. Seeing this the case with myself, I tried to acquire knowledge to make my company agreeable. I see young ladies, and gentlemen, who entertain each other with their silly jokes and gigglings that are disgusting. When I had company I always directed the conversation so that my friend would teach me something, or I would teach him. I would read the poets, and Scott's writings and history. Read Josephus, mythology and the Bible together, and never read a course that taught me as much. I would go to the country dances and sometimes to balls in the City. The church did not object to this: I would teach Sunday school at the same time. No one taught me that this was wrong. One thing was a tower of defense to me. I always, when possible, read the Bible and would pray. After retiring would get up and kneel, feeling that to pray in bed only, was disrespectful to God. If the angels in heaven would prostrate themselves before Him, I a poor sinner should. And right here, I believe in "advancing on your knees." Abraham prostrated himself, so did David and Solomon, Elijah, Daniel, Paul, and even our sinless Advocate. Why did the Holy Ghost state the position so often? For our example, of course. There are no space writers in the Scriptures. I often had doubts as to whether the Bible was the work of God or man. I kept these doubts to myself, for I thought infidelity a disgrace. I wanted to believe the Bible the word of God. I early saw that to close the Bible was to shut out all knowledge of the purpose of life. Without its revelations one does not know why we are born, why we live, or where we go after death. We can see the purpose of all nature, but not of this life of ours, and God had, by revelation, to make this known.

The Bible was a mystery to me. It often seemed to be a contradiction. I did not love to read it, but above all things, I did not want to be a hypocrite. I was determined to try to do my part. I would pray for the same thing over and over again, so as to be in earnest, and think of what I was asking. My mind was distracted by thoughts of the world. I said, if there is a God, he will not hear the prayer of those, so disrespectful as not to think of what they ask. I never seemed to get rid of this, unless at times, when I would have some sorrow of heart. "By the sadness of the countenance, the heart is made better."

I do not believe the Bible because I understand it; for there are few things of revelation that I do understand. Creation is a mystery, still we know everything had a beginning. I do not know why things grow out of the earth. Why they are green. Why grass makes wool on a sheep and hair on a cow, but I know these are facts. I cannot understand why or how the blood of Jesus Christ cleanses from sin, neither do I understand that greatest of all mysteries, the new birth, but nothing more positively a fact in my experience.

God is not perceived by the five senses. The things that are seen are temporal, but those that are unseen are eternal. What a sin of presumption to question God in any of His providences. What God says and does is wisdom, righteousness and power.

The book of Psalms condemned me. I said, I never felt like David. I cannot rejoice. Still I felt that I ought to, but instead, a constant feeling of condemnation and conviction. This was torture to me. I would often have been willing to have died, if I thought it would have been an eternal sleep. My childhood and girlhood were not happy; had so many disappointments. I was called "hard headed" by my parents. I never was free to have what I wished; something would come between me and what I wanted. No one understood me so well as my darling aunt Hope Hill, my mother's sister. She seemed to read me and would talk to me of persons and things, answering the very cry of my heart. My mother would often let me stay with her for months. She had five sons, but no daughters and she was very fond of me. This lesson she taught me: A party of ladies came out from Independence to spend the day with her. Mrs. Woodson and a Mrs. Porter, wife of Dr. Porter, I remember the latter, one of the handsomest women I ever saw, beautiful feet, hands, hair, and a woman who knew it, and, it was a mater of the greatest pride with her, these charms. I was very much captivated by her splendid appearance and could not keep my eyes from her. Next day Mrs. John Staton, a country neighbor of my aunts, came in to make a visit, She was very plain, wore a calico dress, waist-apron, and she was knitting a sock. After she left aunt said to me: "Carry, you did not seem to like Mrs. Staton's society as you did Mrs. Porter's; but one sentence of Mrs. Staton's is worth all Mrs. Porter said. Mrs. Porter lives for this world, Mrs. Staton lives for God." This Lesson I did not learn then, but have since. Oh! for the old-fashioned women.

MY EXPERIENCE WITH SPIRITUALISM.

Just at the close of the war when we were on a farm in Cass County, Missouri, a colony of spiritualists were near us, Mrs. Hawkins, the medium was about 60 years old, very peculiar, and finely educated. My father had some farms he was selling for other people. He took Mrs. Hawkins and several of her company to look at a farm with a view of selling it. When she saw it from a hill some distance off she said: "That is the place I saw in Connecticut." She bought it for a town site. In writing to Washington to give it a name, the word "Peculiar" was selected, and so it has ever been called. Mrs. Hawkins took a great fancy to me. She would tell me of great things she had done, then say: "Could Jesus Christ have done more?" I had never heard of Spiritualism that I knew of, up to this time. This colony brought mechanics, merchants and musicians with them. I was in great confusion about this matter, not knowing what to think, for she did some superhuman things. Up stairs we had a large safe full of old books. I was looking over them one day, came to a little book called "Spiritualism Exposed". I immediately went to the orchard, sat under a tree, as my custom was, when I wished to read, for there I could be quiet. I read the little book through, before I stopped. This blessed lesson showed me to my entire satisfaction, that modern spiritualism is witchcraft. The writer took the instances in the Bible. God told Moses: "You must not suffer a witch to live;" see it at the court of Pharoah, and that they have "superhuman power." There are two kingdoms. One of darkness, and one of light. God rules in the latter; The Devil in the former. Both have powers above the power of man. The magicians at Pharoah's court were wizards; and the woman of Endor was a witch. The Bible speaks of dealing with "familiar spirits." Manasseh, Saul, and other Kings, were cursed for such. Gal. 5th has it as one of the "mortal sins." The Devil can do lying miracles to deceive. He will heal the body, or appear to do it, to damn the soul. I find this in "Christian Science." This is the mark of the "Beast" or carnal mind. Man is but a beast without the new birth, or spirit of God. Carnality always seeks to elevate itself. Grace is humble, and sees nothing good outside of God. The mark of the beast, is the number, or mark of a man; that is carnality or the Beast. Rev. 13:18.

CHAPTER IV.

MY FIRST MARRIAGE.—A BITTER DISAPPOINTMENT.— MOTHER GLOYD.—MY DRUGGED AND WHISKEY MURDERED HUSBAND.—LOSING MY POSITION AS TEACHER.—SECOND MARRIAGE.—LOSS OF PROPERTY.— KEEPING HOTEL.— STRUGGLES FOR DAILY FOOD.—THE AFFLICTIONS OF MY CHILD.—ANSWER TO PRAYER.

In the fall of 1865, Dr. Gloyd, a young physician, called to see my father to secure the country school, saying he wished to locate in our section of the country, and wanted to take a school that winter, and then he could decide where he would like to practice his profession.

This man was a thorough student, spoke, and read, several different languages; he boarded with. I liked him, and stood in awe of him because of his superior education, never thinking that he loved me, until he astonished me one evening by kissing me. I had never had a gentleman to take such a privilege and felt shocked, threw up my hands to my face, saying several times: "I am ruined." My aunt and mother had instilled great reserve in my actions, when in company of gentlemen, so much so that I had never allowed one to sit near or hold my hand. This was not because I did not like their society, but I had been taught that to inspire respect or love from a man, you must keep him at a distance. This often made me awkward and reserved, but it did me no harm. When I learned that Dr. Gloyd loved me, I began to love him. He was an only child. His parents had but a modest living. My mother was not pleased with seeing a growing attachment between us, for there was another match she had planned for me. When she saw this she would not allow me to sit alone in the room with him, so our communication was mostly by writing letters. I never knew Shakespeare until he read it to me, and I became an ardent admirer of the greatest poet. The volume of Shakespeare on his table was our postoffice. In the morning at breakfast he would manage to call the name "Shakespeare;" then I would know there was a letter for me in its leaves. After teaching three months he went to Holden, Mo., and located; sent for his father and mother and in two years we were married.

{illust. caption =
MRS. NATION IS SITTING WHERE SHE STOOD AT HER FIRST MARRIAGE IN THE PARLOR
OF HER OLD HOME IN CASS COUNTY, MISSOURI.}

My father and mother warned me that the doctor was addicted to drink, but I had no idea of the curse of rum. I did not fear anything, for I was in love, and doubted in him nothing. When Dr. Gloyd came up to marry me the 21st of November, 1867, I noticed with pain, that his countenance was not bright, he was changed. The day was one of the gloomiest I ever saw, a mist fell, and not a ray of sunshine. I felt a foreboding on the day I had looked forward to, as being one of the happiest. I did not find Dr. Gloyd the lover I expected. He was kind but seemed to want to be away from me; used to sit and read, when I was so hungry for his caresses and love. I have heard that this is the experience of many other young married women. They are so disappointed that their husbands change so after marriage. With my observation and experience I believe that men have it in their power to keep the love of ninety-nine women out of a hundred. Why do women lose love for their husbands? I find it is mostly due to indifference on the part of the husband. I often hear the experience of those poor abandoned sisters. I ask, Why are you in this house of sin and death? When I can get their confidence, many of them say: "I married a man; he drank, and went with other women. I got discouraged or spiteful, and went to the bad also." I find that drink causes so much enmity between the sexes. Drinking men neglect their wives. Their wives become jealous. Men often go with abandoned women under the influence of that drink that animates the animal passions and asks not for the association of love, but the gratification of lust. Men do not go to the houses of ill-fame to meet women they love but oftener those they almost hate. The drink habit destroys in men the appreciation of a home life, and when a woman leaves all others for one man, she does, and should, expect his companionship, and is not satisfied without it. Libertines, taking advantage of this, select women whose husbands are neglectful, and he wins victims by his attentions, and poor woman, as at the first, is beguiled. Marriage, while it is the blissful consummation of pure love, is the most serious of all relations, and girls and boys should early be instructed about the secrets of their own natures, the object of marriage, and the serious results of any marriage where true love is not the object. I confess myself that I was not fit to marry with the ignorance of its holy purpose. Sunday school teachers, mothers, fathers, and ministers, look into God's word and see the results of sin. God has written of this so as to force you to educate your children. Talk freely. Truth will purify everything it comes in contact with. Ignorance is not innocence, but is the promoter of crime: "My people are destroyed for lack of knowledge."

About five days after we were married, Dr. Gloyd came in, threw himself on the bed and fell asleep. I was in the next room and saw his mother bow down over his face. She did not know I saw her. When she left, I did the same thing, and the fumes of liquor came in my face. I was terror stricken, and from that time on, I knew why he was so changed. Not one happy moment did I see; I cried most all the time. My husband seemed to understand that I knew his condition. Twice, with tears in his eyes, he remarked: "Oh! Pet, I would give my right arm to make you happy." He would be out until late every night. I never closed my eyes. His sign in front of the door on the street would creak in the wind, and I would sit by the window waiting to hear his footsteps. I never saw him stagger. He would lock himself up in the "Masonic Lodge" and allow no one to see him. People would call for him in case of sickness, but he could not be found.

My anguish was unspeakable, I was comparatively a child. I wanted some one to help me. He was a mason. I talked to a Mr. Hulitt, a brother mason, I begged of him to help me save my precious husband. I talked to a dear friend, Mrs. Clara Mize, a Christian, hoping to get some help in that direction, but all they could say, was. "Oh, what a pity, to see a man like Dr. Gloyd throw himself away!" The world was all at once changed to me, it was like a place of torture. I thought certainly, there must be a way to prevent this suicide and murder. I now know, that the impulse was born in me then to combat to the death this inhumanity to man.

I believe the masons were a great curse to Dr. Gloyd. These men would drink with him. There is no society or business that separates man and wife, or calls men from their homes at night, that produces any good results. I believe that secret societies are unscriptural, and that the Masonic Lodge has been the ruin of many a home and character.

I was so ignorant I did not know that I owed a duty to myself to avoid gloomy thoughts; did not know that a mother could entail a curse on her offspring before it was born. Oh, the curse that comes through heredity, and this liquor evil, a disease that entails more depravity on children unborn, than all else, unless it be tobacco. There is an object lesson taught in the Bible. The mother of Samson was told by an angel to "drink neither wine nor strong drink" before her child was born, and not to allow him to do so after he was born. God shows by this, that these things are injurious. Mothers often make drunkards of their own children, before they are born. My parents heard that Dr. Gloyd was drinking. My father came down to visit us, and I went home with him. My mother told me I must never go back to my husband again. I knew the time was near at hand, when I would be helpless, with a drunken husband, and no means of support. What could I do? I kept writing to "Charlie," as I called him. He came to see me once; my mother treated him as a stranger. He expressed much anxiety about my confinement in September; got a party to agree to come for him at the time; but my mother would not allow it. In six weeks after my little girl was born, my mother sent my brother with me to Holden to get my trunk and other things to bring them home. Her words to me were: "If you stay in Holden, never return home again." My husband begged me to stay with him; he said: "Pet, if you leave me, I will be a dead man in six months." I wanted to stay with him, but dared not disobey my mother and be thrown out of shelter, for I saw I could not depend on my husband. I did not know then that drinking men were drugged men, diseased men. His mother told me that when he was growing up to manhood, his father, Harry Gloyd, was Justice of the Peace in Newport, Ohio, twelve years, and that Charlie was so disgusted with the drink cases, that he would go in a room and lock himself in, to get out of their hearing; that he never touched a drop until he went in the army, the 118th regiment, Thomas L. Young being the Colonel. Dr. Gloyd was a captain. In the society of these officers he, for the first time, began to drink intoxicants. He was fighting to free others from slavery, and he became a worse slave than those he fought to free. In a little less than six months from the day my child was born, I got a telegram telling of his death. His father died a few months before he did, and mother Gloyd was left entirely alone.

Mother Gloyd was a true type of a New England housewife, and I had always lived in the south. I could not say at this time that I loved her, although I respected her very highly. But I wanted to be with the mother of the man I loved more than my own life; I wanted to supply his place if possible. My father gave me several lots; by selling one of these and Dr. Gloyd's library and instruments, I built a house of three rooms on one of the lots and rented the house we lived in, which brought us in a little income, but not sufficient to support us. I wanted to prepare myself to teach, and I attended the Normal Institute of Warrensburg. I was not able to pay my board and Mr. Archie Gilkerson and wife charged me nothing and were as kind to me as parents. God bless them! I got a certificate and was given the primary room in the Public School at Holden. Mother Gloyd kept house and took care of Charlien, my little girl, and I made the living. This continued for four years. I lost my position as teacher in that school this way: A Dr. Moore was a member of the board, he criticised me for the way I had the little ones read; for instance, in the sentence, "I saw a man," I had them use the short a instead of the long a, and so with the article a; having them read it as we would speak it naturally. He made this serious objection, and I lost my place and Dr. Moore's niece got my room as teacher. This was a severe blow to me, for I could not leave mother Gloyd and Charlien to teach in another place, and I knew of no other way of making a living except by teaching. I resolved then to get married. I made it a subject of prayer and went to the Lord explaining things about this way. I said: "My Lord, you see the situation I cannot take care of mother and Charlien. I want you to help me. If it be best for me to marry, I will do so. I have no one picked out, but I want you to select the one that you think best. I want to give you my life, and I want by marrying to glorify and serve you, as well as to take care of mother and Charlien and be a good wife." I have always been a literalist. I find out that it is the only way to interpret the Bible. When God says: "Commit thy way unto the Lord; trust also in him he shall bring it to pass," I believe that to be the way to act. My faith does not at all times grasp this or other promises, but there are times when I can appropriate them and make them mine; there are times when I can pray with faith, believing that I have the things I pray for, other times it is not so.

In about ten days from that time I made this a subject of prayer, I was walking down the street in Holden and passed a place where Mr. Nation was standing, who had come up from Warrensburg, where he was then editing the "Warrensburg Journal". He was standing in the door with his back to me, but turned and spoke. There was a peculiar thrill which passed through my heart which made me start. The next day I got a letter from him, asking me to correspond with him. I was not surprised; had been expecting something like it. I knew that this was in answer to my prayer, and David Nation was to be the husband God selected for me. He was nineteen years older than I, was very good looking, and was a well-informed, successful lawyer, also a Christian minister. My friends in Holden opposed this because of the difference in our ages and of his large family. I gave him the loving confidence of a true wife and he was often very kind to me. We were married within six weeks from the time I got the letter from him. Mother Gloyd went to live with us and continued to do so for fifteen years, until she died. My married life with Mr. Nation was not a happy one. I found out that he deceived me in so many things. I can remember the first time I found this out. I felt like something was broken that could never be mended. What a shattered thing is betrayed confidence! Oh, husband, and wives, do not lie to each other, even though you should do a vile act; confess to the truth of the matter! There will be some trouble over it, but you can never lose your love for a truthful person. I hated lying because I loved the truth. I hated dishonesty because I loved honesty. I loved, therefore I hated. I love mankind therefore I hated the enemies of mankind. I loved God and therefore hated the devil. Truth is the pearl of great price. Whoso getteth it has all earth and heaven.

I shall not in this book give to the public the details of my life as a wife of David Nation any more than possible. He and I agreed in but few things, and still we did not have the outbreaks many husbands and wives have. The most serious trouble that ever rose between us was in regard to Christianity. My whole Christian life was an offense unto him, and I found out if I yielded to his ideas and views that I would be false to every true motive. He saw that I resented this influence and it caused him to be suspicious and jealous. I think my combative nature was largely developed by living with him, for I had to fight for everything that I kept. About two years after we were married, we exchanged our mutual properties for seventeen hundred acres of land on the San Bernard River in Texas, part of which was a cotton plantation. We knew nothing of the cultivation of cotton or of plantation life. We took a car load of good furniture with us and some fine stock, hogs and cattle. In packing up to go to Texas there was a widow who assisted me. In paying her for her services, I gave her some worthless things, because I was so avaricious. I would not pay her money, but gave her the things I did not want to carry with me. I remember I left about eight bushels of potatoes in the cellar for her and the night we left they froze. I felt very much condemned the way I treated this poor woman.

We were as helpless on the plantation as little children. The cultivation of cotton was very different from anything we had been used to. A bad neighbor threw all of our plows in the Bernard River and everything seemed to go wrong. We had eight horses die in the pasture the spring after we moved there. Soon the money we took with us was gone and Mr. Nation got discouraged. He went to Brazoria, the county seat, and stayed six weeks during court, for the purpose of entering the practice of law again.

The cotton had been planted before he left. A neighbor named Martin Hanks came over and told me not to allow the cotton to go to waste, said he would lend me his plows, and advised me to get a colored man named Edmond, who was his master's overseer in slave time, to manage this crop for me. I hired five other negroes, paying them with things I had in the house, for I had not a cent of money. The result was a fine crop of cotton. Mr. Nation's daughter Lola, was then eleven years old, and Charlien was three years younger. We lived six miles from a school, and just at a time when the girls needed school most. I began to see what a disastrous move we had made. I became very dispondant and sick at heart. I was young and did not know then how to contend with disappointments on every hand. At one time I was quite sick with chills and fever. I had nothing in the house but meal, some fat bacon and sweet potatoes. There was a poor old man that we took in for charity who was with us, named Mr. Holt. I called him to my bedside and asked him to go to the patch and dig a bushel of sweet potatoes and take them to town and exchange them for a little tea, sugar, lemons and bread. He failed in this and was returning when, he met a dear, sweet woman, Mrs. Underwood, that I called my "Texas Mother." She called to Mr. Holt, and asked him how I was. He told her I was sick and out of anything to eat. She took the potatoes and sent the articles I wanted. I believe I should have died had he returned without them, for I was almost famished for food and sick besides.

I was in Columbia one day and stopped at the Old Columbia Hotel, owned by the Messrs. Park, two bachelors. Mrs. Ballenger a widow was renting it from Messrs. Park. I said to them: "If you ever need a tenant, send for me." In a few months Mrs. Ballenger's daughter died and she left. Mr. Park sent for me to come. We had a car load of good plain furniture and bedding, some handsome tableware, but no money to buy provisions.

Dear old mother Gloyd was a great help to me. She had once kept hotel herself. I did not ask credit, and this is how I got the money to begin keeping hotel: There was an Irish ditcher named Dunn whose wife did my work. She was a good cook. I borrowed of Mr. Dunn three dollars and fifty cents, and with this money began the hotel business. The house was a rattle trap, plastering off, and a regular bed-bug nest. I fumigated, pasted the walls over with cloth and newspapers, where the plastering was off, and made curtains out of old sheets. My purchases were about like this for the first day: Fifty cents worth of meat, coffee ten cents, rice ten cents and sugar twenty-five cents, potatoes five, etc. The transients at one meal would give me something to spend for the next. I assisted about the cooking and helped in the dining-room. Mother Gloyd and Lola attended to the chamber work, and little Charlien was the one who did the buying for the house. I would often wash out my tablecloths at night myself and iron them in the morning before breakfast. I would take boarders' washing, hire a woman to wash, then do the ironing myself. Columbia was a small village of not more than five hundred people. It was the terminal of a railroad called the Columbia Tap. Mr. Painter, the conductor, began boarding with us right off and in three or four days he brought a family there to board by the name of Oastram, father, mother and two boys, having come south to buy a plantation. Mrs. Oastrom handed me a ten dollar bill. I called Lola and Charlien upstairs and showed them the ten dollar bill. We were overjoyed; we danced, laughed, and cried. Charlien said: "Now we can buy a whole ham." For several months my little children and I ate nothing but broken food. I can never put on paper the struggles of this life. I would not know one day how we would get along the next.

The bitterest sorrows of my life have come from not having the love of a husband. I must here say that I have had, at times, in the society of those I love, a foretaste of what this could be. For years I never saw a loving husband that I did not envy the wife; it was a cry of my heart for love. I used to ask God why He denied me this. I can see now why it was. I know it was God's will for me to marry Mr. Nation. Had I married a man I could have loved, God could never have used me. Phrenologists who have examined my head have said: "How can you, who are such a lover of home be without one?" The very thing that I was denied caused me to have a desire to secure it to others. Payne who wrote "Home Sweet Home" never had one. There is in my life a cause of sadness and bitter sorrow that God only knows. I shall not write it here. Oh! how the heart will break almost for a loving word! I believe the great want of the world is love. Jesus came to bring love to earth.

During these severe afflictions I began to see how little there was in life. I wondered at the gaiety of people. Seemed like a pall hung over the earth. I would wonder that the birds sung, or the sun would shine. I might say that for years this was my experience. I would go to God but got very little relief;

yet I never gave up. It was all the hope I could see for me. About this time my little Charlien, who had been such a help to me, began to go into a decline, until she was taken down with typhoid fever. Her case was violent and she was delirious from the first. This my only child was peculiar. She was the result of a drunken father and a distracted mother. The curse of heredity is one of the most heart-breaking results of the saloon. Poor little children are brought into the world, cursed by disposition and disease, entailed on them. How can mothers be true to their offspring with a constant dread of the nameless horrors wives are exposed to by being drunkards' wives. Men will not raise domestic animals under conditions where the mothers may bring forth weak or deformed offspring. My precious child seemed to have taken a perfect dislike to Christianity. This was a great grief to me, and I used to pray to God to save her soul at any cost; I often prayed for bodily affliction on her, if that was what would make her love and serve God. Anything for her eternal salvation.

Her right cheek was very much swollen, and on examination we found there was an eating sore inside her cheek. This kept up in spite of all remedies, and at last the whole of her right cheek fell out, leaving the teeth bare. My friends and boarders were very angry at the physician, saying she was salivated. From the first something told me this is an answer to your prayer. At this time, when her life was despaired of, I had an intense longing to save my child, who was so dear to me. I said: "Oh, God, let me keep a piece of my child." A minister said: "Don't pray for the life of your child; she will be so deformed it were better she were dead." I could not feel this way. After being at death's door for nine days, she began to recover. The wound in her face healed up to a hole about the size of a twenty-five cent piece. Her jaws closed and remained so for eight years. The sickness of my daughter and the keeping up of the hotel was such a tax on my mind, that for six months all transactions would recede from my memory. For instance, if anyone told me something, in an hour afterwards, I could not tell whether it had been hours, days or months since it was told me. I never entirely recovered from this, still being forgetful of names, dates and circumstances, unless they are particularly impressed upon my mind. When I could afford it, I took my child, then twelve years old, down to Galveston, put her under the care of Dr. Dowell for the purpose of closing the hole in her cheek. I had to leave the little one down there among strangers, for I could not afford to stay with her. A mother only will know what this means. After four operations the place was closed up in her cheek, still her mouth was closed, her teeth close together. I suffered torture all these years for fear she might strangle to death. I took her to San Antonio, Texas, to Dr. Herff, and he and his two sons removed a section of the jawbone, expecting to make an artificial joint, enabling her to use the other side of her jaw. After all this, the operation was a failure, and her jaws closed up again. We, in the meantime, moved to Richmond from

Columbia. We became very successful in the hotel business and I saved money enough to send her to New York City, where her father, Dr. Gloyd, had a cousin, Dr. Messinger, who would see that she had the best relief possible. None of the surgeons there gave her any hope of opening her jaws. She went to Dr. John Wyeth to have him perform the plastic surgery; that is, he cut off a flap from under her chin, turning it over the scar on her cheek.

Although Charlien was not a Christian, she had faith in God. Once she complained of my being too strict with her, but said: "Mamma I owe it to you that I have any faith in God, even if you are severe with me." She always believed that her mother had a God. Finding no physician in New York that could open her jaws, she wrote me this: "No one but God can open my mouth, Mamma; ask him to do it." There was a Catholic woman, Miss Doregan, who boarded with me and had a store around the corner from the hotel, and I could think of no one else who had as much faith as this woman. She said she believed that God would heal my child according to prayer, so I went for seven mornings before breakfast
to this saint of God. She taught me many holy truths and she explained the Scriptures to me. I learned from her a prayer that we said in concert, that was written by one of the Old Fathers, and is one of the most complete in devotion I have ever read. I will record it here:
"Come Holy Ghost send down those beams,
That sweetly flow in silent streams,
From thy bright throne above;
Oh, Come Father of the poor,
Thou bounteous source of all our store;
Come fire our hearts with love.
Come thou of comforters the best,
Come thou the soul's delicious guest,
The pilgrim's sweet relief:
Thou art our rest in toil and sweat,
Refreshment in excessive heat
And solace in our grief.
Oh! sacred light shoot home the darts,
Oh! pierce the center of those hearts
Whose faith aspires to thee.
Without thy God-head nothing can
Have any worth a price in man,
Nothing can harmless be."
"Lord wash our sinful stains away,
Water from heaven our barren clay,
Our wounds and bruises heal.
To thy sweet yoke our stiff necks bow,

Warm with thy fire our hearts of snow,
Our wandering feet repair.
Oh, grant thy faithful dearest Lord,
Whose only hope is thy sure word,
The seven gifts of thy spirit.
Grant us in life to obey thy grace,
Grant us in death to see thy face
And endless joys inherit,
Through the same Christ our Lord."
     "Amen."

And now I often use this beautiful and comprehensive petition to my Dear Lord.

Charlien wrote that she had letters of introduction to a physician in Philadelphia, Dr. J. Ewing Mears, but in every letter would say: "Keep on praying." This we did. Oh, the anxiety of my mother heart! My duties as landlady kept me busy all day and part of the night. I often had to do my own cooking.

God was good to me and we were very successful financially, and managed to meet all debts and payments on the property we had purchased.

After I knew the operation had been performed in Philadelphia, I telegraphed to Charlien. The answer came from the physician: "All right," but my anxiety was intensified. I became almost wild with anxiety, and I determined to go to her. I borrowed four hundred dollars from Alex McNabb, the man she was engaged to, and in three hours I was on my way to my precious suffering one. As soon as I got on the train a sense of divine guidance came to me.

When I arrived at the hospital, I had the nurse take me to my child's room. I cannot describe the meeting. She was packing up her clothes. I said: "Why are you doing this?" Then she told me this pitiful story: "Mamma, you did not send me any money, and the Doctor and nurse seemed dissatisfied, so I took most of my clothes down to a soup house and pawned them, that the woman may give me a room and soup until I could hear from you."

This was horrible to think of. I had sent her money, but like some others, Charlien never knew the value of money. I had her on my lap and we were crying together. Just to think, in ten minutes more my child might have been gone, and I might not have found her for some time. Her mouth was opened half an inch, and as she talked, I noticed that the side of her face the jaw bone had been taken from, was moving as she chewed a piece of gum. I placed my hands on each side of her face and said: "Now chew, Well, this is just like God; he has not only opened your mouth, but has given you a new jaw bone.

My darling you know that the bone from this side was taken out." "Yes", she said, "I told Dr. Mears that, but he said it could not be."

I told him I saw the bone and teeth that were taken out. So in answer to prayer, God had wrought this miracle.

I stayed there six weeks with her, She went to see the doctor three times a week. He used a pry to open her jaws, which was very painful to her but she gradually grew better. We were so happy in each other's society. I took her every place to see sights in that grand, philanthropic city. I believe Philadelphia, "Brotherly Love," has more evidence of the meaning of the name than any city I have ever seen. The "Breakfast Association" for redeemed men has no equal in its Christ-like work. When I left New York for Kansas, I bought two tickets, one from New York to Chicago and another one from there on. When I went to check my trunk I found one ticket was gone. I had only about three or four dollars, not enough to get me another ticket. This was at Fulton Ferry. I turned and walked out going toward the elevated road, looking as I went for my ticket. Was praying God to help me find it. I walked about the streets as if in a dream. Wishing to learn where I was, I crossed the street to ask a policeman. Seeing a paper at his feet I picked it up and it was my lost ticket. Joshua made the sun stand still by prayer. Elijah closed the heavens from raining on the earth and raised the dead. It is not strange that God should answer my prayer in this case.

In six weeks I returned home leaving Charlien, who went to Vermont to visit some of her father's relatives, the Gloyds. She was gone six months, came home and married and continued to live in Richmond, Texas. For a year she and her husband lived with me; also Mr. Nation's daughter, Lola, was married and living with me, and mother Gloyd, now eighty-six years old, was there. My cares now were so heavy many times that I could not attend religious worship as I wished. Sunday morning I frequently gathered my servants in the dining-room, and there we read and studied the Bible. I had great heaviness of heart, because I had no time to meditate and study the Scriptures. I saw I was only living to feed the perishing bodies of men and women. I would frequently go upstairs and prostrate myself on the floor, crying to God for deliverance from my present surroundings, telling Him over and over, "if he would free me I would do for Him what he couldn't get anyone else to do." How literally this has been fulfilled, for God held me to my vow, and what Carry A. Nation has done is what no one else has; not only in the instance of smashing saloons, but in every other work. My life beyond dispute has been marvelous and no one that will stop to consider but will know and must admit that an unseen power, one super-human, has upheld me, "not by might, nor by power, but by my Spirit, saith the Lord."

CHAPTER V.

THE BAPTISM OF THE HOLY GHOST.—REJECTED AS A BIBLE TEACHER IN METHODIST AND EPISCOPALIAN CHURCHES.—TAUGHT IN HOTEL DINING-ROOM.— VISION, WARNING AND BLESSING.—ENTERTAINING ANGELS.—THE JEWS.— PRAYER FOR RAIN AND ANSWER.—GOD'S JUDGEMENTS ON THE WICKED.— MOVED TO KANSAS.—DEATH OF MOTHER GLOYD.— SERMON OF A CATHOLIC PRIEST.

In this chapter I will tell of God's leading. I say of my life, "This is the Lord's doings and marvelous in our eyes." A Methodist conference was held in Richmond, Texas, about the year 1884. I attended. The minister read the sixty-second chapter of Isaiah. From the time he began reading I was marvelously affected. Paul said it was not "lawful" or possible to utter some things. There was a halo around the minister. I was wrapt in ecstacy. My first impression was that an angel was talking and that the house was ascending to heaven. I felt my natural heart expanding to an enormous size. I looked to see what impression was made on the people in the audience. I saw one man nodding. I was surprised, for no one seemed at all astonished or delighted.

At the close of the meeting I tried to find out the meaning. No one felt as I did. I went to a saintly woman, Mrs. Ruth Todd, and asked her about the sermon. She had felt nothing remarkable. I had never been taught that anyone but the Apostles in Jesus' time got the gift of the Holy Ghost, or I would have understood this wonderful state. I then and there openly consecrated myself to God, telling my friends that "from henceforth all my time, means and efforts should be given to God." (Mr. Nation in his petition for divorce said that up to this year I had been a good wife.) I was often considered crazy, on the subject of religion. When I spoke to people I would ask them, "if they loved God;" I could not refrain from this; the servant in the kitchen, the guest, the merchant, the market man; I felt impelled by divine love for the souls of men.

God had given me an intense love for souls, and one was as precious as another to me. I now see what the enlarging of my heart meant. Once an old colored man brought in the kitchen some eggs to sell. I said: "Uncle, do you love God?" He turned to my cook Fannie and said: "Hear dat". Fannie said: "Oh! Mrs. Nation knows the Lord." Uncle said: "Thank God one white woman got ligen," clapped his hands and praised God. It used to be and is now the sweetest music to have anyone praise God. I am at church often, when I long to hear a loud shout of praise go up to the giver of every good and perfect gift. It is torture to attend the cold, dead service of most of the churches.

I was a teacher in the Methodist Sunday school and had given perfect satisfaction up to this time; but things changed. The minister said from the pulpit that the teachers should be Methodists, and spoke so pointedly that all knew he meant me. The superintendent at the Episcopal Sunday school asked me to teach in their Sunday school. (This was Judge Williams, the husband of Lola, Mr. Nation's daughter.) I did so, and things went smoothly for a while.

Father Denroach was the minister, and one morning he asked the school questions out of the catechism. My class could not answer. I arose and said: "Father Denroach, I do not teach my class the catechism, I use only God's word." "What objection do you find to the catechism?" he asked. I replied: "I cannot teach the Bible and catechism, for one contradicts the other. The gospel is to be believed and obeyed and a Christian is a follower of Christ. The catechism in the first lesson asks this question: What is your name? 'Bob, Tom or John.' 'When did you get that name?' 'In my baptism, when I was made a Christian.' "Baptism never did make a Christian. Infants cannot be made Christians, they cannot follow Christ, cannot believe or obey the Gospel. Jesus said: 'Of such is the Kingdom of Heaven! Now if I teach my class that the state of being a Christian is something they get without the exercise of their will, I contradict what I have been teaching." The dear old man walked up and down the aisle shaking his robes. I said: "A house divided against itself cannot stand." You must have an Episcopalian teacher to teach your doctrine." So I was shut out from teaching in the only two churches in Richmond.

I could not be satisfied. I tried to get the Methodist church for a Mission school in the afternoon, but failed. I got plank for seats and after dinner on Lord's Day I had my hotel dining-room seated and gathered all the little ones I could. These were largely children who went to no Sunday- School. I got five Catholic children to attend. We had an attendance of from thirty to forty. We bought an organ, had our charts and maps. One poor saloon keeper named Frost came several times and always gave a dollar. He was killed in the fight between the Jaybirds and Peckerwoods in Richmond. This work was a blessing to my soul and I have seen happy results from that little school. I kept this up until I left there for Kansas. The last Sunday we all went to the graveyard to study our lesson. I wished by this to impress the little ones with the purpose of the Gospel.

I have had visions and dreams that I know were sent to me by my Heavenly Father to warn or comfort or instruct me. I notice my dreams, not all, but I can tell the significant ones, usually by the impression they make on me. The dream that comes to me just before waking up generally means something to me. To dream of snakes has always been a bad omen to me. When I first started out smashing, while in Wichita jail, I dreamed of two enormous snakes, one on one side of a road, the other on the other; one raised to strike me, the other made no move. I was impressed that the one that was the most venomous and in the attitude of striking me with its fangs was the Republican party, and this has been my deadly foe.

I will here relate a vision I had. One cold night in March, 1889, I heard a groan across the hall. It was about three o'clock in the morning. I found the sufferer to be an old gentleman who was having very severe cramps, so I went down to the kitchen to make a mustard plaster. The hotel was a number of frame buildings, one having twenty-one rooms, and about five or six cottages around the main building. We carried no insurance, and so many would say we had a "firetrap" there. We had a mortgage on the place, and I was kept in terror constantly for fear of fire, and would often spring out of bed at night in my sleep, expecting to see a fire.

I lit a candle, went down stairs through several dark halls. Then I went upstairs again and gave the old man the plaster; afterwards returned to the kitchen, thinking probably I left the candle burning. Things were all dark, but when I started up the stairs, there seemed to be a light shining behind me, which would come and go in flashes, as I ascended. I looked everywhere to see where it came from, but discovered it to be an unnatural manifestation, for I could not see to step nor move by it. It followed me until I got to my room door. It did not alarm me. I felt the sweet, peaceful presence of God, I prayed to him and I could think of no reason for having this blessing from God, except that I had gotten up in the cold to relieve this suffering man. I stood by my bed for a short time praying to God, and thanking him for his goodness to me. I thought Mr. Nation was asleep, but he afterwards told me that he heard me whispering. I slept until late, and when I did go down to breakfast, Mr. Nation and Alex, my son-in-law, were at the table. I told them I had a warning last night, and if I had a Daniel or Joseph they could interpret a vision I had. The peculiar vision of the light was repeated to them, but they paid very little attention to it; being very busy I thought no more of it that day.

Just about three o'clock the next morning, I was awakened by the cry of fire. Charlien screamed from the next room: "Mamma, the town is on fire." I ran out and the whole heavens seemed to be on fire. It had originated in a drugstore and was sweeping towards the hotel. I immediately ran upstairs and began to pray. I told God "There wasn't a dishonest dollar so, far as I knew in the house, and that He told me "to call on Him in a day of trouble," and said, "this is my day of trouble, and begged He would hear me. Many of the guests passed by, some of them with baggage in their hands and some still dressing. I prayed until I seemed to get an answer of security. One lady, Mrs. Moore, the wife of a physician, who had boarded with me a long time, had a very elegant set of furniture, and she called to me several times to take my things out of the hotel. She had two colored men moving her furniture I heard her say to several persons: "That woman has lost her mind." All the boarders had their trunks out and everyone was saying to me: "Why don't you try to save your furniture?" I would take hold of some things to take out, but it seemed something would intimate, "Let it be." I walked down the street and Mr. Blakely, one of the men who was killed in the Jaybird and Peckerwood battle in Richmond said: "Are you insured?"

I said: "Yes, up there," pointing to Heaven.

All fear was gone, and now in the time of almost certain danger I was confident of deliverance, when before I had been nervous, in time when all was secure. At last the cry came in: "You are saved." I went in the hotel office, sat down by the stove and Alex, my son-in-law, was by me. I said to him: "Oh, Alex, my vision!" He looked almost paralyzed, for I had told him it was a warning and all the circumstances. From that day to this I have never had any fear of fire.

ENTERTAINING ANGELS UNAWARES.

One noon I was busy with the guests and waiting on the tables, and going to the kitchen I saw sitting on the wood-box a poor dejected looking creature, a man about twenty-four years of age. He asked me if I had any tinware to mend. I told him, "No, but you can have your dinner." He said. "I don't want any." He looked the picture of dispair. I said: "Don't go until I can speak to you."

When I had time I told him I wanted some one to wash dishes. He consented to stay, and I felt at that time I must care for that poor creature or he would die. He stayed with us three years and proved to be a jewel. All the rest of my help was colored, and generally speaking, white and colored help do not assimilate, but they all had profound respect for Smith. He soon owned his horse and did the draying for the hotel. Then he got to be a clerk, and bought pecans for the northern market. All his family had died from consumption, and he was traveling for his health. He left us for Pierce's Sanitarium, Buffalo, N. Y., and stayed there some time for treatment. He ran a little booth by the Niagara Bridge, and soon accumulated quite a little sum. He became a Christian and married. I often got letters from him expressing so much gratitude. He was an infidel when he first came, and he said it was my influence that made him a Christian.

I often had the Orthodox Jews to stop with me. They ate nothing that contained lard; their food was mackerel, eggs, bread and coffee. The rates were two dollars a day, but I charged them only one dollar, and allowed them to pay their bills with something that was in their "pack." My other guests would often regard them with almost scorn, but when they were at their meals I would wait on them myself, showing them this preference, for I could not but respect their sacrifice for the sake of their religion. I have always treated the Jews with great respect. Our Savior was a Jew and said: "Salvation is of the Jews." They are a monument to the truth of the Scriptures, a people without a country; and though they are wanderers upon the face of the earth, they retain their characteristics more than any other people have ever done. If an Italian, German or Frenchman comes to America, in a hundred years he becomes thoroughly an American, losing the peculiarities of his descent. But wherever a Jew goes no matter how long he stays he remains a Jew. This can be said of no other people on earth.

I know by experience that the Jews are tricksters, but they have almost been forced into their cupidity in getting money, yet the greatest promise of deliverance in the Bible is for that nation. The foundation stones of heaven and the pearly gates are named for the twelve tribes. No Christian should scorn a Jew.

One day I was driving down the street of Richmond in a buggy, and Mr. Blakely the merchant I dealt so much with, and also a member of the Methodist church, stopped me, saying that he had something to say to me:

"Your friends are becoming very uneasy about the state of your mind. You are thinking too much on religious subjects, and they asked me to warn you." This gave me a blessed assurance, and I laughed very heartily, saying:

"Your words are indeed a blessing to me, for if I have a religion that the world understands, it is not a religion of the Bible."

I was naturally ambitious and was very fond of nice furniture, china and dainty things, but I have lost all taste for these, and stopped making fashionable calls, for I have seen the vanity and wickedness in fashionable society and costly dressing. I educated myself to look at things as I thought God would, and this change came about after that transaction between my soul and God, at the Methodist church, which I know was the "Baptism of the Holy Ghost;" but did not know then what it was. I had been born in the Christian church, and was taught that only the Apostles had received that gift. I never knew what to call this experience until three years after when I went to Kansas, and had it explained to me by the Free Methodists, and where God gave me a witness that it was true.

We had quite a drought in Texas, everything was parched and burning up, and great concern was felt by all. Charlien said to me one day: "Mamma why don't you pray for rain?"

I was so struck with the idea that I went to the church that night and proposed that we pray for rain. So four ladies were elected to appoint a special meeting. The minister's wife, Mrs. Todd, Mrs. Blakely and myself were the four. We met and we said the first thing is to agree. The minister's wife began to cry and said:

"I have read of so many thunderbolts lately, that I am almost afraid to pray;" and Mrs. Blakely repeated the same, but I told the women this was doubting God in the beginning.

" 'If you ask for bread, will He give you a stone.' I am willing to trust God who said: 'Ask and ye shall receive,' and let Him send the rain any way He pleases." This was finally agreed upon, and the next afternoon the citizens of the town were called to the church to pray for rain.

After the meeting, we were standing on the platform in front of the church, and a sprinkle of rain out of a cloudless sky fell on the platform, and on the shutters of the house. This was nothing but a miracle, and was very astonishing to us all. The next day the clouds began to gather in the sky, and the moisture began, at first, to fall like heavy dew. There was no lightning or thunder and the rain came down in the gentlest manner and continued in this way three days. With this marvelous manifestation in direct answer to prayer, many people said "we would have had the rain any way." "Truly the ox knoweth his owner, and the ass his master's crib, but my people doth not know, my people doth not consider."

I began to think what I should do to fulfill my vow to God, for I vowed to return to Him something for rain, to show my gratitude that I had seen done. There was an old man, about seventy years old, entirely destitute, whose name was Bestwick. I went to see him, asked him to come to the hotel and make his home there. There was also a poor German girl, named Fredricka. I also gave her board at the hotel. These two stayed with me free of charge as long as I lived in Richmond.

There were two political factions in Richmond at this time, one called the "Jaybirds" and the other "Peckerwoods". The latter were people that were in favor of the negro holding offices. This party had control of the country for some time. The head of this party was Garvey, the sheriff. The head of the former was Henry Frost, a saloon-keeper, and to this belonged nearly all the young men of Richmond.

Mr. Nation was correspondent for the Houston Post and he wrote a letter speaking of the bad-influence and conduct of these young men the night before; screaming about the streets and disturbing the peace generally. He went down to meet the trains about twelve o'clock at night. The next night after the article appeared in the Post, he came in and woke me up saying:

"Wife get up; I have been beaten almost to death;" and lighting a lamp, I found that his body was covered with bruises. I bathed him in cold water and otherwise tried to relieve him. He was too faint to tell me the trouble, only the boys had beaten him. I knelt down by the window to pray to God. I began by calling on God to send a punishment on people that would do such a mean, cowardly act. I prayed until I received perfect deliverance from that kind of a spirit, and when I got up from off my knees, it was four o'clock in the morning.

In this crowd was a family of Gibson boys, whose father was an infidel, and encouraged his sons in this matter and in all their bad ways. There were also other boys, Peason, Little, Winston; twenty-one in all. A man by the name of Henry George asked Mr. Nation to come and sit on a bale of cotton on the depot platform, and talk with him; another one of these boys came up and threw Mr. Nation backwards on the platform. Then each one gave him a hit with a stick, or a cane. I don't think there are but two or three of those boys living now. After moving to Kansas, a few months after this I returned to Texas for a visit. I then looked, upon the graves of four of the Gibsons. "Truly, vengeance is mine, I will repay," saith the Lord.

Mr. Nation was very unpopular with the "Jaybird" faction, because they said no Republican should stay in Fort Bend County. The bitterness between these two factions broke out in a war. Garvey and Frost with three others were killed. Before this animosity between them arose, Richmond was a very pleasant place to live. A great deal of sociability existed among the people, but from this time business and social relations were almost entirely ruined.

I visited Richmond in 1902, and I never saw such a difference. The Galveston storm greatly damaged many of the houses, and the ruins were still there. A pall of death seemed to be over the whole place, and one coming into the town would feel a desire to leave it as quickly as possible, if there was not some interest independent of the town. God said: "They shall eat the fruit of their own doing." Still in Richmond God has those who have not bowed their knees to Baal.

Mr. Nation's life was threatened and we had to leave. He went to Kansas where he had a brother. After an application he took charge of a Christian church at Medicine Lodge, Barber County, Kansas. This is January, 1904, and we moved to Kansas about fourteen years ago.

We traded the hotel for property in Medicine Lodge. Charlien, Lola and their husbands moved to themselves and mother Gloyd would consent to stay away from me only until we could get settled in Kansas. She had her trunk prepared for the journey. She was now eighty-six years old, but had remarkable vitality. I said:

"Mother you had better stay here the rest of your life, for Kansas is much colder than this climate."

But she replied: "I came from Vermont and it is very cold there."

She followed me to the train, and when I went to leave her she placed her arms around me and her head on my breast. Her last words were: "I have lived with you and I want to die with you." Oh, how I disliked to leave her! This was the last time I saw her dear, sweet face. We had lived together as constant companions for twenty-three years.

Before I left Richmond, I requested of two of my dear friends, Mrs. Connor and Mrs. Todd, that if mother ever got sick, they would stay by her until the last. In a year from this time she died, being sick only three days. These dear friends stayed by her side until the last. A telegram was sent to me when she was first taken sick, and I wanted to go, but I had no money of my own, and Mr. Nation would not consent. I have never ceased to be sorry for it.

I was very much pleased when I first went to Kansas, for it was a great relief from burdens. We boarded six months. After the year was up, Mr. Nation went to Holton, Kansas, and took charge of a church there. He went before I did, and to save shipping our horse and buggy, I drove through. In order to get a good start and directions for my journey, I went to Bro. Ed. Crouce, who lived on a farm about five miles from town. Our horse was not very safe for he had a way of balking. Bro. Crouce told me to give him a severe cut across the back and give him the reins if he attempted to balk. I tried this on two occasions, following his directions. The horse reared up and acted in a way that terrified me, but I conquered and for ten years I drove that horse. He was a noble beast with almost human sense. This journey was four hundred miles. For a hundred and fifty miles I was accompanied by a young girl of sixteen years of age, who was a farmer's daughter and seemed to be afraid of nothing. She was a great inspiration to me, preparing me to drive the two hundred and fifty miles alone. The great difficulty was in finding places to stop at night. I got so I did not look for large roomy houses for entertainment, but the smaller ones. I found out that the friends of the poor are the poor. Mr. Nation met me at Topeka and he was so pleased that he said: "You shall have this horse and buggy for your own."

Holton was thirty miles north and we drove up together.

I began to have a contempt for popular preaching, keeping apart from "clicks" and "sects". I knew that my husband ought not to be in the ministry. I do not believe he was ever a converted man. This made me very miserable, putting us in a false light before the people. It was my desire to serve God in a simple, humble way. Before the year was out because of some dissatisfaction in the church between Mr. Nation and the board, we left

Holton. I then drove back to Medicine Lodge alone, enjoying my trip very much. Mr. Nation never took charge of a church again. He was a man well versed in law, and at one time rendered valuable service in prosecuting liquor cases in Medicine Lodge.

When I lived in Texas and was keeping hotel in Richmond, one cold rainy morning, a lot of men came in from the train.

I took special notice of one man. His hands were that of a woman, his face was very refined, but his clothes were shabby. He was sitting by himself and I said to him: "You must excuse me but you look so much like a catholic priest I once saw." I did not then dream he was one. Next morning I sent one of the boys that waited on the table to see what was the matter that he did not come down to breakfast. He was sick. I went up to see him and he told me he often had attacks of heart trouble; that he had fallen in a faint in the yard the night before. I asked him if he had any friends. He said: "No." I asked him his business? "You guessed it last night," he replied. Then he told me he was a catholic priest. I was very much astonished for he had on a common suit with a red necktie. I then knew he was in trouble somewhere. He told me he had no money. I told him he was welcome to stay as long as he wished. I gathered up some clean garments and did for him all I could. I felt glad to have this catholic priest in my house. I resolved to ask him concerning their faith. He was one of the saddest man I ever saw and it made my heart ache to see him. I knew so well what it was to have "a heart bowed down with grief and woe," and I saw in this poor creature desolation. I asked him if he should die, what sin he would have to repent of. He said: "I may have sinned in trying to fix up a home for poor priests who come into disfavor with the bishops." His words were: "There is no one so helpless as a catholic priest sent adrift. A boy ten years old knows as well how to make a living for himself. I have been from a boy, in a Jesuit College, St. John's, near New York. You do not know the sorrows of a catholic priest. Few know that so many priests are dying from heart disease. I am trying to get to San Antonio, for a priest there may help me some." He stayed at the hotel five days. One evening he came in the parlor where there was quite a company, and I was astonished to see him so changed. He was no longer the shrinking, crest-fallen man, but he seemed bright and joined in conversation; sang and played on the piano. I soon found out he had been drinking. I wanted to shield him from the scandal and made an excuse to call him from the room, and told him what I did this for. Next morning he came down as "sad as night". I said: "Are you going to leave?" "Yes," he replied. I wrote a note to the conductor, whom I knew well; told him the condition of this poor man; told him to pass him to San Antonio. I had just three dollars, this I gave to him. Oh, the gratitude in the face of this poor man. He raised his hands and asked "Christ, and his mother, the holy martyrs, and the angels to bless me."

In a few days I heard of a priest from Cleveland, Ohio, who through gambling and drinking, had spent thirty thousand dollars of the church's money and he was sent adrift. The name of this priest was John Kelly and on our hotel register the name of this priest was written "John Kelly."

CHAPTER VI.

WHY MY NAME IS NOT ON A CHURCH BOOK, AND WHY THE MINISTERS WITHDREW FROM ME.—CLOSING THE DIVES OF MEDICINE LODGE.—CORA BENNETT, AND WHY SHE KILLED BILLY MORRIS IN A DIVE IN KIOWA.—HER RESURRECTION.—RAIDING A JOINT DRUGSTORE.

I soon saw that I was not popular with the church at Medicine Lodge. I testified to having received the "baptism of the Holy Ghost," and the minister, Mr. Nicholson, took occasion to say that I was not sound in the faith. This church at this time had a board of deacons and elders, who I knew to be unworthy, some of them addicted to intoxicating drinks and other flagrant sins. There was one man whose sincerity I never questioned, Mr. Smith, who had a good report from those in and out of the church.

Mr. Nicholson, the preacher, used to go to a drugstore kept by a noted jointist and infidel. He would sit with him in front of his drugstore. I would rebuke him for "sitting in the seat of the scornful and in the way of sinners."

Whenever I went visiting, I went where I felt I could do some good for Jesus, and at Thanksgiving and Christmas I invited the poor, crippled and blind, to a feast at my house as Jesus said to never invite those who were able to make a feast.

There was a Mrs. Tucker, who was quite young and married to an old man. She worked hard, washing, to care for her five children. I would take her to church and it was not long before she joined. There was rejoicing in Heaven, but none in the church at Medicine Lodge. For two years she attended church, and not an officer or member ever called to see her. I would visit her, and often take her clothes for her children, also read the Bible, and prayed with her. I did not wish her to notice the lack of all Christian fellowship, but she saw the cool way in which she was treated and she stopped going to church. A false report of treachery was told to this minister by her unfeeling, jealous husband, and without going to see this poor woman, it was decided to take her name from the church book.

One Lord's Day morning, before Mr. Nicholson commenced his sermon, he said: "It is the painful duty of the church to withdraw fellowship from Sister Tucker, who had been living in open adultery." I was sitting in front, and I rose to my feet.

Mr. Nicholson said: "You sit down, the elders will attend to this."

I said: "No, the elders will not, but I will. What you have said is not true about this woman. She has been a member of the church for two years, and neither you nor the elders or any member of this church but myself have been in her home. I do for that woman what I would want some one to do for me, under the same circumstances. These elders never reclaim the erring or pray with the dying, but this poor little lamb has come in for shelter, and they are pulling the fleece off of her."

All this time Mr. Nicholson was telling me in angry tones to "sit down". He then called on the elders to take me out, came down from the pulpit, took me by the arm intending to put me out himself, but he could not move me. I turned to the audience, told them what the preacher said could not be proven. The Normal was in session and there were many strangers present. I sat down as calmly as if nothing had happened out of the usual, and waited until the close.

Mr. Nicholson came to me after service and said: "We will settle your case."

I said: "Do your worst and do your best."

That afternoon the elders met in the church, and withdrew from me because I was a "stumbling block," and a "disturber of the peace." This was a grief to me, for my beloved father, mother, brothers and sisters belonged to this society of Christians, and I had, since I was a child ten years of age. I wept much over this, but I went to church as usual, not so much to the Christian church, but the Baptist, where they were very kind to me.

Bro. Wesley Cain had charge of that church and this man and his wife were a tower of strength to me. What this man and wife did for the people of Medicine Lodge will receive approbation on "That Day," at the resurrection of the just.

Mrs. Cain was local president of the W. C. T. U. and she was at her post; was self-sacrificing, and had such a sympathizing heart. The poor never applied to Bro. Cain and his noble wife in vain. I have much to thank them for.

I was Jail Evangelist at this time for the W. C. T. U. and I learned that almost everyone who was in jail was directly or indirectly there from the influence of intoxicating drinks. I began to ask why should we have the result of the saloon, when Kansas was a prohibition state, and the constitution made it a crime to manufacture, barter, sell or give away intoxicating drinks? When I went to Medicine Lodge there were seven dives where drinks were sold. I will give some reasons why they were removed. I began to harass these dive-keepers, although they were not as much to blame as the city officials who allowed them to run. Mart Strong was a noted joint-keeper. He and his son, Frank, were both bad drinking characters, and would sell it every chance they got. Mart had a dive and I was in several times to talk to him, and he would try to flatter me and turn things into a joke. When he saw I did not listen to such talk, treated me very rude. One Saturday I saw quite a number of men into his place, and I went in also. Saloons in Kansas generally have a front room to enter as a precaution, then a back room where the bar is. I didn't get farther than the front, for Mart came hastily, taking me by the shoulders and said: "Get out of here, you crazy woman." I was singing this song:

Who hath sorrow? Who hath Woe?
They who dare not answer no;
They whose feet to sin incline,
While they tarry at the wine.

CHORUS:

They who tarry at the wine cup
They who tarry at the wine cup.
They who tarry at the wine cup.

Who hath babblings, who hath strife?
He who leads a drunkard's life;
He whose loved ones weep and pine,
While he tarries at the wine.

Who hath wounds without a cause?
He who breaks God's holy laws;
He who scorns the Lord divine,
While he tarries at the wine.

Who hath redness at the eyes?
Who brings poverty and sighs?
Unto homes almost divine,
While he tarries at the wine?

Touch not, taste not, handle not:
Drink will make the dark, dark blot,
Like an adder it will sting,
And at last to ruin bring,
They who tarry at the drink."

I continued to sing this, with tears running down my face. When I finished the song there was a great crowd; some of the men had tears in their eyes as well. James Gano, the constable, was standing near the door and said: "I wish I could take you off the streets." I said: "Yes, you want to take me, a woman, whose heart is breaking to see the ruin of these men, the desolate homes and broken laws, and you a constable, oath-bound to close his man's unlawful business."

The treatment I got at the hands of this Mart Strong was told to the mayor and councilmen, and there was great indignation. The councilmen went to Mart's place that night. The door was locked and a number of gamblers were in there. The mayor forced the door open and told Mart Strong never to open business in the town again. He left next day; and this closed up one of the worst places in the town. Then there was Henry Durst, another jointist of long standing who was a German and had accumulated quite a lot of property by this dishonest business. He was a prominent Catholic. A Mrs. Elliott, a good Christian woman, came to my home crying bitterly and between sobs told me, that for six weeks her husband had been drinking at Durst's bar, until he was crazy. She had been washing to feed her three children and for some days had nothing in the house but cornbread and molasses. She said that her husband had come in, wild with drink and run his family out and kicked over the table and she said: "I came to you to ask you what to do."

I did not speak a word, for I was too full of conflicting feelings; but I put on my bonnet and Sister Elliott asked me what I was going to do. I told her that I did not know, but for her to come with me. We walked down to Henry Durst's place, a distance of half a mile. I fell down on my knees before the screen and began to call on God. There were five men in there drinking. I was indifferent to those passing the street. It was a strange sight to see women on their knees on the most prominent part of the street. I told God about this man selling liquor to this woman's husband, and told Him she had been washing to get bread, and asked God to close up this den and drive this man out. Mrs. Elliott also prayed. We then told this man that God would hear and that hell was his portion if he did not change. In a short time he closed his bar, left his family there, and went to another state. His property was sold gradually and he never returned, except to move his family away, and I heard afterwards he was reduced to poverty.

Another jointist was named Hank O'Bryan. In passing his place one night from prayer-meeting, I smelled the horrid drink and went in. A man by the name of Grogan was there, half drunk, and I said: "You have a dive here." Mr. Grogan replied: "No, Mother Nation, you are wrong, and I can prove it."

"Let me see what you have in the back room," I asked. "All right, Mother," he said, and took me through several windings, until I came to a very small room with a table covered with beer bottles, that had been recently emptied, and in one corner sat a man, Mr. Smith, a man from Sharon, who the W. C. T. U. had been talking of handling for selling liquor in that town. Mr. Grogan introduced me to him, and he, Mr. Smith, looked terrified and astonished. I took up one of the bottles and asked what it had contained. His reply: "Hop Tea." I asked: "What name is that on the label?" It was "Anheuser-Busch," but I could get neither of them to pronounce it. I turned up one of the bottles and put it to my lips and told them that it was beer, and that I could take an oath that it was. Grogan threw up his hands saying: "Now, Mother Nation, if you get me into trouble I will do something desperate." I had visited this man Grogan in jail about a year before this, where he was put for getting drunk and fighting. I said: "I do not wish to get either of you in trouble, but want to get you out." I had my Bible with me and I opened it to several passages where drink was condemned, and told them where it would lead. I told them I would not speak of this to anyone. When I said I would not "tell on them" the look of gladness on their faces was pitiful to see.

I said, I am going to pray God to have mercy on you. Kneel down, like two obedient little children—they knelt—some may smile at this, but I was deeply affected and felt a compassion and tenderness toward these poor men, whom the devil was leading captive at his will. That prayer I offered, was heard.

In one week from that time this man Grogan came to my house; one Sunday morning, and fell down at my feet crying and wringing his hands, saying: "Oh! Mrs. Nation I am going to hell, but it is not your fault and I came to ask you to pray for me." He was in great agony of soul. He had been drinking until he was almost crazy. He left in about half an hour, saying he "was going to hell," but I told him, no; to have faith in God and He would save him.

This was the last I saw of him, but I heard afterwards that he had a small store in Wichita and was living in the rear of it with his family. The person that told me of him, said that he asked Mr. Grogan if he sold liquor. His answer was: "No, I got enough of that in Medicine Lodge." This Mr. Smith became a wreck for a time, and lost his business in Sharon. After I came out of jail in Wichita the third time, I met a man on the street and he made himself known as the Smith of Sharon. He looked quite well and said he had quit drinking entirely and was a real estate dealer in Wichita.

I soon heard of its being told around in Medicine Lodge that I drank beer in a dive. So I went to Hank O'Bryan's restaurant and said: "Some of these jointists are telling that I drank in a dive. Now if it comes to the ears of the public, I will have to go on the witness stand and tell where I drank beer." Hank turned pale, looked comical and I never heard any more of that.

There was a saloon keeper in Kiowa, named "Billy" Morris and living with him as his wife was a girl whose name was Cora Bennett. This poor girl had been living an irregular life, but was true to this man, who had promised her time after time to marry her, but was only deceiving her. She entered his bar room one day and told him he must fulfill his promise to her now, or she would kill him. He tried to laugh at her. She fired a shot and killed him on the spot; then the poor girl fell on his dead body screaming in a distracted manner. She was arrested and brought to jail at Medicine Lodge; and was there six months. Being Jail Evangelist I went to see her, sometimes twice a week. When I first saw her she was reticent, and did not seem glad to see me. She was so nice, that I fell in love with her and I asked the ladies of the W. C. T. U. to visit her, but they thought her a hopeless case. She bought a Bible and we would read and pray together and talked about the need of Christ in our lives. She was a woman of great sympathy. I asked her once: "Did you ever love anyone." She wept bitterly and said: "Yes, the man I killed."

Toward the last she seemed perfectly delighted when I came to her cell. She, consented to go to a home where she would have friends who would keep her, to make a change in her life. The morning she left I went to the jail and rode with her in the hack to the depot and then to a town about twenty miles east of Medicine Lodge, called Attica. On the train from Medicine Lodge to Attica, the deputy sheriff had some man to give this girl a letter from him, telling her to meet him at Wellington. The girl's father lived at Attica, and an older sister of her's met us. I could see the sister was not a good woman, and she took Cora to a room and exchanged the modest hat and dress for a showy hat and elaborate silk dress; and when I saw her it almost broke my heart. I said to her: "Oh, Cora, all my work to save you is in vain." I had rather have seen her drop dead, and I grieved all the way home. From Attica she went to Wellington, instead of Olathe, Kansas, where she was to enter this home. James Dobson was sheriff of Barber County and his brother kept a saloon in Kiowa, the first saloon I ever smashed.

I heard no good news of Cora for some years; she led a bad life. Five years later, through a W. C. T. U. lecturer, I heard that she was married and living in Colorado; and she was an efficient worker as a W. C. T. U. woman; among fallen women. She told of her past life and of a Mrs. Nation visiting her. This woman said it was so incredible to believe that Cora could have been so bad, and had taken a human life, that she was anxious to see the place in Kiowa and to see Cora's prison cell and myself. I was then in Oklahoma, and I certainly rejoiced over this news from her I had learned to love. I saw in this wayward girl certain qualities that would be a power for good, if once God could have His way with her life.

There are diamonds in the slush and filth of this world. Happy is he who picks them up and helps to wash the dirt away, that they may shine for God. I am very much drawn to my fallen sisters. Oh! the cruelty and oppression they meet with! If the first stone was cast by those who were guiltless, those who were to be stoned would rarely get a blow.

O. L. DAY'S DRUG STORE.

There was a druggist, O. L. Day, in Medicine Lodge who was unlawfully selling intoxicating liquor. He himself was drinking; also his clerk. I got a knowledge of a deposit of this contraband goods. I put a little boy on my buggy horse and sent a letter to our dear Sister Cain, who was president of our local union. She called several of the women together at our W. C. T. V. room and made known to them what I knew of O. L. Day receiving these intoxicants. There was a great deal of discussion, but at last it was decided that we should investigate. At that time I was regarded as a fanatic, and many of these were afraid for me to plan for them, so I kept very quiet. It was finally agreed that Mrs. A. L. Noble and Mrs. Runyan should go first and see how matters were. Sister Runyan finally said before we got there: "Let Mrs. Nation go in my place." I said: "Thank God!" Oh, I was so glad, for I felt that I could handle this case.

{illust. caption =
THIS IS A PICTURE OF A SOCIETY I ORGANIZED IN DEWEY COUNTY, OKLA., WHEN WE
LIVED IN DOUGOUTS. WE WOULD GO FROM HOUSE TO HOUSE, WASH, SEW, CLEAN HOUSE,
AND OTHERWISE HELP THE HELPLESS.}

O. L. Day was a real gentleman by nature. He was the man with one fault, and that was alcoholism. Mrs. Noble said: "You do the talking." While we were in the W. C. T. U. room discussing, Sister Runyan said: "I will not have anything to do with this if Mrs. Nation does." I kept still, praying for the raid to go through, even if I was not in it; and when it came to the point, I had just what I wanted. I felt entirely equal to the occasion. Sister Runyan did not understand me then, for we are the best of friends and she has been true to me in my efforts to defend the homes of Kansas. I told Mr. Day, we, as a W. C. T. U. thought he had not been dealing fairly, and I looked at his little back room suspiciously, as much as to say: "I would like to see what you have in there." He said: "Ladies would you like to go in the room?" I said: "Yes." I knew I could discover the secret. I saw behind the prescription case a ten gallon keg. I said to myself: "That is a find." About this time the rest of the women, accompanied by Sister Cain, came in the front door. Mr. Day was as white as death all the time. As soon as he went to the front I smelled the keg bung. I turned it on one side and rolled it to the front saying; "Women, this is the whiskey!" Mr. Day's clerk caught the end of the keg to turn it out of my hands and on the other side of it was Jim Gano, the marshal, who I think hauled all the divekeepers' goods to them. He was a Republican and in with the whiskey ring and a "rummy" himself. I then placed a foot on each side of the keg and held it firm with both feet and hands. Jim Gano sprang in front of me and with his chest against my head, I thought certainly he would break my neck. I called to the women to help me. Mrs. Noble caught him by one side of the collar and some one the other side and held him back against the counter until I could roll the keg out into the street. All this time Sister Cain, like a general, was saying: "Don't any one touch these women. They are right. They are christian women, trying to save the boys of our state." I called for a hatchet from the hardware store of Mr. Case. He was very angry and said: "No!" He also, was drinking too much. I called to Mrs. Noble to get a sledge hammer from the blacksmith shop across the street. She did and handed it to me. I struck with all my might. The whiskey flew high in the air. The ladies came near to pour it out, but I said: "Save some." So Sister Runyan got a bottle and filled it. Then we poured it out and set it afire. I fell on my knees in the middle of the street and thanked God for this victory. Dr. Gould, a man "fit for treason, stratagem and spoils," was the one to help Day dispose of these drinks, as many doctors do. This doctor gave out that this was "California Brandy", costing seventy-five dollars, that he had advised Day to get it for medical purposes.

Mr. Day was at this time getting a permit to sell it for medical purposes. He appeared in court to prove he was a graduated pharmacist, never drank, and never had a clerk that did. The W. C. T. U. were there in a body. We contested his right to have the permit. Poor man. I pitied him. He was very much under the influence of intoxicants. When asked; "What that was in the keg the ladies rolled out of his drug store on the 16th of February?" he said: "It was California brandy." When asked: "If he knew the taste of whiskey and brandy," he said: "Yes." We handed him a bottle of this that he said was brandy. He pronounced it "a poor quality of sour mash whiskey." Sister Runyan was then put on the stand and said: "It came from the keg that was smashed."

This man was so humbled that he sold out in a month and left Medicine Lodge. There are parties in that town who are more responsible than O. L. Day. They did every thing in their power to have him do that which was his ruin. In retaliation for this the republican rum element one night made an attack on Sister Cain's and my house, broke windows and threw rocks, and broke my buggy. They also sent a negro to my house, named Haskel, a noted bootlegger. He asked for an interview. He had quite a tale to tell me about hearing some men say that if the women appeared against Day that my house would go. I am so well acquainted with the colored race I could read him from the first and knew that these "Rummies" had put this negro up to intimidate me. I listened as if I believed. Then I said: "Haskel you ought to know by this time that such men as these will not prevent me from doing my duty, besides should my home be burned, it would be a lecture in favor of my cause that would be worth more to me than the home. Now Haskel you get in the company of these men and you tell them what I have told you." This negro pretended to me that he came to me as a friend. When I told him what I did, his expression was amusing to see.

CHAPTER VII.

SPIRITUAL LEADINGS.—JESUS A CONSCIOUS PRESENCE THREE DAYS.—LOSS OF LIBERTY BY COMPROMISING.— THE PRICE PAID TO BE REINSTATED.—DISGRACE TO BE A MILLIONAIRE

I had once while in Medicine Lodge, a heavenly rapture for three days. My Savior was my constant companion. I saw no form, heard no word. But His dear face was just behind and looking over my right shoulder. He was a conscious presence and the deep peace was beyond any experience I ever had. I shunned the society of persons. I would talk to Him, would sing and play the accompaniment on the organ. I was particular about my home work. While I saw no face, or form, I realized that His was a sweet, smiling, gratified expression, and it told me I was pleasing Him. I did not seem then to think this anything wonderful, and have often reproached myself for not setting more store by this at the time.

There was a period of from six months to a year that I was terribly haunted by a feeling as if hung over a precipice. I was hanging only by a rope above my head held by a hand out of a cloud. At night or in the day, it was the same uneasy dread of falling. The precipice below was black and horrible. There were banks on each side. At last I swung over, landing on the right side. Oh! the relief!

When I first began to pray in public I was very awkward, never could make any but what one would call a disconnected prayer, that never seems to be impressive in an audience.

I asked an old-fashioned sister, who I knew was a saint, to tell me what was wrong in my testimony. "I do not have liberty when I speak." She said: "You do not praise God enough." I began to pray for a spirit of praise. Shortly after this I was at prayer-meeting, was praying for a spirit of praise. It was put in my mouth I rose to my feet and began to say: "Praise God; Praise God!" repeating it over and over. Oh! how sweet to use and hear those words! I could scarcely repress the impulse to use them all the time. For a long time after this, when the Bible was read or testimony struck me as being just right, I would audibly say: "Praise God!" This was a "gift", for I had never felt the impulse before. I have in a measure left this off, but I use it all the time, when I hear good news, or see what pleases me. "He led captivity (sin) captive and gave GIFTS unto men." Ever since I received the "baptism of the Holy Ghost," I have liked one church about as well as another. I go to all even the Catholic. I fast on Friday and use the sign of the cross. Fast, because my Savior suffered in the flesh on Friday; use the sign of the cross, because in the cross is salvation. Meditations on the cross always lift heavenward. 'Tis the royal way, I want to keep it always in view, want it to be the last I see. We who bear the cross continually in this transient life, will wear the crown continually in the eternal. I love a picture of the cross or a crucifix. I am debtor both to the Jew and the Greek. I do not feel the dislike to the Catholic church that some Protestants do. I believe there are as many honest priests as there are other ministers. God's church is invisible to the world, for it is set up in the hearts of the children of men. I have been greatly edified by conversing with Catholic priests. When I lived in Texas my spiritual condition was such that I wanted some explanation. I went to see Father Hennesy, of Houston, I explained to him my strange leadings, he said a wise and good thing, told me to "read the scriptures and pray and God would lead me right."

I was at church in Medicine Lodge one night, during a protracted meeting held by Bro. Parker and Hodges. Two sisters came to me and complained that I made so much noise, said they could not enjoy the service. I said: "To please you I will try to keep quiet, but remember it is my God and YOUR God I am praising. I would rejoice to hear you praise Him." Next night something was said that was good to me. I said: "Praise God!" caught myself when I saw one of the sisters near, and from that time I felt little impulse and at last none. I went to every meeting but lost my liberty and became so bound, I could not testify or pray. I was very miserable, would weep from a desolation of spirit. This continued for three weeks. The meeting was still going on. My spiritual darkness became so great, I went up one afternoon to the altar. I rose and told of how I had "lost my liberty and peace by withholding praise to God by trying to please two sisters." While I was confessing, the spirit fell in great power and I acted like I was beside myself, was almost wild with delight. I seemed to fly home and back in the evening. One in this state appears crazy to the world, even disgusting. No one sees a reason for this unnatural overflow of feeling. At the beginning of the service, opportunity was given for testimony. I rose eager to tell of my returned joy; told of praying for, and getting what I prayed for, then losing it, by compromise; closed by saying: "That never again would I refuse to do the will of God even if it offended all and made me appear a fool." My testimony seemed to be fanatical, for my manner indicated one greatly moved. When I took my seat a "still small voice" said. "You must sing a song." Bro. Osburn was sitting near. He had the song book "Finest of the Wheat," in his hands. I took it then handed it back. I felt like one in a dreadful dilemma—all joy had given place to fear. Bro. Osburn again handed me the book. I felt then I must go through this trying ordeal. I took the book, walked up to the front, all were standing, the church crowded and Bro. Parker gave out the number of the hymn "40". "No," I said, "We will sing No. 3." This song was, "I know Not Why This Wondrous Grace To Me He Hath Made Known." Bro. Parker gave out the number again. I said, "No," and began to sing. Bro. Allen accompanied me with his cornet. Of course one can imagine what an impression this would make on an audience. I sang, two verses and the chorus. I then took my seat. Then a flood of peace and heavenly companionship took possession of me. I then knew what it was to have angels minister unto you. God took me at my word and made me appear a "fool," and objectionable, to the whole people. What a fatal result there might have been, if I had not obeyed God!

I know why people do not have power with God. They will not abandon themselves to the whole will of God, because they will not suffer the OFFENSE of the cross. Why care for the criticism of men that change and die!

I had an experience once for eight months, when I felt that Christ had turned his face from me, not in displeasure, but this was a trial of faith. My prayers had no response, brought me no hope of having been heard. But I prayed quite as much, if not more. Never got discouraged, although I was in gloom, and my heart was like lead. All at once there was a return of the conscious presence of God. 'Tis a poor servant that serves only for hire. "Though He slay me yet will I trust Him." God has kept me from following any but Him.

One dear friend thought that Haney was the great holiness teacher, another one thought Carodine. They would quote their sayings, but I always found better and clearer teaching in the word of God. I could see errors in all the holiness teachers, but not one in the Bible. The book of Job settled the question of the most perfect experience. Men can be perfect men and not perfect saints. When Job was, "holding fast his integrity" God did not bless him like He did when Job saw the perfection of God and said: "Wherefore I abhor myself and repent in dust and ashes." The Sermon on the Mount is the greatest lesson in holiness and is from the only one that can teach holiness. Great lessons can be taught by all persons, taught of God, but 'tis better to drink at the fountain than out of a stale bucket. Besides all have imperfection. "To the law and to the testimony if they speak not according to this word it is because there is no light in them." "They shall all be taught of God." "If any lack wisdom, let him ask of God who giveth to all liberally and upbraideth not, and it shall be given."

From the time that my Christian experience began, I never wished to be associated with rich people, or rather people that had wealth for display. Would feel uncomfortable to go in a house filled with furniture or bric-a-brac. It would be an evidence to me of the great waste of money and time by the owner. Nothing had value to me only as it could be used for the salvation of men and women, and the glorifying of God. It mortified me to see a "swell dressed" woman. I noticed that those so- called fashionable women really never had time or money to do charity. Of course there are exceptions. The display of wealth to me is an evidence of a depraved nature. The use of wealth, is in relieving the wants of mankind. The time is coming when the millionaires will be the despised of the people, for they are learning fast that people who amass fortunes, and hoard them, are in that condition because they have ground the face of the poor. They are not honest or good. A man or woman now that can hoard money or goods and pass and repass the suffering every day, has a cold, selfish heart, and instead of its being in the future a letter of credit to say: "Mr. So and So is a millionaire," it will be a disgrace as it should be, to live for wealth and self alone. Still 'tis well to get all the money in a good way, that you can and then use it in a good cause. Job was a rich man but he was a friend of the "fatherless and widow." "He dealt his bread to the hungry. He was feet to the lame and eyes to the blind." Such rich men as Job are blessings, but those men who boast of their hoarded treasures, spend their money in the gratification of their lusts, to them God says: "Woe or curses unto you rich men! Weep and howl for your miseries that shall come upon you! Your garments are motheaten, your gold is cankered and the rust shall eat your flesh as if it were fire." Yes, there is a class of rich men that would now HOWL, and weep with all their money, if they knew their fate.

I have never had so light a heart or felt so well satisfied as since I smashed those murder mills. For years I had an aching, weeping heart. I would often put ashes on my head. I felt like wearing sackcloth. I can see the hand of God in my life. From a small child I loved the world, used to be fond of pets. It seemed that my pets always came to grief. Then I was very anxious to be thought smart. Would try to write and wanted a thorough education. I became almost an invalid. Could not attend school. Was hindered on account of the circumstances brought about by the Civil war. The man I loved and married brought to me bitter grief. The child I loved so well became afflicted and never seemed to want my love. The man I married, hoping to serve God, I found to be opposed to all I did, as a Christian. I used to wonder why this was. I saw others with their loving children and husbands and I would wish their condition was mine. I now see why God saw in me a great lover, and in order to have me use that love for Him, and others, He did not let me have those that would have narrowed my life down to my own selfish wishes. Oh! the grief He has sent me! Oh! the fiery trials! Oh! the shattered hopes! How I love Him for this! "Whom the Lord loveth He chasteneth and scourgeth every son whom He receiveth." There are pages in my life that have had much to do in bringing me in sympathy with the fallen tempted natures. These I cannot write, but let no erring, sinful man or woman think that Carry Nation would not understand this, for Carry Nation is a sinner saved by grace and I know He can save to the uttermost, all that come unto Him. "Heaven is made for redeemed sinners and hell for the proud and disobedient." When I see the proud glance, the boastful manner, the display of, "I am better than thou," I feel pity and commiseration for the poor dying creature and see "behind the face a grinning skull". I like the companionship of the servant in the kitchen more than the mistress in the parlor. I covet the humblest walk. I wish for the power, often, to make the rich take back seats, and give the front to the poor, the crippled, the lame and the blind. I will not have a piece of fine furniture. I have no carpets on my floors. I have two small rooms in Topeka in the building I desire to give to the W. C. T. U. for prohibition work. The little cupboard I use is made of a dry-goods box, with shelves in it, a curtain in front. My dishes, all told, kitchen and dining-room, are not worth five dollars. This is what the poor have, and better than some have. It is good enough. It is better than my blessed Lord had. I desire nothing better. I would feel like a reprobate to fill my room with expensive furniture, using money I could feed the hungry with, clothe the naked, doing things that would please my Lord. What a change! I used to delight in cut-glass, china, plush, velvet and lace. Now I can say "vanity of vanity, all is vanity!" There may be almost selfishness in this eager desire I have to give away the means that are at my disposal. What I use or leave behind will never be placed to my credit in the bank of heaven. What we give away for the love of God and our neighbor is all we take with us. I will be so delighted with a home that I can call mine, forever. I like nice wearing apparel but I will not be deceived by spending my time and means for that which will hinder me from having them where moth and rust doth not corrupt and where thieves do not break through and steal. So I wish to make to myself friends of the mammon of unrighteousness and not enemies, for the hoarded dollars are bitter foes that will be witnesses against these rich men at That Day. I am praying that God may send me means to carry out a plan to save Kansas from traitors. The state has made herself a name, that will endure forever, because she began a warfare against a government at a time when few were wise enough to see that this revolution meant defiance to the rum-soaked republican rule. Every moral reform is a protest against this government we live under. What does the W. C. T. U. mean? The mothers banding themselves together to prevent the Government from slaughtering them.

From the beginning of my Christian experience I have devoted myself to the poor. I prayed God to give me opportunity to be helpful to those who were destitute of the comforts of life. The people of Medicine Lodge were so good to aid me. I could go to the stores and ask for flour, sugar and different kinds of eatables and get them. There was one man I never asked in vain, when I wished aid for the poor, that was C. Q. Chandler, a man who was able to help. I have taken poor children to his house and he has given me orders at the dry-goods stores to clothe them, so they could attend school. He has given me money frequently to get fuel and clothes for those who needed them. One Christmas he wrote me a letter, asking me for the names of all the poor ones and asking me to name something they needed. I did, and all got something useful. Such men are worthy to be stewards of God's treasury.

For years I made it my duty, every fall, to go from house to house to gather clothes for the poor families, wash women and others who had not time to sew for their children. I never allowed a child to stay out of day or Sunday school, for want of clothes. I would sort out these clothes and distribute as needed. Persons would say, "I would be afraid I would make people angry." I said if every one feels that way I will say: "You are not the one I am sent to." I never hurt any ones feelings by offering them these things.

There was a family by the name of French who came into a neighborhood about three miles from town. I heard they were destitute. I filled my buggy and went there and sure enough they were sadly in need. I brought the things in just such as was needed. The family was large. The woman cried like her heart would break, just for gratitude; she could not thank me enough. It takes so little to make some people happy.

I read of a miserable miser once who was on the verge of suicide by the side of a river. A little girl came to him saying: "Please sir, my mother is sick and hungry. Please give me something so I can get her something to eat." The man said within himself: "I will do this for the child before I die." He went to a bakershop and got her a full basket. Then she looked so weak he carried it home to her mother. The poor woman on the pallet of straw, kissed his hands and blessed him. He thought of the money he might use to make people happy. He concluded he would use it before he died for he had enjoyed for the first time in his life the peace that comes from giving. After this his life was a blessing to himself and others. He had found the best use of life.

I once read of a beautiful story of one of the early fathers of the church. He gave away everything even to sufficient clothes to keep himself warm. A rich kind hearted woman made him a coat of fur very expensive. Next time she saw him he did not have it. "Where is that coat father," she asked. He replied: "I thought so much of it I laid it up in heaven. Where moth and rust doth not corrupt and where thieves do not break through and steal." He had given it to the first shivering man he met.

CHAPTER VIII.

THE DIVINE CALL.—THE JOINT DRUGGIST OF MEDICINE LODGE.—BEER A POISON.— DOCTORS MAKE DRUNKARDS.—SMASHING AT KIOWA.—ATTITUDE OF SOME W. C. T. U.'S OF KANSAS.—SUIT FOR SLANDER.— SMASHING AT WICHITA.— CONSPIRACY OF THE REPUBLICANS TO PUT ME IN THE INSANE ASYLUM.— SUFFERINGS IN JAIL AT WICHITA.—SLANDERS FROM THE RUM-SOAKED PAPERS OF KANSAS.

At the time these dives were open, contrary to the statutes of our state, the officers were really in league with this lawless element. I was heavily burdened and could see "the wicked walking on every side, and the vilest men exalted." I was ridiculed and my work was called "meddler" "crazy," was pointed at as a fanatic. I spent much time in tears, prayer and fasting. While not a Roman Catholic, I have practiced abstinence from meat on Friday, for Christ suffered on that day, and 'tis well for us to suffer. I also use the sign of the cross, for it is medicine to the soul to be reminded of His sufferings. Jesus left us the communion of bread and wine that we might remember His passion. I would also fast days at a time. One day I was so sad; I opened the Bible with a prayer for light, and saw these words: "Arise, shine, for thy light is come and the glory of the Lord is risen upon thee." These words gave me unbounded delight.

I ran to a sister and said: "There is to be a change in my life."

On the 6th of June, before retiring, as I often did, I threw myself face downward at the foot of my bed and told the Lord to use me any way to suppress the dreadful curse of liquor; that He had ways to do it, that I had done all I knew, that the wicked had conspired to take from us the protection of homes in Kansas; to kill our children and break our hearts. I told Him I wished I had a thousand lives, that I would give Him all of them, and wanted Him to make it known to me, some way. The next morning, before I awoke, I heard these words very distinctly: "Go to Kiowa, and" (as in a vision and here my hands were lifted and cast down suddenly.) "I'll stand by you." I did not hear these words as other words; there was no voice, but they seemed to be spoken in my heart. I sprang from my bed as if electrified, and knew this was directions given me, for I understood that it was God's will for me to go to Kiowa to break, or smash the saloons. I was so glad, that I hardly looked in the face of anyone that day, for fear they would read my thoughts, and do something to prevent me. I told no one of my plans, for I felt that no one would understand, if I should.

I got a box that would fit under my buggy seat, and every time I thought no one would see me, I went out in the yard and picked up some brick-bats, for rocks are scarce around Medicine Lodge, and I wrapped them up in newspapers to pack in the box under my buggy seat. I also had four bottles I had bought from Southworth, the druggist, with "Schlitz-Malt" in them, which I used to smash with. I bought two kinds of this malt and I opened one bottle and found it to be beer. I was going to use these bottles of beer to convict this wiley joint-druggist.

One of the bottles I took to a W. C. T. U. meeting, and in the presence of the ladies I opened it and drank the contents. Then I had two of them to take me down to a Doctor's office. I fell limp on the sofa and said: "Doctor, what is the matter with me?"

He looked at my eyes, felt my heart and pulse, shook his head and looked grave.

I said: "Am I poisoned or in an abnormal state?"

"Yes, said the Doctor." I said: "What poisoned me is that beer you recommended Bro. —— to take as a tonic." I resorted to this stratagem, to show the effect that beer has upon the system. This Doctor was a kind man and meant well, but it must have been ignorance that made him say beer could ever be used as a medicine.

There was another, Dr. Kocile, in Medicine Lodge who used to sell all the whiskey he could. He made a drunkard of a very prominent woman of the town, who took the Keely cure. She told the W. C. T. U. of the villainy of this doctor and she could not have hated anyone more. Oh! the drunkards the doctors are making! No physician, who is worthy of the name will prescribe it as a medicine, for there is not one medical quality in alcohol. It kills the living and preserves the dead. Never preserves anything but death. It is made by a rotting process and it rots the brain, body and soul; it paralyzes the vascular circulation and increases the action of the heart. This is friction and friction in any machinery is dangerous, and the cure is not hastened but delayed.

I have given space in this book to one of the most scientific articles, showing how dangerous alcohol is to the human system.

Any physician that will prescribe whiskey or alcohol as a medicine is either a fool or a knave. A fool because he does not understand his business, for even saying that alcohol does arouse the action of the heart, there are medicines that will do that and will not produce the fatal results of alcoholism, which is the worst of all diseases. He is a knave because his practice is a matter of getting a case, and a fee at the same time, like a machine agent who breaks the machine to get the job of mending it. Alcohol destroys the normal condition of all the functions of the body. The stomach is thrown out of fix, and the patient goes to the doctor for a stomach pill, the heart, liver, kidneys, and in fact the whole body is in a deranged condition, and the doctor has a perpetual patient. I sincerely believe this to be the reason why many physicians prescribe it.

I was doing my own work at the time God spoke to me; cooking, washing and ironing; was a plain home keeper. I cooked enough for my husband until next day, knowing that I would be gone all night. I told him I expected to stay all night with a friend, Mrs. Springer. I hitched my horse to the buggy, put the box of "smashers" in, and at half past three o'clock in the afternoon, the sixth of June, 1900, I started to Kiowa. Whenever I thought of the consequences of what I was going to do, and what my husband and friends would think, also what my enemies would do, I had a sensation of nervousness, almost like fright, but as soon as I would look up and pray, all that would leave me, and things would look bright. And I might say I prayed almost every step of the way. This Mrs. Springer lived about ten miles south of Medicine Lodge. I often stopped there and I knew that Prince, my horse, would naturally go into the gate, opening on the road, if I did not prevent it. I thought perhaps it was God's will for me to drive to Kiowa that night, so gave the horse the reins, and if he turned in, I would stay all night, if not, I would go to Kiowa. Prince hastened his speed past the gate, and I knew that it was God's will for me to go on. I got there at 8:30 P. M. and stayed all night with a friend. Early next morning I had my horse put to the buggy and drove to the first place, kept by Mr. Dobson. I put the smashers on my right arm and went in. He and another man were standing behind the bar. These rocks and bottles being wrapped in paper looked like packages bought from a store. Be wise as devils and harmless as doves. I did not wish my enemies to know what I had.

I said: "Mr. Dobson, I told you last spring, when I held my county convention here, (I was W. C. T. U. president of Barber County,) to close this place, and you didn't do it. Now I have come with another remonstrance. Get out of the way. I don't want to strike you, but I am going to break up this den of vice."

I began to throw at the mirror and the bottles below the mirror. Mr. Dobson and his companion jumped into a corner, seemed very much terrified. From that I went to another saloon, until I had destroyed three, breaking some of the windows in the front of the building. In the last place, kept by Lewis, there was quite a young man behind the bar. I said to him: "Young man, come from behind that bar, your mother did not raise you for such a place." I threw a brick at the mirror, which was a very heavy one, and it did not break, but the brick fell and broke everything in its way. I began to look around for something that would break it. I was standing by a billiard table on which there was one ball. I said: "Thank God," and picked it up, threw it, and it made a hole in the mirror. While I was throwing these rocks at the dives in Kiowa, there was a picture before my eyes of Mr. McKinley, the President, sitting in an old arm chair and as I threw, the chair would fall to pieces.

The other dive keepers closed up, stood in front of their places and would not let me come in. By this time, the streets were crowded with people; most of them seemed to look puzzled. There was one boy about fifteen years old who seemed perfectly wild with joy, and he jumped, skipped and yelled with delight. I have since thought of that as being a significant sign. For to smash saloons will save the boy.

I stood in the middle of the street and spoke in this way: "I have destroyed three of your places of business, and if I have broken a statute of Kansas, put me in jail; if I am not a law-breaker your mayor and councilmen are. You must arrest one of us, for if I am not a criminal, they are."

One of the councilmen, who was a butcher, said: "Don't you think we can attend to our business."

"Yes," I said, "You can, but you won't. As Jail Evangelist of Medicine Lodge, I know you have manufactured many criminals and this county is burdened down with taxes to prosecute the results of these dives. Two murders have been committed in the last five years in this county, one in a dive I have just destroyed. You are a butcher of hogs and cattle, but they are butchering men, women and children, positively contrary to the laws of God and man, and the mayor and councilmen are more to blame than the jointist, and now if I have done wrong in any particular, arrest me." When I was through with my speech I got in my buggy and said: "I'll go home."

The marshal held my horse and said: "Not yet; the mayor wishes to see you."

I drove up where he was, and the man who owned one of the dive- buildings I had smashed was standing by Dr. Korn, the mayor, and said: "I want you to pay for the front windows you broke of my building."

I said: "No, you are a partner of the dive-keeper and the statutes hold your building responsible. The man that rents the building for any business is no better than the man who carries on the business, and you are "particepts criminus" or party to the crime." They ran back and forward to the city attorney several times. At last they came and told me I could go. As I drove through the streets the reins fell out of my hands and I, standing up in my buggy; lifted my hands twice, saying: "Peace on earth, good will to men." This action I know was done through the inspiration of the Holy Spirit. "Peace on earth, good will to men" being the result of the destruction of saloons and the motive for destroying them.

When I reached Medicine Lodge the town was in quite an excitement, the news having been telegraphed ahead. I drove through the streets and told the people I would be at the postoffice corner to tell why I had done this. A great crowd had gathered and I began to tell them of my work in the jail here, and the young men's lives that had been ruined, and the broken hearted mothers, the taxation that had been brought on the county, and other wrongs of the dives of Kiowa; of how I had been to the sheriff, Mr. Gano, and the prosecuting attorney, Mr. Griffin; how I had written to the state's attorney-general Mr. Godard, and I saw there was a conspiracy with the party in power to violate their oaths, and refuse to enforce the constitution of Kansas, and I did only what they swore they would do. I had a letter from a Mr. Long, of Kiowa, saying that Mr. Griffin, the prosecuting attorney, was taking bribes, and that he and the sheriff were drinking and gambling in the dives at Kiowa.

This smashing aroused the people of the county to this outrage and these dive-keepers were arrested, although we did not ask the prosecuting attorney to get out a warrant, or sheriff to make an arrest. Neither did we take the case before any justice of the peace in Kiowa or Medicine Lodge, for they belong to the republican party and would prevent the prosecution. The cases were taken out in the country several miles from Kiowa before Moses E. Wright, a Free Methodist and a justice of the peace of Moore township.

The men were found guilty, and for the first time in the history of Barber County, all dives were closed. Of course it took two or three months to accomplish this and not a word was said about suing me for slander, until after the dives were closed. Then I began to hear that Sam Griffin was going to sue me for slander, because I said he took bribes. The papers were served on me, but I was not at all alarmed, for I thought it would give me an opportunity to bring out the facts of the case. I knew little about the tricks of lawyers, and the unfair rulings of judges.

I will here speak of the attitude of some of the W. C. T. U. concerning the smashing. Most of this grand body of grand women endorsed me from the first. A few weeks after the Kiowa raid, I held a convention in Medicine Lodge. I got letters from various W. C. T. U. workers of the state that they would hold my convention for me. I said: "No, I will hold my own convention."

Up to this time, no one had ever offered to hold my convention, and I fully understood, although I did not say anything, that the W. C. T. U. did not want it to go out that they endorsed me in my work at Kiowa. The state president came to my home the first day of the convention. I believe this was done, thinking I would ask her to preside at the meeting, or convention. I was glad to see her and asked her to conduct a parliamentary drill. She came to me privately and asked me to state to the convention that the W. C. T. U.

knew nothing about the smashing at Kiowa and was not responsible for this act of mine. I did so, saying the "honor of smashing the saloons at Kiowa would have to be ascribed to myself alone, as the W. C. T. U. did not wish any of it. So far as Sister Hutchinson, who is, and has been the president for some time, is concerned, I believe her to be a conscientious woman, and whose heart is in the right place. She and I have been the best of friends and love each other, and she has often defended me and spoken well of my work. But I think the W. C. T. U. would be much more effective under her management, if she had understood that Stanley, the republican governor, wished to handicap her in her prohibition work when he appointed her husband as physician in the reformatory at Hutchinson, Kansas. Be it said to the credit of this christian physician he never used alcohol in his practice. And perhaps other bearings have prevented her from seeing that the republican pressure has injured our work more than anything else in Kansas. Many of the wives of these political wire-pullers are prominent in the Union. A W. C. T. U. must of necessity be a prohibitionist, for her pledge is a prohibition pledge, not a temperance one.

The Free Methodists, although few in number, and considered a church of but small influence, have been a great power in reform. They were the abolitionists of negro slavery to a man, and now they are the abolitionists of the liquor curse to a man. They were also my friends in this smashing. Father Wright and Bro. Atwood were at the convention I speak of. Father Wright, who has been an old soldier for the defence of Truth for many years said to me: "Never mind, Sister Nation, when they see the way the cat jumps, you will have plenty of friends." The ministers were also my friends and approved of the smashing. Bro. McClain, of the Christian church, was at the convention, and he was trying to apologize for the smashing and defend me at the same time, he said: "We all make mistakes and crooked paths, and Sister Nation we all know, tries to do right, and even if she did some crooked things, all the rest of us do the same thing."

I appreciated his motive, but for the sake of others, I replied: "I could not see that the term 'crooked' should be used. I rolled up the rocks as STRAIGHT as I could, I placed them straight in the box, hitched up my horse straight, drove straight to Kiowa, walked straight in the saloon, threw straight and broke them up in the straightest manner, drove home straight and I did not make a crooked step in smashing." This of course was pleasantry, but it was the way I took to justify myself, as but few seemed to see the merit or result of this crusade.

I never explained to the people that God told me to do this for some months, for I tried to shield myself from the almost universal opinion that I was partially insane.

I will now speak of my persecution for so-called slandering the prosecuting attorney. As I said, no one mentioned such a thing until the dives were closed. Closing the joints, called attention to the perjury of the county officials, for it was proven to be their fault, that we have dives in Kansas. In order to direct the attention from themselves, as perjurers, and to me as insane, and to be avenged, they put their heads together to bring this suit against me. Mr. Griffin was no more to blame in this matter than the rest of the republicans. A. L. Noble, Polly Tincher, Edd Sample, and Mr. Herr, the city attorney of Kiowa, were all employed by Sam Griffin. This practically took all the legal ability, leaving one, G. A. Martin, whom I retained. I had witnesses enough to prove gambling and drinking in these dives by Sam, and the sheriff; had sufficient testimony to justify me in saying what I did. The republican judge of Kingman, Gillette, ruled out my testimony right through. If my case had been conducted properly by my lawyer, and proper exceptions taken, I could have taken the case to the supreme court, and had it reversed on several rulings. Judge Stevens and Judge Lacey, who were at the trial, told me they never saw such determination on the part of any judge to cut out the defense as the rulings of Judge Gillette. It was evident that everything was cut and dried before going into court. Judge Gillette had several pages of instructions to the jury, telling them their duty was to convict and that the damages should be a large sum. I had these instructions examined by a good lawyer, Mr. Duminel, of Topeka, and the judge overleaped his perogative. He should have told the jury the facts and the statute governing slander, but his instructions were an appeal and command to convict me. This Judge Gillette has a reputation for being a respected citizen, but his zeal to save from disgrace his republican colleagues led him to thus persecute a loyal woman Home Defender of Kansas, and protect the rum defenders, and republican schemers, who have done more to injure prohibition in Kansas than any other party. If a democrat wanted to carry on a dive, republicans would grant him the permit to do so.

The jury brought in a verdict of guilty; but the damages to the character of this republican county attorney was one dollar, and of course I sent him the dollar, but the cost which was, including all, about two hundred dollars was assessed to me and a judgement put on a piece of property, which I paid off, by the sale of my little hatchets, and lectures. Strange these trials never caused me to become discouraged, rather the reverse. I knew I was right, and God in his own time would come to my help. The more injustice I suffered, the more cause I had to resent the wrongs. I always felt that I was keeping others out of trouble, when I was in. I had resolved that at the first opportunity I would go to Wichita and break up some of the bold outlawed murder mills there. I thought perhaps it was God's will to make me a sacrifice as he did John Brown, and I knew this was a defiance of the national intrigue of both republican and democratic parties, when I destroyed this malicious property, which afforded them a means of enslaving the people, taxing them to gather a revenue they could squander, and giving them political jobs, thus creating a force to manage the interest and take care of the results of a business where the advantage was in the graft it gave to them and the brewers and distillers.

In two weeks from the close of this trial, on the 27th of December, 1900, I went to Wichita, almost seven months after the raid in Kiowa. Mr. Nation went to see his brother, Mr. Seth Nation, in eastern Kansas and I was free to leave home. Monday was the 26th, the day I started. The Sunday before, the 25th, I went to the Baptist Sunday school then to the Presbyterian for preaching, and at the close walked over to the Methodist church for class meeting. I could not keep from weeping, but I controlled myself the best I could. I did not know but that it would be the last time I would ever see my dear friends again, and could not tell them why. I gave my testimony at the class meeting; spoke particularly to members of the choir about their extravagant dress; told them that a poor sinner coming there for relief would be driven away, to see such a vanity fair in front. I begged them to dress neither in gold, silver or costly array, and spoke of the sin of wearing the corpses of dead birds and plumage of birds, and closed by saying: "These may be my dying words." At the close Sister Shell, a W. C. T. U. said to me: "What do you mean by 'my dying words?' for you never looked better in your life." I said: "You will know later." I never told anyone then of my intention of smashing saloons in Wichita.

I took a valise with me, and in that valise I put a rod of iron, perhaps a foot long, and as large around as my thumb. I also took a cane with me. I found out by smashing in Kiowa that I could use a rock but once, so I took the cane with me. I got down to Wichita about seven o'clock in the evening, that day, and went to the hotel near the Santa Fe depot and left my valise. I went up town to select the place I would begin at first. I went into about fourteen places, where men were drinking at bars, the same as they do in licensed places. The police standing with the others. This outrage of law and decency was in violation of the oaths taken by every city officer, including mayor and councilmen, and they were as much bound to destroy these joints as they would be to arrest a murderer, or break up a den of thieves, but many of these so-called officers encouraged the violation of the law and patronized these places. I have often explained that this was the scheme of politicians and brewers to make prohibition a failure, by encouraging in every way the violation of the constitution. I felt the outrage deeply, and would gladly have given my life to redress the wrongs of the people. As Esther said: "How can I see the desolation of my people? If I perish." As Patrick Henry said: "Give me liberty or give me death."

I finally came to the "Carey Hotel," next to which was called the Carey Annex or Bar. The first thing that struck me was the life-size picture of a naked woman, opposite the mirror. This was an oil painting with a glass over it, and was a very fine painting hired from the artist who painted it, to be put in that place for a vile purpose. I called to the bartender; told him he was insulting his own mother by having her form stripped naked and hung up in a place where it was not even decent for a woman to be in when she had her clothes on. I told him he was a law-breaker and that he should be behind prison bars, instead of saloon bars. He said nothing to me but walked to the back of his saloon. It is very significant that the picture of naked women are in saloons. Women are stripped of everything by them. Her husband is torn from her, she is robbed of her sons, her home, her food and her virtue, and then they strip her clothes off and hang her up bare in these dens of robbery and murder. Well does a saloon make a woman bare of all things! The motive for doing this is to suggest vice, animating the animal in man and degrading the respect he should have for the sex to whom he owes his being, yes, his Savior also.

I decided to go to the Carey for several reasons. It was the most dangerous, being the finest. The low doggery will take the low and keep them low but these so-called respectable ones will take the respectable, make them low, then kick them out. A poor vagabond applied to a bar tender in one of these hells glittering with crystalized tears and fine fixtures. The man behind the bar said, "You get out, you disgrace my place." The poor creature, who had been his mother's greatest treasure, shuffled out toward the door. Another customer came in, a nice looking young man with a good suit, a white collar, and looking as if he had plenty of money, The smiling bar tender mixed a drink and was handing it to him. The poor vagabond from the door called out. "Oh, don't begin on him. Five years ago, I came into your place, looking just like that young man. You have made me what you see me now. Give that drink to me and finish your work. Don't begin on him."

I went back to the hotel and bound the rod and cane together, then wrapped paper around the top of it. I slept but little that night, spending most of the night in prayer. I wore a large cape. I took the cane and walked down the back stairs the next morning, and out in the alley I picked up as many rocks as I could carry under my cape. I walked into the Carey Bar-room, and threw two rocks at the picture; then turned and smashed the mirror that covered almost the entire side of the large room. Some men drinking at the bar ran at break-neck speed; the bartender was wiping a glass and he seemed transfixed to the spot and never moved. I took the cane and broke up the sideboard, which had on it all kinds of intoxicating drinks. Then I ran out across the street to destroy another one. I was arrested at 8:30 A. M., my rocks and cane taken from me, and I was taken to the police headquarters, where I was treated very nicely by the Chief of Police, Mr. Cubbin, who seemed to be amused at what I had done. This man was not very popular with the administration, and was soon put out. I was kept in the office until 6:30 P. M. Gov. Stanley was in town at that time, and I telephoned to several places for him. I saw that he was dodging me, so. I called a messenger boy and sent a note to Gov. Stanley, telling him that I was unlawfully restrained of my liberty; that I wished him to call and see me, or try to relieve me in some way. The messenger told me, when he came back, that he caught him at his home, that he read the message over three times, then said: "I have nothing to say," and went in, and closed the door. This is the man who taught Sunday School in Wichita for twenty years, where they were letting these murder shops run in violation of the law. Strange that this man should pull wool over the eyes of the voters of Kansas. I never did have any confidence in him. When he came to Medicine Lodge to lecture a few months before this, I would not go to hear him, telling the people that he was an enemy.

Kansas has learned some dear lessons, and she will be wise indeed when she learns that only Prohibitionists will enforce prohibition laws. That republicans and democrats are traitors, and no one belonging to these parties should ever hold office, especially in Kansas.

At 6:30 P. M., I was tried and taken to Wichita jail; found guilty of malicious mischief, Sam Amidon being the prosecuting attorney, and the friend of every joint keeper in the city. He called me a "spotter" when I wanted to give evidence against the jointists.

The legislature was to convene in a few days and it was understood that the question of resubmitting the Prohibition Amendment would come up. Being a part of the constitution, the people had to vote on it, and it was frustrating their plans to have such agitation at this time, and these republican leaders were determined to make a quietus of me, if possible. The scheme was to get me in an insane asylum, and they wished to increase my insanity as they called my zeal, so as to have me out of their way, for I was calling too much attention to their lawlessness, at this time, when it might prove disastrous to their plots. Two sheriffs conducted me to my cell. The sensation of being locked in such a place for the first time is not like any other, and never occurs the second time. These men watched me after the door was locked. I tried to be brave, but the tears were running down my face. I took hold of the iron bars of my door, and tried to shake them and said: "Never mind, you put me in here a cub, but I will go out a roaring lion and I will make all hell howl." I wanted to let them know that I was going to grow while in there.

Three days after, on the 30th, there was brought in and put next to my cell an old man, named Isaiah Cooper, a lunatic, who raved, cursed and tore his clothes and bedding. He was brought from the poor farm where he was waiting to be sent to the insane asylum. There were some cigarette, smokers in the jail and the fumes came in my cell, for I had nothing but an open barred door. I begged that I might not be compelled to smell this poison, but, instead of diminishing, the smoke increased. Two prisoners from across the rotunda were brought next to my cell.

What an outrage, to tax the citizens of Sedgwick County to build such a jail as that in Wichita. It holds one hundred and sixty prisoners. There were thirteen there when I was put in. I have been in many jails, but in none did I ever see a rotary, except in Wichita, a large iron cage, with one door, the little cells the shape of a piece of pie. Perhaps there were a dozen in this one. The cage rotated within a cylinder. This was for the worst criminals, and the cells were only large enough for a small cot, a chair and a table about a foot square.

{illust. caption =
JUST BEFORE I LEFT WICHITA JAIL A PHOTOGRAPHER CAME TO MY CELL AND ASKED
TO TAKE MY PICTURE. HERE IT IS IN THE POSITION OF KNEELING, READING
MY BIBLE, WHICH WAS MY USUAL ATTITUDE.}

Mr. Simmons was the sheriff and he told the prisoners to "smoke all they pleased," that he would keep them in material, and he kept his word. Tobacco smoke is poison to me and cigarettes are worse. The health- board belonged to this republican whiskey ring, and was in conspiracy to make me insane, so they put a quarantine on the jail for three weeks, and I was a lone woman in there, with two cigarette smokers, and a maniac, next to my cell. John, the Trusty, smoked a horrid strong pipe, and he also was next to my cell. Strange to say, when that jail had so many apartments, and so few in them, that four inmates should have been put next to me; but there was "a cause." Mr. Dick Dodd was the jailor, and for three weeks he was the only one who came in my cell and I was not allowed to see anyone in that time, but Dr. Jordan who called once. I cried and begged to be relieved of the smoke, for I do not think Mr. Dodd realized how poisonous it was to me. I would have to keep my windows up in the cold January weather, and the fire would go down at night. I had two blankets, no pillow and a bed that the criminals had slept on for years perhaps. I would shiver with cold, and often would lay on the cement floor with my head in my hands to keep out of the draught. Oh! the physical agony! I had something like La Grippe which settled on my bronchial tubes, from which I have never recovered, and I expect to feel the effect to my dying day. I had a strong voice for singing, which I lost, and have never been able to sing, to speak of since. Hour after hour I would lay on the floor, listening to the ravings of this poor old man, who would fall on his iron bed and hard floor, cursing and calling out names. One night I thought I could not live to see day. I had in my cell sweetest of all companions, my Bible. I read and studied it, and this particular night I told the Lord he must come to my aid. As I often do, I opened my Bible at random and read the first place

I opened to, the 144th Psalm. I have often read the book through, but this chapter seemed entirely new. It reads, Verse 1: "Blessed be the Lord my strength, which teacheth my hands to war and my fingers to fight. 2. My goodness and my fortress my high tower and my deliverer; my shield and He in whom I trust; who subdueth my people under me."

God told me in this chapter that He led me to "fight with my fingers and war with my hands;" that He would be my REFUGE and DELIVERER; that He would bring the people to me.

David had just such enemies as these when be says in this chapter: "Cast forth thy lightnings and scatter them; shoot out thine arrows and destroy them."

7. Send thine hand from above; rid me and deliver me out of great waters from the hand of strange children.

8. Where mouth speaketh vanity; and where right hand is a right hand of falsehood.

12. That our sons may be plants grown up in their youth; that our daughters may be as corner-stones polished after the similitude of a palace."

Here is the motive: The drink murders our sons, and do not allow them to grow to be healthy, brave, strong men. The greatest enemy of woman and her offspring and her virtue is the licensed hellholes or saloons.

13. "That our garners may be full of all manner of store."

Our grain is used to poison; our bread-stuff is turned to the venom of asps and the bread winner is burdened with disease of drunkeness, where health should be the result, of raising that which, when rotted and made into alcohol, perpetrates ruin and death; Our garners or grain houses are spoiled or robbed.

14. "That there be no breaking in or going out; that there be no complaining in our street."

What is it causing the breaking into jails, prisons, asylums, penitentiaries, alms-houses? The going out of the homes, of hearts; going out into the cold; going into drunkard's graves and a drunkard's hell?

"Complaining in our streets." Oh! the cold and hungry little children! Oh! the weeping wives and mothers! Oh! the misery and desolation of the drunkards! All from this drink of sorrow and death.

15. "Happy is that people that is in such a case; yea, happy is that people whose God is the Lord."

"People whose God is the Lord," will not allow this evil. They will smash it out in one way or another. This blessed word was a "light to my feet and a lamp to my pathway." I rejoiced for the comfort it gave me; for the Lord truly talked to my soul while I read and reread this. I must say that "Little Dodds," the turnkey as I called him, was often kind to me, but he was completely the servant of Simmons and his wife.

Once Mr. Dodds asked me if I would leave the jail; that Sam Amidon would bring a hack to the back door of the jail and he, Mr. Dodds, and his wife, would go with me to Kansas City.

John, the Dutch trusty, said to me one day: "There is something in the wind; people are coming and going and talking to Dodds." Mr. Dodds was supposed to be quarantined in the jail, but he went in and out of the office and he would also go to his home; the prisoners saw him from the window time and time again.

It was agony to hear the ravings night and day of the poor old maniac. He would frequently fall on his iron bed and floor. He was a large man of about sixty years of age or over. He was helpless; but had no one to take care of him, but John, the trusty, who for the sake of mercy, would give him some attention. The sanitary condition of his cell must have been something horrible, from the smell that came into my room.

One night the poor lunatic fell so hard on the floor, or bed that he lay as one dead, for some time. The jailer and others were aroused and before they dare have a physician come in, they had to scrub and clean the cell. Then Dr. Jordan came, and the old man was finally brought to life. This doctor was in the conspiracy to have me adjudged insane; A woman fifty-five years old, who never broke a statute of Kansas.

Mr. Dodds told me that Sam Amidon would have a cab at the back door of the jail and would take me out. I consented. John, the Trusty, said to me, "Don't you leave this jail, there is some plotting going on, and they mean mischief. I asked him to get me a wire to fasten my door, which he did, and I wound it around the open places in the door and to the iron beam it shut on, and then John brought me the leg of a cot. I watched all night, listening for some one to come in my cell to drag me out. With the cot leg I was going to strike their hands if they attempted to open the door. I know what it is to expect murder in my cell. God said, 'He would stand by me, and who but He, has."

I got so many letters from poor, distracted mothers, who wrote so often: "For God's sake come here." In some letters there was money. One letter from a United Brethren church in Winfield, Kansas; the minister, Bro. Hendershot, wrote me that he took up a collection in their church for me of

$7.38. How I cried over that letter and kissed it! I knew that I had some friends who understood me; and just after this letter, one from a Catholic priest came, which was a great comfort. The many letters I got from all kinds of vice was a great encouragement to me. I must say: "All hell got hit, when I smashed the saloons." For I never, until then, knew that people thought, or could write such vile things; letter after letter, of the most horrible infidelity, cursing God, calling me every vile name, and threatening me.

I was not allowed a pillow; I begged for one, for I had La Grippe, and my head was as sore as a boil. Mr. Dodd frequently brought me the papers, and nearly every time that Wichita Eagle would have some falsehoods concerning me, always giving out that I "was crazy," "was in a padded cell," "only a matter of time when I would be in the insane asylum;" that I used "obscene language" and "was raving." The bible says: "All liars shall have their part in the lake that burns with fire;" so the Murdocks of Wichita ought to tremble. I associate the name "Murdock" with murderer. The real depravity of such people was shown, when a lone old woman with a love of humanity, was in a cell suffering so unjustly, that these people should have left nothing undone to prejudice the people against her. Even when my brother died, this Murdock paper spoke of me "raving in jail," and I was not privileged to go to him in his dying hours. Such people drove the nails in the hands and the spear in the side of Jesus.

This Wichita Eagle is the rum-bought sheet that has made Wichita one of the most lawless places in Kansas.

When first arrested in Wichita, in violation of the Constitution, I was denied bail and compelled to bring a Habeas corpus proceeding in the Supreme Court to get a trial or bail. Sam Amidon as attorney for Simmons proposed a return to the writ, and filed a false certificate from Dr. Shults, president of the Board of Health, stating that Board had quarantined the jail. Rather than face the Supreme Court with a false return the case was dismissed. I do not believe that history ever recorded a quarantine of a jail before, for public buildings, such as post office, court houses or jails cannot be made pest houses, and such buildings are cleansed. There was not a meeting of the Health Board. This was a conspiracy, signed by Dr. Shults and the sheriff, for the purpose of keeping me in jail, preventing me from seeing my friends or lawyers, and by persecution to get me in an insane asylum. Below is a copy of this fraudulent notice:

ORIGINAL NOTICE TO O. D. KIRK, JUDGE, WARDEN EBEY, CLERK, CHAS. W. SIMMONS, SHERIFF. SERVED TUESDAY, JANUARY 15, 1901.

To O. D. Kirk, Judge, Harden Ebey, Clerk, and Charles W. Simmons, Sheriff:

You, and each of you, are hereby notified that the following is a copy of a paper purporting to be a statement made by J. W. Shults, President of the Board of Health, of Wichita, Kansas, and attached to the return of Charles W. Simmons in the The Matter of the Application of CARRIE NATION for a Writ of Habeas Corpus now pending in The Supreme Court of the State of Kansas, viz:

"Wichita, Kansas, December 29, 1900.

"At special meeting of the Board of Health, held in the City of Wichita, Kansas, on the 29th day of December, 1900, at the office of Dr. J. W. Shults, President of the Board of Health, the following resolution was adopted and ordered spread upon the minutes kept by the said board. 'Whereas it has come to the knowledge of the Board of Health that the inhabitants of the jail of Sedgwick County, Kansas, have been exposed to small pox and that one Isaiah Cooper confined therein has been exposed to smallpox and is infected with said disease and that the said Isaiah Cooper is a violently insane man and it is impossible to move him from said jail and that all of the said jail have been exposed to the same and that one W. A. Jordan, who is County Physician of Sedgwick County and City Physician of the City of Wichita, Kansas, asked and desired and demanded that said jail be quarantined or that said Isaiah Cooper be removed therefrom and that said jail be fumigated, and whereas it is impossible to remove the said Isaiah Cooper therefrom, the action of said W. A. Jordan in recommending the quarantine of the said county jail and in quarantining the same is hereby approved and the said county jail is hereby declared quarantined and ordered quarantined for the space of twenty-one days from this date and all persons in charge of said jail and the health officer of said city are hereby directed to enforce this said quarantine and the order of the said W. A. Jordan. J. W. SHULTS, M. D. President of Board of Health."

and that the above statement is not true; that there was no meeting of the Board of Health on the 29th day of December, 1900 and that the said jail has never been quarantined by the said board of health on the said 29th day of December or at any other time.

Dated at Wichita, Kansas, January 14, 1901.
            W. S. ALLEN,
            RAY & KEITH,
            ROBT. BROWN,
        Attorneys for Carrie Nation, an Inmate of said Jail.
    Served on O. B. Kirk, 9:20 a. m., Tuesday, January 15, 1901.
    Harden Ebey, 9:20 a. m., Tuesday, January 15, 1901.
    Chas. W. Simmons, 9:35 a. m., Tuesday, January 15, 1901.

I could tell of many interesting incidents in jail.

There were five singers, one a graduate of the conservatory of music in Boston, and Mr. Dodd was a fine singer himself; he would often sing with the prisoners and it was a great pleasure to me. One song he would have the boys sing was: "My Old Kentucky Home." We had a genuine poet there, and I here give you a poem he sent up to me one day, by the trusty:

SOLEMN THOUGHTS.

'Twas an aged and Christian martyr,
Sat alone in a prison cell,
Where the law of state had brought her,
For wrecking an earthly hell.

Day by day, and night she dwelt there,
Singing songs of Christ's dear love;
At His cross she pray'd and knelt there,
As an angel from above.

In the cells and 'round about her,
Prisoners stood, deep stained in sin;
Listening to the prayers she'd offer,
Looking for her Christ within.

Some who'd never known a mother,
Ne'er had learned to kneel and pray,
Raised their hands, their face to cover,
Till her words had died away.

In the silent midnight hours,
Came a voice in heavenly strain,
Floating o'er in peaceful showers,
Bringing sunshine after rain.

Each one rose from out his slumber,
Listening to her songs of cheer,
Then the stillness rent asunder,
With their praises loud and clear.

Praise from those whose crimes had led them,
O'er a dark and stormy sea,
Where its waves had lashed and tossed them
Into "hell's" captivity.

Wine it was, the drink that led them,
From the tender Shepherd's fold,
Now they hear His voice call them,
With His precious words of gold.

Like the sheep that went astray,
Twice we've heard the story told,
They heard His voice, they saw the way,
That leads to His pastured fold.

The first time I was put in jail, after everything was quiet, I heard some prisoner down below, swearing, and I called out: "What do you mean boys by asking God to damn this place? I think he has done so and we don't want any more damns here. Get down on your knees and ask God to bless you." And all the rest of time I never heard an oath. In a week or so I heard them singing hymns; and I called to them: "How are you boys?"

"We have all been converted since the first of January," was their reply.

One of those young men got out while I was there, and came to my cell and told me that it was true about their conversion.

Oh! the sad hearts behind the bars! Oh! the injustice! I am glad I have been a prisoner for one thing, I never see a face behind the bars that my heart does not pity. I have heard so many tales of ruined lives; have seen men with muscles and brain, bowed into tears. Oh, if we would only love each other more; if we would feel as Paul: "To owe love to all we meet, and pay the debt. 'Tis the most pleasant debt to pay and the indebtedness blesses both parties, especially the one who pays." I used to think that birth and other circumstances made one person better than another. I do not see it that way now. The man with many opportunities is not entitled to as much consideration as one with fewer. I am the defender of the one who needs help most. The great need of the world is Love.

CHAPTER IX.

OUT OF JAIL.—EGGS AND STONE.—SMASHING STILLING'S
JOINT AT ENTERPRISE.— WHIPPED BY HIRED
PROSTITUTES.—PLOT AT HOLT BY HOTEL KEEPER AND
JOINTIST TO POISON AND SLUG ME.—AT CONEY
ISLAND.—HAND BROKEN AND HANDCUFFS.

I got out of Wichita jail about the last week in January, 1901, under a writ of habeas corpus. I got bail,—I forget who went my bail, but God bless them; and left on the evening train about seven o'clock.

While in jail I got a letter asking me to come to Enterprise, Dickinson County, and break up saloons there. I said the name ENTERPRISE, is good and I will go; so I left jail with the intention of going there. It was dark when I started for the train. Many of the Salvation Army were near me. The streets were almost impassable, and the whole city seemed to be on the streets marching down to the station, yelling and laughing.

Many said: "Are you not afraid?" Perfect love casteth out all fear I love the people, I do not fear them.

There walked by my side, a man keeping the crowd back. "Are you one of the Salvation Army?" I said to him.

He said: "No, I am only a tin horn gambler."

I asked him: "Why do you seem to be such a friend of mine."

He answered: "Because I intend that no one shall hurt you, for you are a good woman, and I will see you safe. They all know me, and they will not hurt you." He carried my valise and put me on the train.

There were several thousand at the depot and the crowding was dangerous. I wanted to see the crowd, so I raised the window, waved my hand and as the train pulled out, the eggs began to come; the window fell down and I did not get a spatter. God said: "I'll stand by you." explains this. In two minutes a rock the size of my fist came crashing in at the window; shivered the glass, and the rock fell down at my side; which was a miracle. Not once did I feel alarmed but smiled; while all the passengers were on their feet with fright.

I got to Enterprise at night. I stayed all night with Mrs. Hoffman and next morning, I went down to a dive kept by a man named Stillings. He had closed to go out to a baseball game. The door was locked, so I broke the front glass and climbed in. Several ladies were on the outside, and were friendly to my smashing. I broke the place up. There were twelve cases of beer and I destroyed them and piled them up in the center of the room on the floor. At the close, the marshal came in, took me out and would not let me break up the other dive near by. Neither did he arrest me.

I came down on the corner of the street that night, to tell the people why I did this, when Stillings passed, cursing and shaking his fist at me, saying: "My wife will settle you." Just then a furious woman came around the corner, rushed up to me and struck me a fearful blow in the eye, then ran to her husband, Stillings, and in a frantic manner said: "I have done what you asked me, now let us go home." I stopped speaking long enough to go into a meat shop and have a piece of fresh meat bound on my eye, which was already very dark and painful. Then I finished my address on the street, and went up to a meeting in the church, gave an address, and we organized a society to smash saloons, if they did not close. Next morning we went down the street in a body, Mrs. Hoffman and other women, and the other dive keeper talked to us and promised to go out of business. This Stillings came to me again cursing and threatening, saying: "His wife would fix me." Although this man was disturbing the peace, disorderly and dangerous, no one offered to arrest him. He held me, while four women ran from some place with whips and sticks. One beat me with her fist, another with a whip, one with a raw-hide, while one pulled my hair and kicked me into the gutter, nearly killing me.

I said: "Women, will you let me be murdered." For although there were men and women present, not one did a thing, until at last, an old lady, the mother of the saloon-keeper's wife, picked up a brick and said: "If anyone strikes that woman again I will hit them with this." Then all rushed to defend me.

I was almost breathless. My hair was down, much of it being pulled out. I went home with my friend, Mrs. Hoffman. These parties were arrested. The trial brought out the fact that this dive-keeper, Stillings, had hired these women. To the gambler's wife he was to give twenty- five dollars, to use the raw-hide. Two women were prostitutes, whom this Stillings had brought to town for this purpose. They were fined a small sum, and the whole of them given a few hours to leave town.

My body was bruised and sore. My limbs were striped with bruises; but I was only disabled two days.

While in Enterprise I got a telegram from Holt, signed by the "Temperance Committee," it read: "Come here and help us break up dives." This little town was only twelve miles from Enterprise. In going to the train that night there seemed to have been some one hiding on every corner throwing eggs. My dress was covered with them. I got to Holt at midnight. When I got off the train, I then knew it was a plot to injure me for no one was there to meet me, and I saw some suspicious men keeping in the dark. I got in a hack and went to a hotel. I asked for the women but all had retired. I went up to my room, which was very small. It had one window which was raised an inch with a lath under it, and I thought it strange at the time that the landlord should have let the window down, but I was very tired and dropped asleep almost as soon as I touched the bed. About two o'clock I was awakened with a smothered feeling, struggling for breath. I jumped for the window, which I threw up, for the room was full of the most poisonous odor, as of cigarettes, and other smells. I knew that there were persons at the door puffing the poison in. I sat at the window and listened and in about fifteen minutes I heard some one whistling and saw through the transom that a light was coming. A man stopped at my door and knocked.

"What do you want?"

"I want to speak to you," he replied.

"What is it?"

"I want to speak to you."

God showed me in a vision two men crouched on each side of the door ready to either catch or slug me, if the door was opened.

"I see you sluggers on each side of the door. You villain, you have tried to murder me by throwing poison in my room and now you are trying something else."

"There is a mob here after you."

"You are a liar," I answered.

"There is a committee wants to speak to you."

"You are telling lies in order to have me open my door."

He left and went down below, and for ten minutes there was a great tramping of feet and I could hear the landlord making out as if he was dispersing a crowd. I watched from my window and saw two men walking away. I certainly was thankful for a lock on my door. Next morning when ready to leave my room, I looked up and down the passages well; then I hurried and did not feel safe, until I got on the outside. I asked a little boy if there were any Christians in Holt.

"No, but there are some in the country."

I got my breakfast at a restaurant, and I called out on the streets that I would hold a meeting in front of this hotel where I had stopped. There was a crowd and I then told of the telegram and of how I was treated. I pointed to the landlord, who was the picture of a villain, and a coward. The two dive-keepers of Holt were at this meeting. They asked me if I intended to smash the saloons there.

"Of course, I didn't come to Holt to do anything else."

One man told me that he would shoot me if I came into his place.

"I am not afraid of your gun. Maybe it would be a good thing for a saloon-keeper to kill Carry Nation. It might be the means of causing the people to smash the dives."

The one that talked to me was white with fear and anger, but at last the color came back to his face, and soon he was in good humor; he told me he never expected to open that saloon again. In less than ten days from that time, the people of the county became so aroused, that the prosecuting attorney closed every saloon in the county, which were twelve in number.

From Holt I went to Topeka. I stopped with the United Brethren minister there, and spoke in his church. The saloons were all over Topeka. I went down town after dark, to see the condition of things. It was soon learned that I was on the streets, and a crowd gathered. I went to some dives and joints. I could not get in. One had his mistress stationed at the door with a broomstick. She gave me four blows before I could get away, poor creature. I met her niece after that, who told how the saloon-keeper cast her off and that she died a miserable death.

While I was there the State Temperance Union had a meeting in the First Presbyterian church. Capt. Cook, from Chetopa, got up in the meeting and said: "Here is ten dollars towards giving a medal to the bravest woman in Kansas, Carry Nation." One hundred and twenty dollars was raised.

I said: "I would prefer that the money be used to pay my lawyers, rather than be put into a medal as I did not wear gold in any way."

We held a good many meetings. I spoke in several churches and held meetings in Dr. Eva Harding's office, where we prepared to take measures to break up saloons in Topeka, where sworn officials were perjuring themselves from governor down to constable. About this time a certain woman pretended to be a friend of mine, but was a spy and a traitor. I believe she was hired by the jointists to find out our plans. She told me she knew where every saloon in the city was and would show them to me. It was understood by a few of us that we would make a raid one morning in February, 1901, and I called on this woman to show us where the places were. We wandered around from street to street, and I soon discovered that she was keeping me away from them. One young boy said: "I'll show you a place."

I came to one dive. I lifted my hatchet to smash the door and this woman grabbed at my hatchet and so did the man. He slammed the door and left his hat in my hand. I passed on down to the "Senate" saloon and went in. This was about daylight. The bartender ran towards me with a yell, wrenched my

- 80 -

hatchet out of my hand and shot off his pistol toward the ceiling; he then ran out of the back door, and I got another hatchet from a lady with us. I ran behind the bar, smashed the mirror and all the bottles under it; picked up the cash register, threw it down; then broke the faucets of the refrigerator, opened the door and cut the rubber tubes that conducted the beer. Of course it began to fly all over the house. I threw over the slot machine, breaking it up and I got from it a sharp piece of iron with which I opened the bungs of the beer kegs, and opened the faucets of the barrels, and then the beer flew in every direction and I was completely saturated. A policeman came in and very good-naturedly arrested me. For this I was fined $100 and put in jail. Mr. Cook was sheriff and I was treated very nicely by him and Mrs. Cook. Mrs. Cook's mother was visiting them at this time, a woman thoroughly in sympathy with my work, and I believe that the influence of this good woman was the cause of my being treated so well, for after she left things were very different.

That republican conspiracy in Topeka determined to put me in the insane asylum. One of them, Judge Magaw, swore on the witness stand that he believed me insane. His examination brought out the fact that I compelled him to turn some obscene pictures to the wall once, when I called to see him in his office.

I had received ever so many letters from all over the country justifying smashing as being reasonable, right and legal. I also saw that the republican newspapers of Kansas and other states were determined to put me in a false light before the people. I conceived the idea of editing a paper. I tried to get the Journal to edit the paper, but it seemed that I could not get anyone to take hold of it. Some one suggested to me Nick Chiles, a negro, who had a printing outfit. I knew but little of this man. I sent for him to come and see me at my cell. All the money I had in the world was from the sale of ten cows which was $240. This negro, Chiles talked very fair and promised to print my paper in a creditable way. I gave him the $240. I wrote the editorials while in the jail, and also gave him bundles of letters which I had received and a great many poems that had been written on Carry Nation and smashing. This negro finally cheated me out of my money and papers also. I closed with him after three weeks, he put the papers out, collected for them and never paid me a cent. I believe he paid Mr. Nation some and when I would have made him account for his wrong dealings, I found that the contract between he and I, which was drawn up by Mr. Nation, made this negro my partner. This, of course, was done to prevent me from having any legal redress. My paper was called THE SMASHER'S MAIL. I called it this for it was largely composed of letters which I had received on the subject of smashing. I had no one to read the proofs and was at the mercy of this negro, who was not in sympathy with my cause, but to the reverse. I was often humiliated at the way my articles were tortured. I afterwards got The Kansas Farmer to publish the paper and I then bought a press of my own, but found that I could not conduct a paper and lecture, so after the 13th edition, I closed. The paper accomplished , this much, that the public could see by my editorials that I was not insane.

THE SECOND TIME IN JAIL AT WICHITA.

I was in a meeting of the W. C. T. U. in Wichita, of which Mrs. Summers was president. I wanted to have these women go with me and destroy the places there that were murdering their sons. Many present were in favor of it, but Mrs. Summers was bitterly opposed. Three went out in the hall with me, Mrs. Lucy Wilhoit, Miss Muntz and Mrs. Julia Evans. The husband of the latter was a great drunkard, otherwise a capable physician. Those three women said they would go with me. We went to Mrs. Evans' home and then, for the first time, I took a hatchet and Mrs. Evans a piece of iron. We marched down to the first place, kept by John Burns. We walked in and began to smash right and left. With my hatchet I smashed in the large plate glass windows and also the door. Sister Evans and I then attacked the show case, went behind the bar and I smashed everything in sight. The bartender came running up to me with his hands up, "Don't come near my hatchet, it might fall on you and I will not be responsible for the results."

After we were through for no one resisted us, Mr. Burns was asked. "Why did you not knock that woman down?" he replied, "God forbid that I should strike a woman." ("a man's a man for a' that.")

I did not see what the other two women were doing, but heard Sister Wilhoit talking to the crowd and telling why we had done this.

We were put in one cell, the one I occupied before and were given a cot apiece. This was one of the glorious heavenly and refreshing times. We sang hymns, repeated scripture, would often laugh and cry by turns for joy to think we were worthy to suffer for His sake. "The table was prepared before us in the presence of our enemies, our cup runneth over." This happy condition was not what our persecutors wished, and Mrs. Simmons and her husband, whom we called "Jezebel" and "Ahab," were determined to separate us. Mrs. Simmons was telling that I used obscene language to her husband.

{illust. caption =
THIS PICTURE TAKEN BY A MAN WHO CALLED FOR THE
PURPOSE, TO SEE ME IN
TOPEKA JAIL. I NEVER WANT A PICTURE TAKEN OF ME
WITHOUT MY BIBLE, MY
CONSTANT AND HEAVENLY COMPANION.}

These two were very much interested in having me adjudged insane, for Mr. Simmons had in several ways laid himself liable to criminal prosecution, especially in the matter of the quarantine. Mrs. Simmons came to our cell door, and in the presence of Sister Wilhoit, to whom she had told that I used "obscene language," I asked her if she said this? She had to acknowledge that she did. I told her she spoke a "lie," for I had never done such a thing. She sent her husband and son up to the cell and they dragged me into the rotary and put me in one of those little triangular cells, which was indeed a place of filth. The faucet leaked, and kept a continual spatter, which made the foot of my cot damp. I stayed there five days and while it was not as bad as Jeremiah's dungeon, it was similar. The dampness and poison of this cell added to the already deep cold on my lungs. Dear Bro. Schollenberger! Who has not heard of this great hearted man of Wichita? He brought us little treats and in many ways relieved us of our afflictions and bonds. I was not allowed to be with my lovely sisters again in prison they would write notes and send them by a "trusty," for they were very uneasy about me, fearing foul play.

As soon as the sisters could get bonds, they got out, but I was not allowed to give bond. I was not a meek prisoner, did not act like a criminal. This vexed my prosecutors and they tried to humble me, but I felt that I was right and that God would stand by me and I wanted Him to look down and always find me brave and true and in nothing to be terrified by my adversaries.

I had some money sent me while in jail and this I divided, often to the last, with my fellow prisoners. To one I gave four dollars, for his poor wife was soon to be confined. To the "trusty" John, I gave three dollars for his destitute wife, and often bought little treats, such as fruits and butter. The meals were meat and beans one day, then potatoes and meat all cooked tip into a mush. I became very much attached to my fellow prisoners and I found some with noble sentiments. What do people do who have no hope of heaven, I often ask. What a joy to have a place in view where there is no sickness, no death, no jails, no suffering of any kind.

THE THIRD TIME IN TOPEKA JAIL.

I had become so disgusted with jail food that my stomach refused it. As soon as I was put in jail I told Mr. Cook to send the milkman to my cell. He came and was very kind. He agreed to bring me some bread and milk, ten cents worth a day. This I lived on for the eighteen days. In the cell with me was a woman named Mrs. Mahanna, who was put in for selling beer. She did not happen to have a government license. Poor creature! She bad been the mother of fifteen children; had a broken hip caused by a kick of a drunken husband. She was very ignorant but kind-hearted. The heat was intense and we were next to the roof. Sometimes I would feel like I was suffocated. The windows slanted so that but little draught came in. One pane of glass was partly out and we would sit by that to get a breath of air. While in this jail I had many offers from different theatrical, circus, and museum managers, who tried to tempt me with all kinds of prices; one as high as $800 a week, and a palace car and a maid. I never for one moment thought of taking any of them until two managers came from New York City. The sheriff, Mr. Cook, brought their cards up. I said: "Tell them to wait until morning." I prayed over the matter nearly all night and before day all seemed settled. (This was a test to try my faith.) The cloud was lifted and I told Mr. Cook to tell the men that a "million a minute would not catch me." My dear friends especially Mrs. Goodwin, Dr. Eva Harding and others used their influence to have Stanley, the governor pardon me, this he refused to do, the joint-keepers were those he favored more than me.

I had never thought of going before the public as a lecturer. I knew those people only wanted me as they would a white elephant. I did not at this time see the stage as a missionary field.

At this time I was entirely out of means, was in debt and the duns I got while in jail were a terrible trouble to me. The ten cents I got for my bread and milk came in almost daily for copies of my papers. I paid my milkman sometimes in stamps.

I never wanted to get out of jail so badly in my life, as I did at this time, when the offers to make engagements were so many. Two days after the New York managers were there, I got a letter from James E. Furlong, a Lyceum Manager of Rochester, N. Y., who had managed Patti and many of the great singers. He told me if I would give him "some dates", he would assist me in getting out of jail. I hardly knew what he meant by "dates". Mrs. Goodwin of Topeka called to see me, I showed the letter to her and asked what this man meant by "dates?" She said: "He may want you to lecture or you could tell of your experience."

"I wonder if the people would like to hear me, I can tell my experience," I said. I asked her to tell Mr. Duminel, my lawyer, to come to my cell. I told him of it, and he said he would call the commissioners together and would have them let me out by paying my fines by monthly installments. This he did. So Mr. Furlong sent the money needed and Dr. Harding and Mrs. Goodwin collected seventy dollars from my friends to help me out. When I got to Kansas City, I lacked fifty cents of having enough money to pay for my ticket east, so I borrowed that of the man at the fruit stand in the depot. In about a week from that I spoke at Atlantic City for the Philadelphia American, the proceeds being used to give the poor children an outing. Thousands of people were present. I never made a note or wrote a sentence for the platform in my life. Have spoken extemporaneously from the first and often went on the platform when I could not have told what I was to say to save my life, and for several weeks God compelled me to open my Bible at random and speak from what my eyes fell on. I have literally proved that: "You shall not think of what you shall speak but it shall be given in that hour." The best thoughts have come to me after being asleep, waking in the night or in the morning.

The way I happened to think of a hatchet as a souvenir, some one brought me one and told me I ought to carry them. I then selected a pattern and got a party in Providence, R. I., to make them. These have been a great financial aid to me; helped me pay my fines and expenses. People have often bought them from me, at my prison cell window. I sell them everywhere I go.

The summer of 1902 I was at Coney Island, speaking in Steeple- Chase Park, and a man was very insulting to me, and always took occasion to say something against women. I can scarcely remember how it was, but I broke or smashed his show case of cigars and cigarettes. I knew I would have to pay for it, but I did not mind paying for the object lesson that it would be, for tobacco is a poison, and the use of it is a vice. I was arrested, stood my trial and was being sent to jail, when Mr. Tilyou, Manager of Steeple-Chase Park, took me from the "Black Maria." The policeman who had the prisoners in charge was purple and bloated from beer drinking, he wanted me to go in a place in the front that was already crowded with women. I refused and he struck me on the hand that was holding to the iron bars of the little window and broke a bone, causing it to swell up. I said: "Never mind, you beer-swelled, whiskey- soaked saturn faced man, God will strike you." In six weeks from that time this man fell dead on the streets of Coney Island. This was the first time I every had handcuffs on. I saw in this experience in Police Courts in Coney Island what I never saw before, eight or ten women sentenced for drunkenness; one the mother of five children, and the others nice looking young ladies, and most of them were weeping. When they received their sentences there would be a smothered laugh from the audience of bloated men present, and I turned and said: "Shame on you, for laughing at the sorrows of these poor women." I thought how heartless it was for men to laugh at the disgrace of women. I got out by paying for the destruction of the cigar case.

I was very successful and made enough money to pay $125 a month to have my SMASHER'S MAIL published in the form of a magazine, but having no one in Topeka that could edit the magazine, doing justice to me, I returned and closed the business.

CHAPTER X.

LEGAL STATUS OF PROHIBITION AND JOINT SMASHING,

The very highest judicial authority, the Supreme Court of the Nation, has made a most radical ruling, towit: "No legislature can bargain away the public health or the public morals. The people themselves cannot do it, much less their servants. Government is organized with a view to their preservation and cannot divest itself of the power to provide for them."—101 U. S. 816.

No state, therefore, can license or legalize immorality, vice or crime. All such efforts are treason to society and organized government.

Again, the Supreme Court of the United States has declared: "If the public safety or the public morals require the discontinuance of any manufacture or traffic, the hand of the legislature cannot be stayed from providing for its discontinuance, by any incidental inconvenience which individuals or corporations may suffer."—97 U. S. 32. Thus the legislature of any state can confiscate property by wholesale if necessary for the protection of the community. Powder mills, slaughter houses and pest houses, necessary institutions, are frequently so condemned and rendered absolutely worthless.

The Federal Supreme Court gives ample power to all states to enforce this great fundamental principle. It says: "The state cannot by any contract limit the exercise of her power to the prejudice of the public health and the public morals."—111 U. S. 751.

Speaking specifically, a sweeping decision of the highest tribunal of the land, is as follows: "There is no inherent right in a citizen to thus sell intoxicating liquors by retail; it is not a privilege of a citizen of a state or a citizen of the United States."—137 U. S. 86.

No state or citizen of the United States then has any power, authority or right to vend intoxicating liquors at all.

That there may be no misconception or misconstruction, in a case from Kansas, this final court of appeal in American jurisprudence, said: "For we cannot shut out of view the fact, within the knowledge of all, that the public health, the public morals, and the public safety may be endangered by the general use of intoxicating drinks; nor the fact, established by statistics accessible to everyone, that the idleness, disorder, pauperism, and crime existing in the country are, in some degree at least, traceable to the evil,"— Mugler vs. Kansas, 123 U. S. 623.

And again: "The statistics of every state show a greater amount of crime and misery attributable to the use of ardent spirits obtained at these liquor saloons than to any other source."—137 U. S. 86.

Hon. Justice Grier said: "It is not necessary to array the appalling statistics of misery, pauperism, and crime that have their origin in the use and abuse of ardent spirits. The police power, which is exclusively in the state, is competent to the correction of these great evils, and all measures of restraint or prohibition necessary to effect that purpose are within the scope of that authority, and if a loss of revenue should accrue to the United States, from a diminished consumption of ardent spirits, she will be a gainer a thousand-fold in health, wealth and happiness of the people."—5 Howard 532.

These far-reaching decisions settle forever the disloyalty and un-Americanism of any state or citizen presuming to authorize or condone liquor selling. The whole license system of the United States is clearly illegal and unconstitutional.

Abraham Lincoln interpreted the Constitution right, when he wrote the Emancipation Proclamation. The Presidents of the United States are oath bond to enforce it, and the license to vend intoxicating liquors as unconstitutional. Mr. Roosevelt is violating his oath to allow this business to continue. He has the same right and more cause than Abraham Lincoln to cancel every license, and shut up every brewery and distillery in the United States. God says, "Woe to the crown of pride, to the drunkards—Yes, this thing at the head of the nation is cursed—Look at the assassinated Presidents, since the license was given by the Republican Party in 1863. Lincoln refused to put his name to the bill at first, but was over persuaded to do so by those parties who said it was to pay a war debt, and when that was done, the license would be revoked, but poor, honest Abe Lincoln was not suffered to undo the wrong he was persuaded to commit. Every drunkard's wife and drunkard's mother and child ought to bring suit against the Government, for the durgging, poisoning and murdering of their loved ones. A man can recover if his wife's affections are alienated from him, a person can recover damages even, if he injures his foot on a defective sidewalk—the inference is clear.

And now let us look at the Legal Status of Joint Smashing. Let every lawyer, judge and law-abiding person read carefully the following: Kansas, true to the doctrines enunciated above, and loyal to the best welfare of her populace, enacted constitutional prohibition forbidding the sale of ardent spirits.

Section 14 of the Prohibitory Law reads: "It shall be the duty of all sheriffs and constables, in their respective counties and townships, to file complaints and make arrests for violation of this act, whenever they shall be informed of the violation thereof, and any such officer who shall neglect or refuse to file such complaint or make such arrest, upon being informed of the omission of such offense, shall be subject to a fine not exceeding $100, and his office shall be vacant:

Providing that no such officer shall in any event be liable for costs of such prosecution."

Hence, it is not necessary that the private citizen drum up evidence, swear out warrants and prosecute liquor drug-stores and joints. That is what officials are elected and paid for and if officers fail to abate these liquor venders, then the duty devolves back on the patriotic citizen.

This decision of the Supreme Court of the United States, carried up from Vermont, Spaulding vs. Preston, 21 p. 9, towit: "If any member of the body politic instead of putting his property to honest uses, converts it into an engine to injure the life, liberty, health, morals, peace or property of others, he can, I apprehend, sustain no action against one who withholds or destroys his property with the bona fide intention of preventing injury to himself or others."

In Kansas every liquor selling place is not only a declared nuisance, but a constitutional outlaw. And in the case from Pennsylvania where a private individual had abated a nuisance, the court held: "We consider it also well settled, as is claimed by this defendant, that a common nuisance may be removed, or, in legal language, abated by any individual. Any man, says Lord Hale, may justify the removal of a common nuisance, either by land or by Nyater, because every man is concerned in it."

It is not only the privilege of the patriotic citizen to abate a dangerous nuisance but it is commendable. Bishop on Criminal Law, paragraph 1081, says: "This doctrine (of abatement of a public nuisance by an individual) is an expression of the better instincts of our natures, which lead men to watch over and shield one another from harm."

"The buildings, premises and paraphernalia of a nuisance are not legitimate property and have no rights in law. Damages cannot be recovered for their destruction by an individual. The question of malice does not enter into the case at all."

I Bishop's Criminal Law 828; I Hilliard on Torts, 605.

"At common law it was always the right of a citizen, without official authority, to abate a public nuisance, and without waiting to have it adjudged such by legal tribunal. His right to do so depended upon the fact of its being a nuisance. If be assumed to act upon his own adjudication that it was, and such adjudication was afterwards shown to be wrong, he was liable as a wrong-doer for his error, and appropriate damages could be recovered against him. This common law right still exists in full force. Any citizen, acting either as an individual or as a public official under the orders of local or municipal authorities, whether such orders be or be not in pursuance of special legislation or charter provisions, may abate what the common law deemed a public nuisance. In abating it, property may be destroyed, and the owner deprived of it without trial, without notice and without compensation. Such destruction for public safety or health is not a taking of private property for public uses without compensation, or due process of law, in the sense of the constitution. It is simply the prevention of its noxious and unlawful use, and depends upon the principle that every man must so use his property as not to injure his neighbors, and that the safety of the public is the paramount law. These principles are legal maxims or axioms essential to the existence of regulated society. Written constitutions presuppose them, are subordinate to them, and cannot set them aside."

These great principles of civil jurisprudence and popular government apply alike in every state in the Union. An eminent jurist, Judge James Baker, of Evanston, Ill., formerly a resident of Missouri, gives his professional opinion of the late crusading by the women there. He maintains that it was legal; he points out that the saloons raided, at Denver and Lathrop, were unlawful and that they were "nuisances at common law." He quotes Illinois law as follows: "As the summary abatement of nuisances is a remedy which has ever existed in the law, its exercise cannot be regarded as in conflict with constitutional provisions for the protection of the rights of private property and giving trial by jury. Formal legal proceedings and trial by jury are not appropriate and have never been used in such cases." Judge Baker sums up the case thus: "The women who destroyed such property are not criminals. They have the same right to abate such common nuisances as men have to defend their persons or domiciles when unlawfully assailed. As the women of that state are denied the right to vote or hold office, I think they are fully justified, morally and legally, in protecting their homes, their families, and themselves from the ravages of these demons of vice in the summary manner which the law permits."

More citations might be given proving the legality of joint smashing by the crusaders, but the foregoing is ample, for all fairminded, loyal people. Had the joint smasher's cases been tried on their merits, not one would have been convicted of a misdemeaner. They were arrested, tried, convicted, imprisoned and fined for disturbing the "peace" of a common nuisance, and "malicious" destruction of rebel paraphernalia. Their only intent was against the treasonable liquor traffic. Had there been no liquor dispensing there had been no smashing. This the liquorized courts would not admit for a moment. Every ruling was a burlesque on civil law, a travesty on justice and a contemptible farce. The whole proceedings from beginning to end were a miserable outrage.

DECAY AND DECLINE OF THE AMERICAN REPUBLIC.

Today the country is ringing with the cry of political bribery, boodle and official corruption, from the highest to the lowest. The rum traffic is the principal factor in demoralizing and destroying the dignity, honor and integrity of civic life. It is the insidious foe that is hatching and nursing crime. Startling complication of statistics, obtained from the replies of over 1,000 prison governors in the United States to a circular letter addressed to them, and a summary shows that the general average of 909 replies received from the license states, gives the proportion of crime due to drink at no less than seventy-two per cent; the average from 108 officials in Prohibition states giving the per centage at thirty- seven. A considerable number of the latter were "boot-leggers" in jail for selling whiskey. Out of the 1,017 jailers, only 181 placed their estimate below twenty-five per cent, and fifty-five of these were from empty jails in prohibition territory. The relation of drink to pauperism is much the same as that of drink to crime. Of 73,045 paupers in all the alms- houses of the country, 37,254 are there through drink.

According to official statistics as gathered by Commissioner Carroll D. Wright, of the Bureau of Labor, there are 140 cities in the country having a population of 30,000 and upwards.

In these cities there were in 1898, 294,820 people arrested for drunkeness, almost ten times as many as now comprise our army in the Philippines.

If this great army of drunkards were marshalled for a parade, marching twenty abreast, it would require four and one-half days, marching ten hours a day, for them to pass a given point. And these 295,000 drunks do not include the arrests for "disorderly conduct," "assault" and a dozen other offences which grow out of the licensed rum business. The total arrests for all causes in these cities was 915,167. Counting the moderate estimate of three-fourths of these as being the victims of the lawful saloons, it would require more than a week's marching twenty abreast, for the great procession to stagger past a reviewing stand, and the rum product of only 140 cities heard from.

These appalling statistics are the common property of every citizen, and any political party pretending to financial improvement that ignores the sixteen hundred million dollars worse than squandered in liquor and tobacco annually in the United states, is untrue to itself and false to the nation. Gambrinus, the god Bacchus, the Rum Power, this Moloch of perdition, must be destroyed. Prohibition is the only remedy. Kansas is to be the battle ground. Her constitutional prohibitory law and statutory enactments are all right, properly administered. But in the hands of a republican whiskey "machine" with the governor belonging to the Elks, a liquor fraternity; a confessed defaulter as state treasurer; a United states senator under indictment for bribery; officials from the state house to every county in complicity with the whiskey rebels, it will not be enforced. The liquor men and joint keepers subscribe large sums to campaigns with the tacit, implied or open understanding of immunity from prosecution and punishment on the part of candidates and officials. This has been going from bad to worse for twenty years. Yet the law is so plain that he who runs may read. How many ever saw it in print. The revised statutes of Kansas, 1901, Article 14, Section 2462, reads: "It shall be the duty of all sheriffs, police officers, constables, mayors, marshals, police judges and police officers of any city or town, having notice or knowledge of any violation of the provisions of this act to notify the county attorney of the fact of such violation and to furnish him names of witnesses within his knowledge by which such violation can be proven. If any such officer shall fail to comply with the provisions of this section, he shall, upon conviction, be fined in any sum not less than $100 or more than $500, and such conviction shall be a forfeiture of the office held by such person, and the court before whom such conviction is had shall, in addition to the imposition fine aforesaid, order and adjudge the forfeiture of his said office. For a failure or neglect of official duty in the enforcement of this act, any of the city or county officers herein referred to may be removed by civil action."

Also Article 6, Section 2212, says: "Any officer of the state or of any county, city, district or township, after his election or appointment, and either before or after he shall have qualified or entered upon his official duties, who shall accept or receive any money or the loan of any money, or any real or personal property, or any pecuniary or other personal advantage, present or prospective, under the agreement or understanding that his vote, opinion, judgment or action shall be thereby influenced, or as a reward for having given or withheld any vote, opinion or judgment in any matter before him in his official capacity, or having wrongfully done or omitted to do any official act, shall be punished by a fine of not less than $200 nor more than $1,000, or by imprisonment for not less than one year nor more than seven years in the penitentiary at hard labor, or both such fine and imprisonment at the direction of the court."

Enforce the statute and thousands of officials in Kansas would soon be behind prison bars. When the officiary administrative of any government become corrupt, it is on the highway to disruption and ruin. Greece and Rome are notable examples. The sworn government report is that nearly eighteen gallons of liquor to every man, woman and child, is consumed by Uncle Sam's subjects every twelve months. This republic cannot long survive half sober and half drunk. The immortal Abraham Lincoln in a speech at Springfield, Ill., Feb. 22nd, 1842 said: "Turn now to the temperance revolution. In it we shall find a stronger bondage broken, a viler slavery manumitted, a greater tyrant deposed—in it, more of want supplied, more disease healed, more sorrow assuaged. By it, no orphans starving, no widows weeping; by it, none wounded in feeling, none injured in interest. And what a noble ally this to the cause of political freedom! With such an aid, its march cannot fail to be on and on, until every son of earth shall drink in rich fruition the sorrow-quenching draughts of perfect liberty! And when the victory shall be complete— when there shall be neither a slave nor a drunkard on the earth—how proud the title of that LAND which may truly claim to be the birthplace of and the cradle of both those revolutions that shall have ended in that victory! How nobly distinguished that people who shall have planted and nurtured to maturity both the political and moral freedom of their species!"

William Windom, when Secretary of the U. S. Treasury under the Arthur administration, said: "Considered socially, financially, politically or morally, the licensed liquor traffic is, or ought to be, the overshadowing issue in American politics, and the destruction of this iniquity stands first on the calendar of the world's progress."

By Bible authority and by the common law of our land I have proved to the satisfaction of all who will see the right, that I am a loyal American, a loving Home Defender, doing the will of Him whom I serve and whose I am.

CHAPTER XI.

MY TRIAL FOR DIVORCE.—THE LICENSED RUM TRAFFIC THE CAUSE OF SO MANY DIVORCES.—DIFFERENT TIMES AND PLACES I HAVE BEEN IN JAIL.—AT THE CAPITAL OF CALIFORNIA.—WIDE OPEN TREASON.—AT THE UNIVERSITY OF TEXAS.—WOOLLEY CLUB AT ANN ARBOR, MICHIGAN.—CATHOLIC PRIEST AND CIGARETTES.

Mr. Nation brought suit for divorce against me while I was in jail. I was very much astonished at it, for I never thought that our disagreement would result in his desiring a divorce. We had lived together twenty-four years, and while we could not agree, I never wanted a divorce. His petition stated the reason for this was "extreme cruelty and desertion." He sued for all the property and wanted the court to have me pay for the cost of the trial. I shall always believe he was induced to do this by the republicans, thinking to hinder my work.

The people of Medicine Lodge were shocked at this, for they knew I had been faithful to my duties as a wife, up to the time I went to Wichita, and when I went to Topeka I told Mr. Nation if he would stay there with me, I would pay his board and room rent, which I did. He came to Topeka and the first thing that he took offense at was my objecting to his opening my mail, for when he did I never saw a dollar sent for a subscription and sometimes would find parts of letters destroyed.

On the day of the trial, Mr. Nation could not produce a witness to prove I was other than kind, except the affidavit of a man who could neither read nor write. Mr. Nation wrote out what he wanted this man to swear to, and the man signed it, for he could just write his name. This man was in Oklahoma at the time, My neighbors came of their own accord and testified to my having done my cooking and housework; frequently cooking meals and taking them to Mr. Nation, who was still in bed. Judge Gillette, the same man who was on the bench in my slander suit presided. Mr. Nation did not get his divorce because of my "extreme cruelty," but because I testified that I could not, nor would never live with him as a wife. I could not. I was very much grieved to bear this reproach, of a divorced wife. I made my home during the trial with my dear friend, Mrs. Judge Howe, who is still living, and she knows how bitter this was to me.

The home was given me, and the divorce and a small piece of property in Medicine Lodge to Mr. Nation. I shortly after sold this home for $800. It was part of the payment for "Home for Drunkards' Wives" in Kansas City. It was as I expected, a means used by my enemies to hinder me in my work. I was blamed for the divorce. It was said, "I broke up a home." That if I was in a good work I would not do these things. And while delivering my lectures, it was often called out; "Why don't you go back to your husband? No wonder he got a divorce from you," and all such sayings. But I learned to expect and was prepared for such treatment.

We hear, "A woman's place is at home." That is true, but what and where is home. Not the walls of a house. Not furniture, food or clothes. Home is where the heart is, where our loved ones are. If my son is in a drinking place, my place is there. If my daughter, or the daughter of any one else, my family or any other family is in trouble, my place is there. That woman would be selfish or cowardly who would refuse to leave her home to relieve suffering or trouble. Jesus said, "Go out into the highways and hedges." He said this to women, as well as men. If the women of Galilee had not left their homes they would not have followed Jesus. If Phoebe had not left her home, she would not have gone on the business of the church to Jerusalem. We would have no woman missionaries—Women now, are forced to go out to save the homes.

D. L. Moody once said, and which I hardly understood at the time: "When a wife knew that the man that should be her husband was unfaithful and corrupt, she was as bad as he if she lived with him." I have thought much of the meaning of husband. He is one who is a man who provides and cares for his family, as much as it is in his power to do, but when he refuses and will not do this, he breaks his marriage vow and becomes his wife's enemy. A husband is not an enemy. This will place many women in the roll of living with men who are not their husbands, and this is so. I do not favor divorce, but it is better to separate, than bring up children of drunkards or licentious fathers. There is nothing which is making so much enmity between the sexes as intoxicating drink. This is the cause of so many divorces. Men who go into saloons generally visit houses of prostitution. The women they meet there have been deceived and lost their self respect, become discouraged because men have made them their victims through treachery and in turn these women revenge themselves by taking all means to drag these men down. Prostitutes do not like men; they often hate them. The man who goes there generally loses respect for the virtues of women, and from associating with bad women they judge other women to be vile. These men hate the very women they go to see. Married men who drink are bad husbands, for they deceive their wives, who soon find it out; and the husbands and wives cannot be happy. A woman leaves all others for one man and she wishes his society. In the evening the clubs and drinking places take up men's time when their families should have it. These things destroy love and confidence between husbands and wives. 'Tis not all men's fault, for there are some drinking women.

A man came to me just before I went on the stage at Newport, and said: "Carry Nation, step aside here, I must speak to you. I am in so much trouble.

Give me some advice. My wife is at home drunk; she is that way most of the time. We have six children and they feel disgraced. What can I do? I am almost wild."

I asked: "Did you ever drink with your wife?"

He looked confused. I said: "Women do not usually go to saloons but you men bring it home and use it on the table and women are just as apt to catch the disease of alcoholism as men. This may be the way your wife learned to be a drunkard. Wives have been nursing their drunken husbands for years; now the chickens have come home to roost, and you are nursing your drunken wives."

Poor man! He, indeed, seemed distracted; and he is not alone, there are hundreds of cases.

I met a lovely creature on the train, who had been married a few months. Her husband was a lumber merchant in Chicago. She sat by me and told me her sad story. She had been a poor girl and dearly loved a man whose mother opposed the match and prevented the marriage. The young lumber merchant, left rich by the death of his father, proposed and she married him. In a month, the mother of the man she loved first, died and the obstacle was removed. In telling me this story I smelled liquor on her breath. She would say a few sentences and then say: "Oh, Carry Nation I am so miserable! If Charlie would only be true to me I would not grieve for the man I love, but Charlie drinks and he goes with other women, and leaves me alone. He gives me all the money I want. I have everything that money can buy; but, Oh! I almost hate these things! I had rather have a hut with someone to love me." She kept talking this way until it was enough to break my heart. She said: "Charlie will be in from the smoking car, and please Mrs. Nation speak to him. I want to be a good wife and I will do all I can to make him a good man. But he laughs at me when I talk to him, he never takes me in earnest. Go speak to him."

So I did. I found him to be a young man about twenty-three, with the marks of dissipation on his face. I said: "I have something to say to you privately. You have a beautiful young wife. If you wish to make her happy you can do so. There is one thing that will ruin the happiness of both. That is intoxicating drink. Did you know your wife is under the influence of some drug?" He said: "Oh, don't say a word to her about that, I am the cause of it. I drink and have persuaded her to, because she has a right to do what I do."

I told him of the fatal results and asked him to quit or it would be the ruin of both. Here were these two on the brink of ruin, so young, so attractive. I never shall forget the pathos of that woman's story. The yearning of that heart for love. Of course in her unhappiness she would turn to the benumbing fascination of the poisonous drug.

On every hand I see the desolation of homes and hearts. There are no five things that make so much enmity between the sexes as this one— the licensed saloon. The home life is destroyed. Men and boys are taken from home at the very time they ought to be there, after their work is done. Families should gather in the evening to enjoy each other's society. It is said that Germans are the cruelest husbands on earth. Their beer gardens have taken the place of firesides. There are more insane and suicides in Germany than any nation on earth. Alcoholism is a disease. Men go to the Keeley cure and take different treatments to get cured. This disease is killing more every year than the deadliest epidemic, and still not one of the senators or representatives will discuss this. Roosevelt toured this country moralizing on different questions. The nearest he ever touched on the subject was "race suicide;" but he did not wish to intimate that drinking intoxicating liquors was the cause. He wished to reproach women for not raising larger families. What protection has a mother if she does? She has to produce the grist to make these murder-mills grind, and I for one, say to women, refuse to be mothers, if the government will not close these murder-shops that are preying on our hearts, for our darling sons are dearer to us than life.

If I had a family to raise and had to live in a city, I know of no place as desirable as Topeka. I was once lecturing in Lincoln, Neb., and made this remark. A wife said to her husband, "Let us take our boy and go to Topeka." So they came. The husband was D. L. Whitney, manager of the Oxygenor Company, and both he and his wife have been a great help to me. I say to fathers and mothers, move to Kansas, where your sons are taught that it takes a SNEAK to sell, and a SNEAK to drink, intoxicating liquors in that state.

I was arrested in Topeka for going into the dives. The officials were determined to keep them open, and the police arrested me for even going in. They did not arrest the keepers. I was thrown out and called names by the proprietors, in the hearing of the police, still they were let go. This was during the time that Parker was mayor.

The voting citizens of Kansas will soon find out that no one but prohibition officers can be trusted to enforce prohibition statutes. I am glad at the present writing there is said to be not a dive in the beautiful city of Topeka, and that she has passed the Rubicon. God grant that no more criminal dens be opened by Republicans, Democrats or any other Anarchists.

I was arrested in Wheeling, West Virginia, winter of 1902, for going in a saloon and telling the man he was in a business that would send him to hell as well as others. The facts are that the police never knew what I was going to do and they were so frightened and rattled that they of course thought they would arrest me to prevent trouble. I have been a terror to evil doers. I was in jail there two nights. No pillow. The bed bugs bad. Col. Arnett, my lawyer, said I had a good case of malicious prosecution. I have begun several suits but the "laws delay" and the condition of dishonest courts has prevented me. I desire to compel Murat Halstead to be shown as he is, a liar, almost equal to the "Murdocks of Wichita."

I was arrested in Bayonne, N. J., the summer of 1903, because I was talking to a poor drunkard. A policeman came up and ordered me to "walk on". I said: "I have a right to speak to any one on the street." He said: "I will arrest you if you do not move on." I said: "You do not wish this poor man to have one warning word to keep him out of a drunkards hell." He arrested me, took me to the police headquarters, where I was sentenced for disturbing the peace. I was put in a cell with a hard board, no cover. There were only two other prisoners, both put there for getting drunk. The partition door was by accident left unlocked and I heard someone creeping, looked up and there was one of the poor creatures in my cell. I called loudly. He ran back. The turnkey came and fastened the door. All night through I was handing water to these poor creatures. The bed bugs were thick and kept me quite busy knocking them out of my face. I lay on the plank but could not sleep a wink. Next morning I was called in court. That police officer in order to make it a case of disturbing the peace said there were one hundred and fifty people around. There was but five and I so testified. I never have seen such false swearing as there is with the police. I got a fine of ten dollars. Of course this judge was a republican.

Here is a list of the times and places I have been in jail:

In Wichita three times. Sentenced December, 1900, thirty days; January 21st, 1901, twenty-one days and January 22nd two days.

Topeka seven times; once thirty days; twice each eighteen days; then twelve days; fifteen days, seven days and three days.

Kansas City once, part of a day; also once, part of a day at Coney Island, once at Los Angeles; once at San Francisco; Scranton twice, one night and part of two days; Bayonne, New Jersey a day and night; Pittsburg three times, one night and part of two days; Philadelphia once, one night.

I was also put in jail in Cape Breton, and in 1904, when five of us attacked the Wholesale House of Mahan Bros., in Wichita, of which I speak elsewhere, making a total of twenty three times.

I spoke at Sacramento, Cal., to the legislature when in session. I got a letter from one of the officers in the capitol, telling of the joints run in the capitol building and patronized by the members of the legislature. A reporter went with me. He tried to get me an opportunity to speak, but he was told I could not do so, and that I had better leave as the crowd prevented them doing business. I did not leave. The reporter said: "You will not be able to speak." I said: "I will speak." I waited until the speaker adjourned for noon, and as quick as a flash I took the stand, and began my address. I saw impatience in the faces of many, but there was a great cheer from visitors and pages. I spoke about as follows: "I am glad to speak to the law-makers of California. I not only believe in making laws, but enforcing them." I called their attention to the most needed legislation on the lines of prohibition of evil. I could see that all seemed rather pleased at this point, I drew out the letter which read as follows: "Dear Madam: I see you are to visit the capitol tomorrow, I wish to call your attention to the flagrant violations under the dome of California's capitol. In the Bill filing room is a place where liquors are kept, also in the Sergeant-at-Arms room in the senate chamber, behind a screen, is stored beer and whiskey, in room 56 there is a safe where bottles of beer and whiskey are kept. These unlicensed bars are patronized by the members, and with their full knowledge and consent." It was certainly a sight to see the faces of these men. After reading each charge, I would stop and say: "Now gentlemen this must be a grave slander, and I want you as a body to rise and down this outrage." I waited, no one rose up. I said: "certainly there must be a mistake, is it possible that the law-makers of this state are the law-breakers, if so, then who is capable of punishing the criminals?" I continued, "I hope that at least there are some of the members of this body that are ignorant of this and that some one if only one will rise and say, "I know nothing of this;" not one arose; Both the houses were adjourned and the aisles and lobbies were packed. These men looked at each other grinning and looking silly, some heartily enjoying it, reminding me of a lot of bad boys that were caught stealing watermelons. The pages and visitors yelled and waved and clapped their hands, but was this not a shame? This is but a sample of the legislatures of the states. Washington's capitol is a reproach to common decency, this government like a fish, "stinks worse at the head."

I spoke in Austin, Texas, at the state university. When I arrived in the city I was met by "Uncle Tom" Murrah. "Uncle Tom" is a true type of the old fashion gentleman. Had it not been for the chivalry of this dear friend I expect I would have had some trouble with the police of Austin.

I went into a saloon and was led out in very forcible manner by the proprietor, who was one of the city council. I stood in front of this man's man-trap and cried out against this outrageous business. The man kept a phonograph going to drown my voice. The police would have interfered but "Uncle Tom" told me to say what I pleased, and he would stand by me. I went up to the state university with students who tried to get a hall for me to speak to them but they could not. I spoke from the steps. In the midst of the speech and the cheers from the boys I heard a voice at my side. I looked and there stood the Principal, Prexley Prather. He was white with excitement, saying: "Madam, we do not allow such." I said: "I am speaking for the good of these boys." "We do not allow speaking on the campus." I said: "I have spoken to the students at Ann Arbor, at Harvard, at Yale, and I will speak to the boys of Texas." The boys gave a yell. The mail man was driving up at this time. The horse took fright, the letters and papers flew in every direction. The man jumped from the sulky; the horse ran up against a tree and was stopped. I offered to pay for the broken shafts but the mail carrier would take nothing. There was no serious damage and all had a good laugh, except, perhaps, the dignified principal.

When I visited the students at Ann Arbor, Mich., I was given a banquet by the Woolley club of the university. It gave me new life to look at such men of intellectual and moral force. Oh! for such men to be the fathers of the rising generation. Just such men as these will save the Nation. THESE are the hatchets that will smash up evil and build up good.

One cannot help but compare the tobacco smoking dull brained sot- tish students with these giants of moral and physical manhood. These young men were the greatest argument in favor of prohibition. God will bless the Woolley club of Ann Arbor and all such as they.

AT HIGH MASS, BUFFALO, OCT. 27

I attended High Mass in St. Joseph Cathedral. One of the priests, Mr. Percell, was taking up the collection. He came to where I was sitting but the smell of cigarette smoke was so strong about him that I could not refrain from a rebuke, so I said: "You smell so bad from cigarette smoke."

He said: "Who?"

I said: "You!"

He said: "You are a liar!"

I said: "No I am not, you do smell bad!"

He said: "I will have you put out of this church!"

I said: "I dare you! You are the one that should be put out!"

He passed on and after Mass I went into the house of the priest's and asked for him. He could not be found but two priests tried to make excuses and treated me well. Said they smoked. I told them God said for them to cleanse themselves from all filthiness of the flesh. That they were making provisions for the flesh to fulfill the lusts thereof. I said: "What a shame for a man to dress like a saint and to smell like a devil!"

One thing I have noticed—that the Catholic schools taught by the Brothers are saturated with vile tobacco smoke. I would not like to send a son to such a place for that reason alone. There are many things I like about the Catholic church, but why, oh, why is it so silent as a general thing on the liquor traffic? Why are so many of its members in this devil's work? Oh! what a retribution will be theirs when it will be proven that instead of clothing the naked they have robbed children of clothes. Instead of feeding the hungry they have allowed them to starve because their bread was taken to buy drink. They sent souls to prison and did not minister to them!

CHAPTER XII.

WOMAN'S SUFFRAGE

In all ages woman has taken an active part in the defense of man. She is the best defender he ever had on earth, because she is his mother. True mothers think more of the interest of their children than of their own. God intended it so, All animals have a care for their offspring. The hen will fight the hawk or dog, even man, to defend her little chicks. The farmer's wife will not set a hen the second time that will not fight for her little chickens. Such hens are taken to market. I have heard my mother say: "I must set that hen again for she is such a good mother." The mother bear will die fighting for her cubs. The hunters say they dislike to kill her, because of her mother love, that never yields up those two little cubs that she places behind her, and then fights until she dies. This is the mother love of a brute,—what ought to be that of the human family?

If a man starts a ranch to raise cattle he protects the females in raising their young. He will kill the animals that will destroy his stock, and if he produces the pelt or scalp of these animals the state pays him a bounty. How is it with the human mothers? They produce the most valuable offspring, but this licensed traffic is defended, while children are murdered before our eyes and our hands are tied so we cannot rescue them. No one will say but that woman represents more morality than man, also that the mother is more interested in the children than the father; then of course, the party who has the most care and love should be allowed the largest privilege to exercise it.

America claims more civilization than any other nation on earth. In the main this is so. But certainly she is not true to the motherhood, and THIS is her peril.. Some of the best reigns have been those of queens. All nations have had their women rulers, but the mothers of America are not allowed to say who shall be the ones to help them make good citizens of their own children, while their bitter foes prey upon their offspring as cannibals. A widow with six sons has a little home. She is taxed the same in proportion as the brewer, who carries on the human butcher-shop that grinds up the six sons of the widow. He and his crowd (republicans and democrats) have the ballot that smashes the poor widow's boys and takes her substance to prosecute her boys after they are made criminals, to pay for their arrest, to build a jail for them. Her heart is broken, home is gone, and disgrace is hers. To accomplish this she is rendered helpless by having no voice or ballot to protect herself. God never made an animal that he did not give it some means of defense. While I am writing this I am in Bridgeport, Connecticut. I find this a city of eighty-two thousand. The PRESIDENT of the board of education is P. W. Wren, who is president of the Connecticut Breweries and owner of one of the largest wholesale whiskey houses in the state. This is as consistent as if one were to start a ranch to raise chickens, ducks, pigs and calves and then place a wolf to guard them from harm, The business of the brewer is to sell beer. No animal but mankind will use this rotten slop, for the others by instinct know it is poison. No man would let his horses drink it, for they would be dangerous instead of being useful. The only way to make the brewer's business profitable is to have boys and girls as consumers. The brewer is not the worst to blame. It is the voter. Mothers would never vote for such a man to be the public guardian of the morals of their children. All liquor men, or liquor license men, are opposed to woman's suffrage, for the reason that should women vote, we would have prohibition or abolition of the vice. The women saved prohibition in Topeka in the year 1903 by five hundred majority, while it would have been lost by two hundred if men only had voted. The contest was between the WET and DRY mayors. Where women have the ballot, even in municipal affairs, no state has resubmitted or brought back the saloon. God said: "It is not good for man to be alone. I will make him a helpmate, a partner, a companion, a guardian." When man elevates a woman he elevates himself. A degraded woman means many degraded men. Free men must be the sons of free women. This land cannot be the land of the free or home of the brave, until woman gets her freedom and men are brave and just to award it to her. No man can have the true impulse of liberty and want his mother to be a slave.

The constitution of the United States starts out by saying. "We, the people of the United States." Women are people as well as men. Therefore I advise all women to go to the polls and vote in spring and fall elections. We want the moral, intellectual electorate. The brewer, distiller, saloon man, their agents, even the colored man was given a vote, and never asked for it. The foreigners in a few months, or a year, after landing, are given the ballot, but the loving, true defenders of God, home and all the best interests of humanity, are compelled to see their sons, husbands, and fathers, murdered before their eyes, without the sign of a protest from the government under which they live. The outrageous unfairness of this is quite evident when we consider that the ballot is represented and controlled by the worst element, when it should be by the best. The women are more affected by oppression than man. She is the mother, the rest are the children.

The mother would vote to save the boy.

The mother would do nothing to injure her boy.

The mother makes a good citizen of her son.

The saloon man votes to make drunkards.

The saloon man does all to injure.

The saloon man makes bad citizens.

The best voters are cast out for President, the vilest are put in, no wonder we have a snob and brewers choice.

A boy's best friend is his mother. Boys and girls go wrong when they do not obey their mothers. God has always used women as a mighty factor in salvation. The promise was given her in the garden, after the fall, that she should produce the Savior, who would give the deadly wound to man's great enemy, the devil. It was the "seed of the woman," not the seed of the man. Christ was born of a woman and the Holy Ghost.

No man has ever been greater in God's estimation than Abraham. Yet when he and Sarah had a dispute and Abraham went to God to decide the matter, God said: "In all that Sarah thy wife hath said unto thee hearken unto her voice." Rebecca understood the will of God, contrary to the will of Isaac. She carried out the plan of God. Jacob sent for Rachel and Leah to consult with them before he left Laban, and he took their advice. "Moses, Aaron and Miriam were chosen by God to lead the people out of Egypt." The Bible so states it. Huldah and Deborah were prophets. Rahab was the first convert in Canaan; she and her family were all that was blessed in that cursed city of Jericho. Esther saved the whole Jewish nation. A woman smashed the head of the wicked Abimelech as did Jael the wife of Heber also. In the Psalms, 68:11, the original says: "The Lord gave the word.—Great was the army of women who published it."

Jesus did his first miracle at the request of a woman, still he rebuked her. He felt her powerful influence and would know no higher will except his heavenly Father's. Christ defended woman, saying: "Why trouble ye the woman, she hath wrought a work on me," hereby rebuking men to interfere with any woman's work when it is good. Christ never rebuked even the harlot. There was not a greater preacher than the woman at the well that brought out the city of Samaria to see Jesus. Philip had four daughters that prophesied. Women were the first disciples, they followed Christ from Galilee. He chose the men, the women chose Him. Pheobe was a deaconess of the church of Cenchrea. The Bible records no act or word of woman against Christ. With sufferings not one was caused by a woman. The poor prostitute bestowed the most loving service when she wept at His feet, kissing them.

This gives some of the Bible women. There have been others in all ages. One instance in the early history of Rome. There was a band of men who first settled Rome. They wished to get wives for themselves and this was the plan by which they got them.

The Romans made a great feast; had games; invited the Sabine nation to come with their wives and daughters, which they did. In the height of the footraces and archery, the Romans rushed in among their invited guests and each snatched a woman. The Sabines returned and prepared for war. The lines of battle were drawn. The stolen women had a conference and decided to stop the war. They rushed in between the Sabine men, their former husbands and fathers, and the Romans, their last husbands, and forebade bloodshed by saying: "You will have to kill each other over our dead bodies."

If those heathen women by their act could reconcile two nations, is it not a rebuke to women in this Christian age for their cowardice in not coming forward and demanding recognition in the matter of being a go-between, for one class of men are arrayed against another..

A hundred thousand of our sons are being sent to drunkard's graves and a drunkard's hell every year. By a bold stand for the right, to defend our loved ones, let us rush between and stop this deadly strife, with the same heroism of the women of Rome, "over our dead bodies." Women will get the ballot in time, but it can be hastened only by women themselves. It will be a great victory for mankind when women can veto the curse of mankind. The mother impulse is stronger with women than any, and when she can protect her offspring, she will make a greater effort to do so than now. She will not then do as many now do, make her body a manikin to hang the fashions of the day on. She will not then display her form to attract the vulgar gaze of the world. She will not place the corpses of cats or birds on her head. She will not wear mops at the bottom of her dress to sweep up the filth of the earth. She will not wear shoes that injure her as the heathen do. She will not put her body in the vice of a corset, displacing the organs of her body, unfitting her to be a mother, causing more than half the surgical operations in the hospitals. She will then discuss character more than fashion. She will be ashamed of her silly, giggling and meaningless conversation. God said, "a man shall not wear that which pertains to a woman neither shall a woman put on a mans garment for all that do such things are an abomination unto God" women will then see the vulgarity and immodesty and sin in dressing in male attire or in any other form of indecent exposure of her person.

Young men often say to me: "Mrs. Nation, if I go to see young ladies I can learn nothing from them. They are not interested in the subjects that are improving to young men. They read only trash." Also they say: "I cannot afford to marry. I cannot support a woman. Their wants are so many.' Dress is a remnant of barbarism. The Indians delight in different colors, the plumage of birds, the skins of animals, even rattle-snakes. We retrograde to their level when we attract the vulgar gaze to such vanities.

God said: "I will make man a HELPMATE," a partner, a helper, not a hinderer to success in any way. What kind of mothers will this class of women make? It is said that a mother does more to mold the mind and heart of the child before it is born than can be done by any one from its birth up to twelve years. God sent an angel to the mother of Samson; told her "not to drink wine or strong drink" before the child was born. Why? God wishes here to teach that mothers can injure their children or entail on them vices before they are born.

Women will triumph in this battle. The devil knows it and has put forth every effort to forestall this great reform. Look at the shop windows, loaded with every style and fashion to attract the eyes of the passing woman. Things that will be but a burden to her, will cause her to use the earnings of her husband and the patrimony of her children and destroy her mother influence and bring upon her just censure of her husband. This is not the rule but the exception, for women, if they are not false, spend more for the advancement of their families than themselves. There never will be a club or other organization of women that will ever make any regulation that will in any way injure the welfare of their offspring. And the interests of men are safe in the keeping of good women.

Woman is also a power for evil. Solomon, the wisest, was not wise enough to keep out of the toils of bad women; and Samson, the strongest, was not strong enough to break away from the bad influence.

Oh! the degradation among women from intoxicating drinks! These degrade women and she degrades men. "Rise up ye women who are at ease in Zion!" The drinking places in the cities, especially in New York, by every device get women in their dens that they may entice men.

Suffrage is not to give woman greater opportunities to be bad but to strengthen their powers to resist evil and help men to do the same. To cause her to think more of the inmates of her home than her raiment. Woman's greatest sins and vices are those of vanity of appearance and dress to attract or please their male companions. The prostitutes do the same thing. Women should be taught to avoid the arts of such. When I see a woman arrayed as I do these women in these homes of sin I think, "There is sympathy."

CHAPTER XIII.

ECHOES OF THE HATCHET.
MRS. NATION AND THE SALOON.

It was a crisis in prohibition enforcement in Kansas. The first smashing was like the opening of a battle. The crashing glass sent a thrill through the community and resounded o'er the land a talisman of destruction to the liquor traffic. It set everybody to talking, even the public school children and students in all the higher institutions were profoundly interested. The press and the pulpit broke their silence and from all over the state came the echo. It was the firing of the signal guns. The response came desultory, as the rattle of musketry in a skirmish, then heavier from the bigger guns, as is the case in all reformatory work. The criticisms and comments were varied, often amusing, reflecting the agitation from far and near and everywhere.

A few months ago and the name of Mrs. Nation was unknown outside of Medicine Lodge, Kansas, but within the limits of sixty days she has achieved notoriety, if not fame, by her unique crusade against the Kansas saloon. Many methods have been adopted during the last two decades for the abatement of the liquor nuisance, but it remained for an American woman, under the spur of bitter memories, and a sort heart, to originate a method, at once so bold and radical as to sharply focus public attention upon the utter villainy and lawlessness of the Kansas saloon.

As was to be expected, Mrs. Nation has been subjected to unhandsome treatment. A section of the press and the pulpit have joined forces with the rum brigade in holding her up to ridicule. She has been burlesqued, abused and belied; but when all the facts are soberly and fairly weighed, it will be found that the scale of justice inclines, very positively, toward this sorely tried woman and her hatchet. I do not pose as Mrs. Nation's champion or apologist; she needs neither. History that corrects the blunders of contemporary critics, will assign to her an honored place long after the paltry penny-a-liner and ranting pulpiteer are forgotten. It is a simple task for those to whom the curse of rum has never come close home, to condemn the methods of a woman, who, as a drunkard's wife and widow, drank to the dregs the bitter cup of woe. Mrs. Nation saw her brilliant and handsome young husband slowly transformed into a demon by rum. She saw him land in an early and dishonored grave. She saw her baby cursed by the father's sin. She saw her early hopes blighted, and poverty haunting her door. She saw a favorite sister grieving her heart out over a fallen husband—fallen in purse, in character, and station. With this black catalogue of domestic griefs "deep printed on her heart," is there a man—surely there is no woman!—who could blame Mrs. Nation, if she turned upon the guilty gang who had blighted her life and smote them right and left. When the infernal record of rum is recalled, it is not so surprising that there is one Mrs. Nation, but that there is not one in every home in the United States. M. N. BUTLER.

A CONTRIBUTION TO HOME FOR DRUNKARD'S WIVES.

Dear Madam:—I see you have purchased property to make a home for drunkard's wives. I send you five dollars to aid you.

                    Yours very truly,
Oakwood, Ills. JACOB F. ILER.

I hope thousands will follow the example of this man. Oh! how the cry comes in: "I want a place in your Home. My husband or son is a drunkard." Help the poor innocent results of the licensed curse.

Persons have often remarked, "How did you feel, when you went in these places?" Imagine a burning house, a frantic mother, for her heart treasures, her babes, arc in that building. She hears their cries, she sees their little arms, waving behind the closed window, amid the smoke that soon will be a flame. She seizes an axe or hatchet near at hand, with which she breaks open door or window to let her darlings escape. Is there a mother in all the land that would not act thus? The mighty ocean, in its anger is lashing a frail vessel, storm tossed, the captain orders the cannon to boom! boom! boom! arousing and calling for help to save the crew. We amputate the diseased limb with a knife, we pull the aching tooth with an instrument of steel. Why? In order to save. Just so, the people are asleep, while our precious ones are in danger of being engulfed in ruin. The smashing is a danger signal, and I kept it up, to prevent the people from relaxing into indifference, just as a frantic, living mother would think only of the salvation of those she loved.

AN APPEAL TO THE NATIONAL PROHIBITION COMMITTEE TO CONCENTRATE THE FORCES IN KANSAS.

(Emmett L. Nichols, Wilkesbarre, Pa.)

It is a fact beyond dispute, that wherever prohibition is carried in a state, the liquor dealers' association of the nation in a menacing manner demands the dominant party in such state that she sees to it that liquor is allowed to be sold in enough places, at least, to make it appear that prohibition is a failure, they knowing that the people once made to see the beneficial effects of prohibition will adopt it generally, as the true solution of the liquor question, as it really is, all other methods having been proven to be absolute failures. The politicians fearing the influence of the power of rum, organized as it is, for self defense yield to the demands of liquorocracy. Mrs. Carrie Nation has shown this to be the true state of affairs in Kansas in her hatchet raid upon the joints of that state. She has shown up to public ridicule the officials of that state, in different places, in demonstrating the fact that they not only refuse to enforce the prohibition law, but screen and protect the violators thereof, and arrest any citizen who attempts to perform the duty which they were sworn to perform. This state of affairs is most exasperating to every lover of country. I contend that Mrs. Nation's hatchet has been the means of bringing about the most critical period of the prohibition reform movement in its history. It has laid open before the world the fact that prohibition does not prohibit in certain portions of Kansas, simply because public officials in violation of their oath of office will to have it so. Now I further contend that unless these officials are forced to prohibit in Kansas, prohibition will eventually be repealed in that state, and the way thereby made all the more difficult for the triumph of the truth if the officials of Kansas are allowed to continue their work of perfidy in refusing to enforce the prohibition laws there, prohibition will not only be repealed in that state, but the securing of national prohibition by peaceful means will be an impossibility. Viewing the conditions in Kansas as I do, I am moved to make this appeal to the National Committee of the prohibition party to concentrate its forces in that state, with the view of arousing sufficient sentiment among the people there to drive every "joint" from within her borders. "On to Kansas" should be the battle cry of the prohibitionists of the nation. It is more important that the will of the sovereign power in Kansas be enforced in the matter of prohibition than it was on the principle of the squatter sovereignty there during the days of slavery. It seems to me that it is the bounden duty of the National Prohibition Committee to make this fight. I fail to see any work within its grasp comparing in importance to it. The agitation which Mrs. Nation created with her hatchet is bound to subside unless some organization, having the cause at heart will take the matter in hand and add fuel to the fire of righteous indignation which has been sweeping the state. The National Prohibition Committee can not afford to look on letting matters take their course. The time has arrived for action on its part, that it may set the example before the world what the party it represents will do if placed in power. The very soul of every prohibitionist in the nation ought to be on fire in a determined fight for the triumph of prohibition in bleeding Kansas. I believe the struggle being had there now means more, either for the weal or woe of this country, than did the struggle against slavery on the same soil by John Brown and his followers.

National Prohibition Committee, I repeat, "On to bleeding Kansas!"

A CO-LABORER IN TEXAS WRITES.

Columbia, Texas, February 23, 1901. Mrs. Carrie Nation, Topeka, Kansas.—Dear Madame and Co- Laborer in the Cause of Humanity—I have thought for some time that I would write to you, but knowing that you were burdened with correspondence I have put it off from time to time, but at last I venture to consume a little of your valuable time in reading a letter from me. I have been fighting the liquor devil going on nine years. Constantly have been called here by the citizens of this place to deliver a series of lectures. I learn that you once lived here and I see from today's Houston Post that you once lived at Richmond, Texas. I find that the lady with whom I am stopping while here knows you (Mrs. G. W. Gayle). Now Dear Mrs. Nation, I wish to say to you that I believe that God has called you to a great work—a work that is much needed, and that is calling the attention of the people of the United States to the magnitude of the liquor traffic—the devil's great agent in peopling hell—and I believe you commenced at the right place, the capital of Kansas—the battlefield. Kansas being somewhat the center of the United States, the eyes of every state in the union is fixed on it as a guiding star relative to prohibition. If prohibition could be proven to be a success in Kansas it would not be long until other states would follow in its steps and on and on until our nation would be free from ruin, but I doubt whether that will ever come, short of a great war such as we have not seen or read of. If it is God's will, let it come, for there is greater cause for war on this line than there was for the liberation of the Cubans from the Spaniards. Now we see published in the papers down here that you have gone into a newspaper enterprise to defend the Negro race. I don't believe this for I know that there will be many things reported by the liquor traffic to destroy your influence. I shall deny this report as far as I can until I hear from you, for I know that the liquor traffic is as wise as serpents and as harmless as the devil, and will do anything they can to sidetrack you from the main issue, and that through your supposed friends, so keep both eyes wide open. Then when they fail in that they will lie on you. God, give you wisdom and may you stick to your bush is my prayer. Oh, pray much and look out for enemies in the guise of friends. They will fool you if you don't look out, for you are doing more good than all the temperance workers combined. God bless you; keep at it, and nothing else, for your work is only the beginning of the greatest temperance and prohibition reform that has ever been. Now it all depends on your not being sidetracked by supposed temperance reformers. Don't allow any mortal person to stop you, but push the battle to a finish. I have known of so many reformers making a good start but about the time the thing begins to boil right well and a prospect of doing something, some supposed helpers come in and capture the whole outfit and put a stop to the move. But I trust in the Lord that this is not a case of that kind. If you have time I would appreciate a reply from you. Write me here as I will be here for about ten days, after that my mail will be forwarded. My permanent address is Fort Worth, Texas, care Polytechnic College. Yours for liberty from rum, J. G. ADAMS.

AN OLD SOLDIERS APPEAL.

Old Soldier's Home, Leavenworth, Kan., February 14, 1901.—Mrs. Carrie Nation:—As I have read of your grand success in Topeka, and elsewhere I wish to congratulate. For God's sake come to the Soldier's Home and save the Old Veterans. Bring your hatchet along and clear out the Canteen in the Home. Congress recently passed a law for all Canteens to be closed on United States reservations, the officials of the Home claim the law does not apply to the Old Soldiers' Home. Last year the officials of the Home were very anxious to have the saloons closed in the Klondike near the Home, for the protection of the Veterans; as it did not bring the revenue into the Home, we are to be paid in one week. Come at once and close the joint in the Home. Over 70 half- barrels of beer are sold in on day at the Home after Pension day. Respectfully, OLD SOLDIER.

A TRAVELING MAN'S LETTER.

Indianapolis, Ind.—"Mrs. Carrie Nation, Wichita, Kan:—As a preface I feel it my duty to extend to you my sincere apology for encroaching these lines for your consideration during the trying hours of your incarceration, but as the purport of my letter undoubtedly differs, materially in text, from the countless hundreds you have received, I feel assured that the sentiment involved, originated as it has, solely from the spirit and intrepid aggressiveness you have exploited in the suppression of that paramount curse of mankind, Drink! will, in a measure, justify you in condoning these lines.

For years the writer has been a traveling salesman, occupying positions of trust and responsibility. As is the universal trait among the larger element of my class, I contracted the indulgence of liquor. From its inception and social intercourse, it gradually developed until I became an irresistible slave to those base affinities—lewd women and whiskey. The result, inevitable as death, produced its dregs; shattered health, separation of family, and social and business ostracism. Prior to a month ago, reparation and redemption from medical arid spiritual aid, had proven valueless; with no alternative, I became resigned to the results of a mis- spent life, when, from the West came the voice and heroic deeds of a woman. Simple yet fervent, intrepid yet unique. You aroused the press and the people. Your mission was born. Thousands, you may have "influenced," but me you have "redeemed." I have read your words with intenseness. Your forcible acts have impressed me. I resolved and have conquered. God bless you! I am now organizing a temperance league among my brother traveling men, paradoxical as it may sound, and am meeting with a fair support, yet I believe an impetus and a stronger influential lever can be extended through the expression of your well wishes and any timely topics you care to extend in furtherance of the cause. Asking your kind indulgence, and with best wishes for your ultimate welfare, believe me. Your loyal supporter, W. S. SANFORD.. Care Terre Haute House, Terre Haute, Ind.

FROM A HEART-BROKEN MOTHER.

Patterson, New Jersey, Sept., 2nd, 1901—Dear Mrs. Nation:—Will you come to this city before going home? The conditions here are worse than in any place in the whole country. One thousand saloons run day and night, every day in the year. Come for God's sake. You can do so much good, and if you smashed fifty or sixty of the hell holes here you would be called an angel. Do Come! and save the young of both sexes. Yours, A HEART-BROKEN MOTHER.

CHAPTER XIV.

CHRISTIAN EXPERIENCE.

The life of a soul moved on by the Holy Spirit is beyond human expression, as well as human understanding. "He that is spiritual judgeth (examines) all things. Yet he himself is judged or examined of no man." The spiritual man can see the condition of the unregenerate for he was once in darkness, but the unregenerate can never understand the condition of the regenerate. The impulses that move one born of God is one of the puzzles not possible to be known by the wisdom of the wise of this world. 'Tis a secret, 'tis hidden, and can come only by Divine Revelation and is always a miracle, the greatest ever performed. It raises from the dead, never to die again. It opens the eyes never to be closed again, 'tis an armor that causes us to handle serpents (devils) without harm and we can hear or drink deadly poisons, or doctrines but they will not kill our soul. "These signs shall follow them that believe. The real Christ life is and always will be hateful to the world. I have often heard it said of me; "I cannot bear that Carry Nation!" I would only to do the people good. I do not blame these as I once did; "For the natural man is not subject to the law of God, neither indeed can be." "Marvel not that the world hate you, ye know that it hated me before it hated you." I know that when I was ten years old I felt the movings of God's spirit—got an answer of peace, but like a little infant pined away, for lack of care and nourishment. Nothing but the divine mercy of Almighty God could have directed the affairs of my tempest-tossed life. I now know there are no accidents. A sparrow falls by a special providence. There are no sins or temptations that I can not say: "My God delivered, saved and forgave me for that." I go to prisons and all kinds of houses of sin. I say: "I can tell you of one who can save and forgive you for that, he forgave me, and he will forgive you, for I was as bad, or worse, than you." I have never seen anyone whom I thought had committed more sin than I. Many will lift up horrified hands at this but 'tis true. I never saw the corruption of but one life, one heart,—that was mine. I was never so shocked, so disgusted, so distracted with remorse over any life, so much as my own. My heart was the foulest place I ever saw. I do not know what is in other people's hearts. Paul meant this when he said: "Christ Jesus came into the world to save sinners of whom I am chief;" Said, this, "is worthy of all acceptation" or was, a good testimony. Because one can never see how bad the heart is, until God sheds the light to see it. So many people are deceived, as a blind man. They may be in filth, and do not know it. It is there, but not seen, for lack of light.

I was first condemned by reading the Psalms. I said: "If Christians have impulses to "rejoice", clap their hands, and "shout", I do not know what it is. I find no response of gladness in my heart." I trembled with fear to think of

God and the judgement day. This continued from youth up to the age of forty. At this time I received from Christ the "Gift of the Holy Ghost", the "Unction", that which "leads unto all truth." There are many names for this; I call it the Bible name. "Hold fast the form of sound words." Before this I had never spoken a word for God or prayed in public. At one time I was called on to do so, and was terrified and mumbled out something, that was no prayer. Now all was changed: "I was glad when they said unto me, let us go into the house of the Lord." I was anxious for my time to come to tell how good Jesus was to me. When I met my neighbors I would be heavy-hearted, because they talked of servants, house cleaning, the new fashions, and these seemed so vain, so frivolous. I liked to direct their minds to speak of the Scriptures, and of the ways of doing work for God. I soon found out I was not welcome, I was looked upon as an intruder, was often avoided, I could see the frowns and glances of impatience at my presence. These would cause me many a cry and mortification. My best companion was the Bible. I then knew what David meant when he said: "More to be desired are they, than gold, yea than much fine gold; sweeter also than the honey and the honey comb." I often kiss and caress my Bible; 'tis the most precious of all earthly treasures.

I wonder how people can live any kind of Christian life without reading the Scriptures and prayer. If I neglect this one day I feel impatient, restless,—a soul hunger. Spurgeon is my favorite of all ministers. I read where he said, "Being a Christian was something like taking a sea bath. You go in up to the ankles and there is no pleasure, then to the knees is not much better, but if you wish to know the pleasure of a bath take a 'HEADER' and plunge. Then you can say, How glorious." Christian life is like a journey. There are flowers and fruit and streams; thorns, dark valleys and fires; rocky steeps from whose summits you can see beautiful prospects. There is rest, refreshment, sleep and bitter tearful watchings. 'Tis a great pleasure to me to be in a spiritual meeting. To know by the testimony how far they have traveled. Some one in the garden of delights; he wonders why that one tells of the dark valley. One at the base of the hill cannot understand why others see what he cannot. The young beginner tells of the beautiful sights and songs; and maybe the one who has been on the road almost a life time will tell of the "continual heaviness, hours of darkness, and the smoking furnace, and the lamp." I have found that the warrior is never as bouyant as the new recruit, in his dress parade. We humor children, and call on men to labor. Few, comparatively, get to the place where they prefer hard labor; to endure desolation of heart; to seek self in nothing; to see all loved but himself; to see others exalted but only abasement for self; to "endure hardness as a good soldier; to lay on the ground; to eat hard tack; to make long, weary marches; footsore and still fight on; to suffer traveling over rocks and thorns; to endure the loss of all things." I will take this last for mine. 'Tis the best, Oh my God, give me this! "He that goeth forth and WEEPETH bearing precious seeds shall doubtless come again rejoicing, bringing his sheaves with him." I do not ask this because I enjoy suffering but to prove my love and gratitude to Him who loved me, and gave Himself for me.

After we moved to Medicine Lodge the Free Methodists came there and held a meeting. I had never heard the doctrine of the "second blessing" or "sanctification" taught. It was very interesting to me. Three women called to see me in my home, to ask me if I had ever "had the Gift." I told them I had something peculiar given me from God in Texas; asked them to pray to God to give this great blessing to me or a witness that he had done so. These sisters were Mrs. Painter, Green and Marvin. I also prayed for myself. In about ten days from that time I was in my sitting room. It was raining. A minister and his daughter were at our house (Mr. Laurance, a Baptist). We were all quietly reading in the room. I was in meditation, praying and saying: "Just now, blessed Father, give me the witness." Then a wonderful thing took place, which it is not "lawful" or possible for me to utter. Something was poured on top of my head, running all over and through me, which I call divine electricity. The two persons who were in the room, Mr. Laurance and his daughter, were very much startled, for I jumped up, clapped my hands, saying: "I have this from God, this divine Gift." I went below in the basement that I might give vent to my gratitude, and under my breath I walked up and down, thanking, praising, crying and laughing.

Like the woman that found the piece of silver that was lost, I had to tell my neighbors. I wrapped myself up to be protected from the rain, and ran to Sister Painters, near by, then to Sister Dollars and Marvin's and several others, to tell them of my great blessing.

When I returned I opened my Bible. Every word and every letter was surrounded with a bright light. I turned over the leaves, and I saw the meaning on the pages at a glance. There was a new light and meaning. I have never been able to express that experience in any other way than to say I was "eating" the word of God. I could now understand why we do not understand the figures and expressions used in the Bible, because I have had several experiences, that were impossible to explain by human language.

I told Mr. Nation that the Bible was a new book to me, tried to explain to him; told him I now saw the meaning of everything. He said: "Explain Lazarus and the rich man." I turned to it instantly. The divine light gave a new meaning to me. I commented thus as I read it: "This rich man is the Jewish nation, with its gorgeous temple service. The poor man is the Gentile nations called dogs, no temple, no altar, no God, no healing; like a man with an incurable loathsome disease. These begged from the Jews the crumbs that fell to their dogs. This rich man had much goods. He could have shared to bless, but through lack of charity he withheld.

The beggar died, and angels took him to Abraham's bosom, the very place the Jews thought was only for them. This is a figure of the death to sin, and the life to righteousness. The natural must die before the spiritual can live. The rich man died, and was buried. The Jewish nation died as it is here predicted, and in hell, he lifted up his eyes, being in torments. It is not said that the Gentiles, or Lazarus were buried. The Jews as a nation are dead, never to be resurrected. They have been scattered abroad in torments, a people without a land, a hiss and a by- word, as God said. The Jew sees the Gentiles with the good things, he once had. Has time and time again begged relief from them. The Jews wish no companionship in their misery, have no missionaries. Five is a number applied to humanity.—five senses, five fingers, five toes. The gulf spoken of as being impassable, is the separateness of the Jews from all others.

The rich man wants one from the dead to go to his five brethren, or humanity. Abraham or the Gospel reminds the Jew that Moses and the prophets were as convincing; they would not believe them. Christ said: "If ye had believed Moses, ye would have believed me for he wrote of me. If ye believe not him, neither will ye believe, though one arose from the dead." Christ in this parable prophesied of his own death and resurrection, they did not believe when he arose from the dead.

Scripture was given a meaning I had never heard of before. This light continued for about three days. Oh! if I had devoted all my time then to reading while I had this divine light! We never know the value of any blessing, until it is gone. Persons almost universally say of me: "You have studied and remember so much of the Bible," but this is a gift from God. I know why God gave this to me. Because I have always been a reader and a student of holy teachings, even when it was sealed, and often to me, contradictory. "If any will do His will, they shall know of the doctrine." Jesus said: "Search the Scriptures." "Study to show thyself a workman well approved unto God, that needeth not to be ashamed, rightly divining the word of truth." 'Tis a sweet love letter by an independent God to a dependent people. "Oh! the depth of the wisdom, both of the knowledge and power of God! How unsearchable are his judgements and his ways past finding out." Yet His love can be felt and known by all. Not one of the severe judgements of God but they reflect this tender love of God, in destroying that which love hates, because sin is the enemy of love, the bitter foe to the happiness of mankind; therefore 'tis an evidence of the intensity of love to destroy sin. Take for instance the destruction of the Amalekites. This people was a curse to the earth and the enemy of all good. "Remember what Amalek did unto thee, by the way, when ye were come forth out of Egypt." "How he met thee by the way, and smote the hindermost of thee, even all that were behind thee when thou wast faint and weary; and he feared not God. Therefore it shall be when the Lord thy God hath given thee rest from thine enemies, thou shalt blot out the remembrance of Amalek from under heaven." God waited four hundred years from this time. They still were murderers. Then he told Saul to utterly destroy this cruel nation. The state kills a man now. This is not a cruelty but a mercy, "And those which remain shall hear and fear and shall henceforth commit no more any such evil." "'Tis a righteous retribution to recompense tribulation to those who trouble you."

Persons often argue that the books of the Bible are written by man and cannot be said to be written by God. I illustrate the way God wrote the Bible by this: You have a package of letters from your mother. Some are written with red ink, some with black, some with a stub pen, some with a fine point, some with a pencil, etc. You do not say, the pen wrote me this letter and the pencil wrote me that. No, this is not spoken of or considered. You say: "My mother wrote these letters to me." Just so, Moses is God's pen, with which he wrote the five books of the Pentateuch. Joshua was also a pen, and Ezra, Job, David, Solomon, and so with the writers of the New Testament. God guided them as we do our pen. The Bible carries within itself its own evidence of divinity. It requires no proof. It but weakens its own evidence, to appeal to human aid. The fulfilled prophesy, its inimitable poetry, is proof to the natural man to KNOW it to be above the human mind, and to a child of God it speaks with life, and love more potent than an earthly parent to their child. The Holy Spirit only can interpret his own words: "'Tis foolishness to those who perish, but unto us who are saved it is the power of God."

I have a great benediction on my work. Wherever I go the dear mothers shake my hand and kiss my face, saying: "God bless you. I want to help you. You did what I wanted to do." It is the heart of motherhood running over with love. "The gentle are the brave, the loving are the daring."

I got a telegram from a man saying: "Your article in Physical Culture on the use of tobacco has cured me of the vice." One man from Omaha, Nebraska, wrote: "Three years ago I was a drunkard. I had a drug store. I was losing business and going to ruin generally. When I heard of what you did, I said: 'If that woman can do that to save others, I ought to do something for myself.' So now I am a changed man. My wife is a changed woman. I have to thank you and Almighty God. My business is growing every day."

Upon several occasions I have had people to put five dollars in my hand. While I was lecturing in Pasadena, California, for the Y. M. C. A. one young man put in my hand what I thought was a silver dollar, but on looking it was a twenty dollar gold piece. I said: "I will lay that up in heaven for you." And so I have. I never learned his name but he will certainly find that twenty dollars in the bank of heaven with interest.

When I first started out in this crusade I was called crazy and a "freak" by my enemies, but now they say: "No, Carry Nation, you are not crazy, but you are sharp. You started out to accomplish something and you did. You are a grafter. It is the money you are after." Jesus said: "John came neither eating or drinking and ye say, Behold a wine bibber and a glutton." So it is the world never did understand an unselfish life. It is a small thing to be judged by a man that withers as grass. "If I yet please man, I should not be the servant of Christ."

CHAPTER XV.

SPIRITUAL AUTHORITY FOR MY CHRISTIAN WORK.

There have been from the first time I started out persons who understood that God moved me. These were students of the Old Scriptures. Jesus told the people before the New Testament was written to "search the Scriptures—these are they that testify of me. ALL Scripture is given by inspiration of God and is profitable for doctrine, for correction, for instruction in righteousness, that the man of God may be thoroughly furnished unto every good work." To be thorough one must know the old as well as the new. In all the sermons of Paul, Peter and the rest, they quote from old Scripture. So did Jesus. Read Peter's first sermon on the day of Pentecost. There is a tendency to study the New Testament more than the Old. It is not possible to understand the New, unless we first study the Old. One of my favorite books is Deuteronomy, the dying words of Moses. He here repeats the great mercy, consideration and power of God's dealings with his people. Tells the kind of characters God will bless. How God loves the pure and good. How He hates the wicked. We here see that God creates good and evil, and holds us responsible for the choosing. While God rules in all things we have the power to bring on ourselves blessings or cursings. This book declares the man or woman invincible that abandons himself or herself to do God's will.

> "True merit lies in braving the unequal.
> True glory comes from daring to begin.
> God loves the man or woman, who reckless of the sequel,
> Fights long and well, whether they lose or win."

In the seventh chapter of Deuteronomy, God commanded the children of Israel to "destroy the images," "break down" the altars and "burn the graven images" of the Gods of the heathen. This was smashing. Also said to them: "If you do not drive them out they shall be thorns in your sides." God gave them power and ability to do this, then he required them to do it. God supplies man's cannots, not his "will nots." In Numbers twenty-fifth chapter, Phineas was given God's covenant of peace and the priesthood, because he slew the woman and man that were committing sin: "Because he was jealous for his God and made an atonement for the children of Israel." This was smashing. God himself smashed up Sodom and Gomorrah. In the seventeenth chapter of Deuteronomy, God says: "The idolator and blasphemer shall be stoned with stones till he die. So shalt thou put away evil from you." This is smashing. I could write a book recounting the incidents recorded in God's Word.

"What is in thine hand, Abel?"

"Nothing but one wee lamb, O God, taken from the flock. I purpose offering it to thee, a willing sacrifice."

And so he did. And the sweet smell of that burning has been filling the air ever since, and constantly going up to God as a perpetual sacrifice of praise.

"What is it thou hast in thine hand, Moses?"

"Nothing but a staff, O God, with which I tend my flocks."

"Take it and use it for me."

And he did; and with it wrought more wondrous things than Egypt and her proud king had seen before.

"Mary, what is that thou hast in thine hand?"

"Nothing but a pot of sweet-smelling ointment, O God, wherewith I would anoint thine only One called Jesus."

And so she did; and not only did the perfume fill all the house in which they were, but the Bible-reading world has been fragrant with the memory of this blessed act of love, which has ever since been spoken of "for a memorial of her."

"Poor woman, what is it that thou hast in thine hand?"

"Only two mites, Lord. It is very little; but then it is all I have, and I would put it into thy treasury."

And so she did; and the story of her generous giving has ever since wrought like a charm, prompting others to give to the Lord.

"What is it that thou hast in thine hand, Dorcas?"

"Only a needle, Lord."

"Take it and use it for me."

And so she did; and not only were the suffering poor of Joppa warmly clad, but inspired by her loving life. "Dorcas Societies" even now continue their benign mission to the poor throughout the earth.

"What is it in thine hand, Shamgar?"

"Only an ox goad, a stick with which to drive oxen. I slew six hundred enemies of God and man delivering from slavery God's people."

"What is it in thine hand Samson?"

"The jaw bone of an ass which was a power in the hand used by God, to slay a thousand wicked cruel infidels."

"David why do you lay aside the armor of Saul and meet the giant, with only a sling?"

"My God will give me the power to slay the foe to mercy and truth."

"Carry Nation, what have you in your hand?"

Sometimes a rock; sometimes a hatchet; God told me to use these to smash that which has smashed and will smash hearts and souls. The sound of this loving deed will stir conscience and hearts and while I can not finish the smashing, the voter of this nation will use their ballots that will, and this impulse will Carry A. Nation.

God sent an angel from heaven to tell Gideon to smash up the altar and image of Baal. By divine command Achan and family were smashed. God would not give Joshua victory until this was done. Saul was commanded by God (through his prophet Samuel,) to utterly destroy the Amalekite's nation, and all their substance. He was disobedient and saved the king. Samuel hacked or smashed up Agag, although Saul was the regularly appointed one. This is a case directly in point. The officers in Kansas were oath-bound to do what Carry A. Nation did.

Our Savior's mission on earth was to "break (smash) every yoke and set the captive free." Upon two occasions he made a scourge, of small cords and laid it on the backs of wicked men who were doing unlawful things. He came into this world "to destroy the works of the devil", to "bruise" or crush the "head of the serpent". We are told to "Abhor that which is evil", to "resist (or fight) the devil and he will flee'". We are not to be "overcome with evil but to overcome evil with good". How? Resist the devil. God blessed the church at Ephesus, because they "hated the evil workers, tried them and found them liars". The hatred of sin is one mark of a Christian. Just in proportion to your love for God will be your hatred of evil. I will here give you a Bible reading on the subject. These are some instances of smashing. The ten plagues of Egypt and the overthrow of Pharaoh, were smashing. The death of of the first born also.

Gen. 19:24 30:15-19 6:25 9:5,6
Josh. 7:25, 26 7:20 4:7-11 7:10,11 15:15
Lev. 19:17 10:24-26 9:53
Num. 33:55,56 23:7
1 Sam. 15:33
Deut. 7:2-5 7:10-13
2 Chron. 34:4,5 21:1-9 19:20
Neh. 13:8-25 21:18-21
Judg. 2:3
Isa. 28:21 13:12-18 3:10 54:16 17:5-7 3:31

Matt. 21:12 19:13-20 4:21
John 2:13-23 25:17-19 5:7
Acts 13:8-11.

If I could I would turn the key on every church in the land, so as to teach some preachers to go out, and not stay in, and compel poor sinners to stay out. I yield no territory to the devil. Let us take every saloon, every house of prostitution of men and women for God. "There shall not a hoof be left behind." "The kingdom of heaven suffereth violence, and the VIOLENT take it by force," which means that where the evil is aggressive, we must be more so, and take, compelling surrender by the determination never to yield.

I feel that I have been peculiarly favored to go into these places, to "cry aloud and spare not and show my people their sins." I find this class so hungry for something better. These poor actresses, who dress in tights and sing indecent songs, are a weary, tired, heart-sick lot of slaves. I mingle with them as a sister. When I can say a warning word I say it. I call them affectionate names and mean it. God will judge both of us. He knows who loved much; he can forgive much. Christ said to a lot of men who took the amen pews: "The publicans and harlots will go into heaven before you." Why? They "repented when they heard". "How are they to bear without a preacher?" I never see a man or woman so low but as a sculptor said of the marble: "There is an angel there." Oh, God, help me to bring it out!

Jesus received sinners and ate with them. He left a command that Christians should invite these to feasts in their homes. Oh! what a revival of religion there would be if the homes of Christians were opened to the lost and sinful, who are dying for some demonstration of love. If the Son of God, the lovely, the pure, the blessed ate with sinners, ought it not to be a privilege to follow Him. We are commanded to "warn, rebuke, and reprove with all long suffering and doctrine." People will work in a revival to get sinners saved, and will pass them day after day on the street and not a word of Scripture, do they use to remind them of God's judgements. Jesus said: "The world hateth me because I testify that the works thereof are evil." I have had men to swear at me, call me names and threaten to knock me down. At first this caused me to feel mortified but that passed off. These very men have afterward told me I was right and they were wrong. The devil "threw some on the ground and they foamed at the mouth" before he was cast out. I have often taken cigars and cigarettes out of men's and boy's mouths. I wished to show them the wrong and that I was a friend. Would you let one you love take a knife to open a vein or cut himself? Oh! the sweetness and force of that promise: "Your LABOR is never in vain in the Lord." This covers all cases, if you, for the love of God, do anything. I often say to myself, after rebuking for sin: "You made a mistake in the way you did this or that, and are you sure it was done for the love of God and your neighbor?" "Yes."

Then "your labor is never in vain in the Lord". It is not WHAT we do that prospers, but what God blesses.. "He that planteth is nothing and he that watereth is nothing, but it is God that giveth the increase." And it matters not how awkward the work, if it be done from love of God, it will prosper. Like other things, the more you do, the better you can do.

All the Christian work I ever did seemed to meet with severe opposition from church members. This is a great stumbling-block to some. The church crucified our blessed Christ, that is, it was the hypocrites; for the church is the light and salt, the body of Christ. "If I yet please men, I should not be the servant of Christ." There is no other organization but the church of Christ that persecutes its own followers. The hierarchy in the church told Christ "He had a devil," but they could not meet the argument when He said: "A kingdom divided against itself will not stand." "If I, by the spirit of Beelzebub, cast out devils, by what kind of a spirit do your children cast them out." The devil never destroys his own work. If the saloon is of the devil, the power that destroys it is the opposite. If a mother should see a gun pointed at her son would she break the law to snatch the gun and smash it? The gun was not hers. It may have been worth a thousand dollars. The saloon is worse than the gun which could only destroy the body.

It is a great blessing to know your mission in life. I know why Christians are waiting with folded hands, not being able to see their mission. They are not willing to pay the great price for their commission. The rich young man could have been a follower of Jesus, the greatest honor in earth or heaven, and could have had eternal treasure in heaven for the transient gain of earth. He would not pay the price. You must give all, to get all. The effect of smashing has always been to cause the people to arouse themselves. The Levite that severed his dead concubine and sent parts of her body to the different tribes of Israel was to cause the people to "consider, take advice and speak." Then they acted and four hundred thousand men presented themselves to redress this wrong.

The smashing in Kansas was to arouse the people. If some ordinary means had been used, people would have heard and forgotten, but the "strange act" demanded an explanation and the people wanted that, and they never will stop talking about this until the question is settled. Let us consider the character of Moses. It is said this man disobeyed God but once, and he was the "meekest of all men". We are first attracted to him peculiarly because he "refused to be called the son of Pharaoh's daughter, rather suffering afflictions with the people of God than to enjoy the pleasures of sin for a season." Rather be counted with the poor despised, afflicted slaves under the taskmaster's lash than be a king or an absolute monarch. This brought out his characteristic prohibition of sin,—the renouncing of every worldly ambition, He here made the choice, at the time when the temptations were greatest, for all that the world could offer was his. He gave all and paid the price it requires to get all. On the banks of the Nile he sees one man oppressing another. That spirit of prohibition of this great wrong caused him to strike (smash) the oppressor.

Here is a lovable trait of this great man. Moses, could not look on and see the helpless suffer at the hands of another, even though it brought death to himself. Forgetful of his own safety, defying the absolute power and authority of this despot, so far as it lay in his power, against all these odds he redressed the wrong of a fellow creature. God saw in Moses a man whom He could use. From the golden throne he sought a retreat, and for forty years was an humble shepherd, learning the lesson of caring for the flocks of Jethro, before he should be called to take the oversight of the flock of God. "He that is faithful in that which is least is faithful also in that which is much." God called this man out of the wilderness to go to the greatest court on earth as His ambassador. Not one compromise would he make, still true to his prohibition principles. God never used or blessed any man or woman that was not a prohibitionist. Eli was one of those conservatives and said only, "Nay verily my sons." And he got his neck broke and both of his sons killed in one day, because he "restrained (or prohibited) not his sons in the iniquity which he knew." Moses, although the meekest of all men, he said to Pharaoh, "There shall not a hoof be left behind." True to the uncompromising spirit of a great leader. When in the Mount, seeing the idolatry, smashed the two tables of stone. Why? He would not deliver the holy laws to a people who were insulting God. This smashing was a demonstration of Moses jealousy for his God. After this I can see him striding down to the place of this "ball" or "hugging". The round dance of the present day is but a repetition of those lascivious plays, and with his ax or hatchet he hacked up that malicious property, shaped into a golden calf. This did not belong to Moses. It was very valuable but he smashed it and ground it to powder and then to further humiliate these rebels, he made them drink the dust mixed with water, then to absolutely destroy and stamp with a vengeance this insult to God, he divided the people and those who were "on the Lord's side" fought with these rebels and slew (smashed) three thousand men. In one of the canonical books of the Catholic Bible we have the story of the holy woman Judeth who cut off the head of Hollifernese to save God's people. Esther the gentle loving queen had the wicked sons of Haman hanged. Our supremest idea of justice is a reward for the good and a punishment for the wicked. We amputate the arm to save the body. David says: "I will not know a wicked person; he that telleth lies shall not dwell in my sight."

The devil has his agents in the churches, and among those who are doing his work the best, are a class of professors who testify that you must not speak ill of any one, not even the devil. They are the "non- resistives". The devil is delighted to be respected, and not fought. He gets his work in just as he wants to and he can imitate true conversion, if he can place in the church those who hinder a warfare against sin. Paul said: "I tell you even weeping they are enemies of the cross of Christ." They are the devils in light. "But there must needs be heresies among you that they who are approved may be manifest." Persons often propose to do something. I may not see the advisability, but because there is action in it, I never object. Oh! for somebody to "do with their might what their hands find to do." "Well DONE" is the best commendation. Faith is like the wind, we cannot see it, but by the quantity of motion and commotion. There are workers "jerkers" and "shirkers"; but through much tribulation and temptation must we enter into the kingdom of heaven. The counterfeit proves the genuine dollar; counterfeits are not counterfeited. So hypocrites prove the genuine Christians. If there were not a genuine there would not be a hypocrite. Our mother and grandmothers who went into saloons praying and spilling the poisoned slop of these houses of crime and tears were blessed in their DEEDS. Oh! that the W. C. T. U. would do as they did, what a reform would take place. I love the organization of mothers. I love their holy impulses but I am heart-sick at their conventionality, their red tape. This organization could put out of existence every drinking hell in the United States if they would demand it and use the power they have even without the ballot. I intend to help the women of the Kansas W. C. T. U., but not one that has any respect for either Republican or Democratic parties shall ever be called on to aid me in my work, women who are not wise enough to know that the rum voting parties are traitors, can be nothing but a hindrance to the interests of mothers. One said to me, "You will cause many women to leave the organization." I said: "Good riddance to bad rubbish, the quicker they get out the better." As Nehemiah, that grand prohibitionist, said: "What have you to do to build the walls of our God."

CHAPTER XVI.

IN NEBRASKA.—WHAT I DID WITH THE FIRST MONEY I GAVE TO THE LORD.— AT CONEY ISLAND.—WHAT I SAID OF MR. MCKINLEY.—IN CALIFORNIA. "CRIBS" AT LOS ANGELES.—ARREST IN SAN FRANCISCO.—CONDEMNED BY SOME MINISTERS.—WHISKEY AND TOBACCO ADVERTISEMENTS,

I told my manager James E. Furlong, to give W. C. T. U. and Prohibitionists the preference, and not to charge them as much. I tried to get into churches, but only a few would open to me. I had many inducements financially to go on the stage but I refused to do so for sometime. Like a little child I have had to sit alone, creep and walk. I paid my fines by monthly installments and in December, of 1902, I settled with the court at Topeka for the "Malicious destruction of property," when, in fact, it was the "Destruction of malicious property."

In the spring of 1902, I went to Nebraska, under the management of Mrs. M. A. S. Monegan. This woman had also made dates for J. G. Woolley and other prominent prohibition lecturers. She was a thorough prohibitionist and by conversing with her I for the first time found the remedy for the licensed saloon. This is "National Prohibition".

I held a debate in Lincoln with Bixbee, of the Journal, a rank republican, who used only ridicule and satire, for he had no argument of course. I lectured for and with the "Red Ribbon Alliance" there who were so faithfully working and praying for the abolition of the saloon. The spring election in Lincoln was for prohibition but lost by sixty votes. William Jennings Bryan lives there and if he, the man who poses as a friend of the people, had opened his mouth against the saloon he could have made this great cause more than the sixty votes. From that time forth I knew Bryan was for Bryan and what Bryan could get for Bryan.

I lectured at the parks and chautauquas in the summer and fairs in the fall, and at the end of the year of 1902, I had the sum of five thousand dollars which I used to build a mission on Central Ave., Kansas City, Kansas. In that vicinity were several dives and I told those poor criminals that we would soon run them out. I had my brother, Campbell Moore, to manage the erection of this brick building. The liquor men tried to buy the ground to hinder the work, but at last the building was finished. I was offered seventy-five dollars rent for the hall but refused it. Then I went to the Salvation Army barracks in Kansas City, Mo., and offered to give it to them free of rent if they would start a mission. They did not see their way clear to accept it. My brother told me of a property that would suit me better for the purpose of a "Home for

Drunkards' Wives and Mothers", which I was trying to arrive at through the mission. I went to see this property, and found it to be about two acres, with a twenty room brick house and a good brick stable on it, nice drives and forest trees, and while it is in the city, it is on a high elevation and as much retired from the dust and crowd as in the country. Mr. Simpson, the owner, sent me ten dollars while I was in jail at Wichita, and he was anxious to let me have this home of his that he had improved himself. I purchased this with the money I got from the other place, paying him five thousand five hundred dollars, owing the rest. This place is situated on Reynolds and Grandview Aves. It was not possible for me to begin this enterprise myself, and in speaking to Myron A. Waterman, of the Savings Bank of Kansas City, Kansas, he suggested that the "Associated Charities" of Kansas City, Kansas, would put it to the use I intended. I liked the idea. The society became incorporated so they could receive the deed, which was a trust, for should the property be used for other than what it was given for, it will revert.

The society took possession in December, 1903, and at this writing, February, 1904, it is full, the Home of many poor and destitute, who now have a good shelter, warmth and light free. They are expected to make their own living. Mr. Simpson gave forty dollars to furnish one room. The local W. C. T. U. have furnished their room and have their two drunkards' wives in it. I here make a plea of help to enlarge this Home. As stated there are two acres of ground and one who would give money to this would fulfill the command to feed the hungry and clothe the naked; these are the orphans and the widows; every dollar will be put in the bank of Heaven.

My motive for doing this was twofold. I wanted to furnish a home for these, the innocent results of the saloon, whose sad condition is beyond words to describe. The people burden themselves with taxes to build jails, penitentiaries, alms houses, insane ayslums, and reformatories to care for the guilty results of the saloon. They pay millions to prosecute these criminals, the result of the saloon, but no one has ever thought of a building, or shelter for these women who are worse than widows, who are free from any fault in this matter, but are the greatest sufferers.

I have been asked by my friends not to call it a "Home for Drunkards' Wives and Mothers", for it would be a reflection on the inmates. Not at all. The condemnation is on the party which makes a demand for such a home, by voting for saloons. The question, Why? will arise in the minds of all who see on the arch over the entrance to this place, "Home for Drunkards' Wives and Mothers". Why? "Because of the saloon. Let us smash the saloon and not these women's homes and hearts." Miss Edith Short is the secretary and is at the home all the time, and she is the right woman in the right place.

There are many persons who would like to donate to such a place. We are waiting for funds to enlarge the place, making rooms or flats for these dear ones. A letter directed to "Drunkards' Wives Home", Kansas City, Kansas, will reach the place, for there is no other of the kind in the world. It was such a relief to me when I saw that what means I could control was used in a manner God would bless, and it was a great source of joy to me to do something for this class. I have been a drunkard's wife myself and I know the desolation of heart they have. This is a worse sorrow than to have one's husband die. A wife always feels that she might have done something to cause her husband to drink or to quit. I believe that some men have been led to drink by women, but it is a cowardly resort, or excuse, and the man who would make this as an excuse is as bad as the woman that caused him to drink, if not worse. The thief, the murderer, or any other class of criminals could just as well blame others for their own wrong doings.

{illust. caption = Mrs. Carry Nation's "Home for Drunkards' Wives and Children" One of two fine properties in Kansas purchased by Mrs. Carry Nation with the money she earned on her lecturing tours. In this way she believes she can bring comfort into the lives now darkened and saddened by the saloon curse.}

When I was at Coney Island, I was asked, what I thought of William McKinley's administration? I said: "I was glad when McKinley was elected for I had heard that he was opposed to the liquor traffic. I did not know then that he rented his wife's property in Canton, Ohio, for saloon purposes, and after his election he had been a constant disappointment to me; that he was the Brewers' president and did their biddings; that we as W. C. T. U. workers, sent petitions, thousands of them to Mr. McKinley to have him refuse to let the canteen run. That we were willing to give our boys to fight the battles of this nation, to die in a foreign land, but we were not willing that a murderer should follow them from their home shores to kill their bodies and souls." This was said at the time that he was thought to be convalescent from his death-wound. I said: "I had no tears for McKinley, neither have I any for his assassin. That no one's life was safe with such a murderer at large." This roused hisses; some left the hall and there was a murmer of confusion. One man threw a wad of paper at me, but I said: "My loyalty to the homes of America demand that I denounce such a president and his crowd." It was a common thing to be hissed. Once I spoke in Sioux City, Iowa, in the church where the martyred Haddock preached. The crowd was so large, the church was filled and emptied three times. I had cheers and hisses at the same time. At the first meeting I was talking at the top of my voice, the audience was clapping and hissing and a good evangelistic brother by my side kept pounding his fist of one hand into the palm of the other and shouting: "She is right! She is right!" That was a great meeting, and I shall never forget it, neither will anyone who was there. I spoke three times to audiences that night. I have been hissed, and after giving the people time to think, have been applauded by the same parties. "Oh, fools and slow of heart to understand," Jesus said.

Murat Halstead, who wrote the book called, "Our Martyred President or the Illustrious Life of William McKinley", wrote some positive falsehoods concerning me. This Halstead has always been a defender of anarchy or the licensed saloon.

William McKinley was no martyr. He was murdered by a man who was the result of a saloon and could not tell why he murdered the President.

I could tell of many amusing incidents, indeed. I could fill a book of interesting anecdotes. Once when I was among the Thousand Islands of the St. Lawrence, in the summer of 1902, a characteristic woman with a very low dress, with a very long train, the whole a mixture of paint, powder, lace, flashy jewelry and corset stays, with as much exposure of person as she dare, came to me in an affected manner, handed me a roll saying: "I am a temperance lecturer, here is one of my bills." I replied: "If you are such, you had better make a practical application of temperance and cover up yourself." The change of her countenance was instantaneous and she with a queer almost startled look said: "You go to He—l."

Once in Elmira, N. Y. the streets were so crowded that we had to leave the Salvation Army Hall. I climbed in a farmer's two horse wagon. He came out of a saloon and gathered up the reins and laid the whip to his horses, which were caught so as to let me out.

Mr. Furlong, my manager, had a keen sense of the ridiculous and would let me alone when I started out. He said he knew I could take care of myself. Often when I would rise to speak to the thousands in the parks, there would be yells and groans, and a manager at Youngstown, Ohio, said to Mr. Furlong: "She will not get a chance to speak." Mr. Furlong said: "You watch how she will handle them." I would always quiet them for at least a time. Once they were determined not to let me talk. I at last went to one side of the stage and began talking very explanatory to some parties in front. The rest wanted to hear, so they were quiet. Then I gave them the hot-shots of truth. I always invited interruptions by questions. I had no set speech and these questions would bring out what the crowd wanted to hear. I like especially the questions from those who oppose me. I have bad men to shake their fists at me saying: "You are an anarchist and ought to be in the lunatic asylum." One agent of a brewer in Hartford, Conn., kept on disturbing the meeting; at last he said: "Why did Christ make wine?" I said: "the wine that He made did not rot. His was the unfermented juice of the grape. God made healthy fruit and grain. The devil rots them and makes alcohol, which rots the brain, rots the body and rots the soul, and that is what is the matter with you."

When I first began my lectures I was not taken seriously by the people. They did not see the great principle back of the work. My manager said: "We must make all the dates this year, for next year it will not be so easy." I said: "You will find it easier, for I will be more popular." He shook his head, but sure enough it was easier. We could not fill the dates, and now the calls are more and more all over the country.

In the winter and spring of 1903, I was in California. I was employed by the theatrical manager of the "Chutes." Beer was sold at this resort. Some W. C. T. U. were very much horrified that I would go to such a place. Mrs. Hester T. Griffith, the president of the Federation of Unions in Los Angeles, came to see me. She had been a staunch friend of mine from the first and she went with me to the "Chutes" and introduced me. This she did time and again saying: "If she had the opportunity to speak at the "Chutes" she would do as Carry Nation does." This woman was a blessing to me. She helped me to see that the stage was a mission field. I was severely criticised by the newspapers, and especially by some of the ministers. One from Rockford, Ill., a Rev. Dr. Van Horn wrote a very slanderous article which I heard of through my friends there. I was arrested in Los Angeles for some advertising my manager did which was contrary to a city ordinance.

In Los Angeles I saw what was called the "Cribs", one of the most disgraceful conditions. No one stayed there during the day; they were there just for the night only. These poor degraded girls would pay two dollars a night to the owners. I said to the women: "These city officials are at the bottom of this. Let us go to the Chief of Police," whose name was Elton. He would not talk to me at first. He said: "If we close these places, these degraded girls will be over the town," when in fact the girls only stayed there at night. I have seen so much of the corruption of the officials that when conditions are bad in any place I know it to be their fault.

We went as a band of missionaries to these dens of vice. At first an officer would go before us and have the girls pull their blinds down to prevent us from seeing or speaking to them. We found hundreds of them who could not speak the English language, they had been brought over by procurers for the purpose of swelling the ranks of this vice. Mrs. Charlton Edholm who wrote "Traffic in Girls", was there helping to rid the city of this disgrace. Her book should be in the hands of every girl in the world. This grand woman has devoted her life work to the rescue of girls. She is in Oakland, California, where she has a "Rescue Home". Any one can get the book by writing her. I also met Mrs. Sobieski, wife of Col. John Sobieski. Sister Sobieski is one who never tires in the work for God. She is a terror to evil doers. God bless these women for their zeal. I found some of the most aggressive christian W. C. T. U. women I have ever seen in Los Angeles, California. I am glad to say that in less than a year from the time I was there the "Cribs" were closed.

I was arrested in San Francisco and spent most of the night in jail, was put in for destroying a bottle of whiskey on this wise: A certain saloon-keeper had just finished a very fine "criminal factory" and he wanted to advertise it. He sent me word by my manager to call and smash this place up. He had a fine mirror he paid one hundred and fifty dollars for that he wanted me to smash. I knew that all he wanted was an advertisement, but I went, not saying what I would do. He had reporters and the house was crowded. I got up on a table to make a speech, which, I did in this fashion: "This man has opened a place to drug and rob poor victims. There are no clothes, no food, no books here, nothing but what degrades men and women." Some one handed me a large empty bottle. I said: "No I want a bottle that has some of that fiery poison in it." I was given a quart bottle of whiskey. I held it up and said: "None but God knows the sorrows in this bottle, the headaches, the heartaches, the desolation, but there is no blessing or happiness connected with it. I will do with this what ought to be done with all its kind." So I threw it as quickly as I could behind the bar on the floor. It fell in with some others and made a great smash. I said: "The man wished me to make a hole in that large mirror so that curiosity would draw others into this snare to catch our boys." I gave the best rebuke for the occasion I could, then I went to my hotel, retired, and about twelve o'clock an officer came to my door. I dressed and went with him to the station. I stayed there until nearly three in the morning. While there I saw one continual stream of poor, drunken wretches, men and women, brought in. My manager came and took me out on bail. Next morning I appeared in court, was my own lawyer. The case was put off two days, then I was discharged. The saloon keeper withdrew the charge. This was done, to advertise this man but the way that I advertise has never done the whiskey business any good.

There is a great art in advertising. Jacob was the first one I read of in the Bible who was aware of this art and science, when he placed the rods before the cattle. The eye is the window by which the inner man, who does not think, is mostly taught. There is no business in America so much advertised as the whiskey and tobacco business. Both are destructive in their influence on the morals and the health of the people. We would be better off without these articles. The interest of these manufactories are built up in proportion as they can catch the unwary who see these signs that are suggestive. One of the most notorious signs is "Wilson's Whiskey That's All". Yes that is ALL it takes to ruin your homes. That is all it takes to break a mother's heart. That is all that is needed to build houses of prostitution and that is ALL that it requires to break up every impulse of justice and love and happiness. That is

ALL that it takes to fill hell. How my heart is stirred when I see this: "Remember me, Oh, my God!"

Whiskey or tobacco never introduce their products by reason or arguments, they never appeal to thought, but suggestion or temptation, and as oft as the eye is lifted, as one walks up the streets of our cities there are hundreds of advertisements to meet the gaze; most every one has a false basis. For instance there is a sign: "Old Crow Whiskey." This is slandering the crow, for there is not a crow or vulture that will use a drop of this slop. There is: "Chew Bull-dog Twist," and "Bull Durham Tobacco." There is not a dog or bull that uses tobacco. There is the, "Royal Bengal Tiger Cigarettes." This is taking advantage of these animals because they can not defend themselves. There is the: "Robert Burns and Tom Moore cigars." There was not a cigar in England when Burns or Tom Moore lived. I have seen a life-size picture of Abraham Lincoln advertising cigars, when Lincoln was a teetotaler from cigars or any intoxicating drink. He promised his mother that he would never use them and kept his promise to his death. This is slandering the dead. I never remember seeing the "Grant Cigar". He died with tobacco cancer. It is said that Mr. McKinley would have recovered but his blood was bad from nicotine.

CHAPTER XVII.

MY VISIT TO WASHINGTON, D. C.—ARRESTED IN THE SENATE CHAMBER.— TAKEN OUT BY OFFICERS.—THE VICES OF COLLEGES, ESPECIALLY YALE— ROOSEVELT A DIVE-KEEPER.

In February, of 1904, I went to Washington, purposely to call on Mr. Roosevelt, the President. Was refused an audience. While in the office of Secretary Loeb, a delegation of politicians, republicans and democrats, came out of the president's apartments with their mutual admiration compliments and suavity of political tricksters.

I asked them what difference there was in their parties? They looked silly and said nothing. Mr. Loeb said: "We do not wish any questions on the subject." I said: "It is a civil question, it ought to have a civil answer." Mr. Loeb called to a police to take me out. I said: "If I was a brewer or distiller I could have an interview. As a representive mother, I ought to be received. I wished to ask him why he practiced the vice of smoking cigarettes? Why he has never said a word against the licensed saloon when it is the greatest question that ever confronted the homes of America? Why he had a coat of arms on his flag? Why he brought a dive into Kansas? I was taken outside in a very orderly manner by two policemen, something unusual, for I am hustled and dragged generally.

Then I went to the Capitol. I called to see Senator Cockrell from Missouri. I asked him his opinion on the liquor traffic. He got excited immediately. He said: "I want no one to mention that subject to me." I said: "It is strange to me that you do not want to converse on the greatest subject before the American people." He became so indignant that he stamped his foot and threatened to have me put out of the building. I also became indignant, and stamped my foot, and said: "Down with your treason! Down with your saloons! You are sent here to represent the interest of the mothers and their children, and you insult a representative mother because you are representing the interest of the brewers and distillers." During this speech of mine he was making tracks up the corridor. Then I went to the House of Representatives and the Senate Chamber. My "spirit was stirred within me", to see at the head of the American people the bitterest enemies to the defense of the homes of America, the very thing our forefathers intended to secure to this people. I wanted to do some "Hatchetation", that not being possible, I thought I would do some agitation. I took a position in a lobby near a door. I rose to my feet, and with a volume of voice that was distinctly heard all over the halls I cried aloud: "Treason, anarchy and conspiracy! Discuss these!" I knew that I would be put out, but I selected these three words to call the attention to the fact that these were more necessary to be discussed than any other subjects. And these were the very ones they were avoiding most. I was taken down to the police station. Court was in session. I had my trial and was fined twenty-five dollars. I made my own plea before the judge, as I had no lawyer. I justified myself upon the same principle that a man would to give a fire alarm. The judge said that he sympathized with my cause but he gave me the maximum fine. I have had just such sympathy as this from all republican judges. The kind of sympathy that a cat has for a mouse when she crushes the bones between her teeth.

I am a loyal American. We want true Americans to represent the principles of Americans. I had my prejudice increased against Mr. Roosevelt when I heard of the "coat of arms" on his flag, in violation of every principle of American citizenship. We have no "my lords" in this country. The people rule here and not the president, for he is the servant. The brewers of America are mostly German and Dutch, and of course the Dutch president is their friend. Roosevelt is also a member of the Order of Eagles, the strongest liquor organization in the United States. Oh, shade of American heroes look down and condemn this outrage to your ashes. I have it from three eye witnesses that Roosevelt smokes and did smoke cigarettes. His secretary, Mr. Loeb, denied this to Mrs. Dye Ellis, but Mr. Roosevelt dare not deny it. The minister for Mr. McKinley denied he rented his property for saloon purposes, but the Chicago New Voice proved he did. I am so true a Daughter of the Revolution that such a president as Theodore Roosevelt is an insult to my sires. And last March when he came to Topeka, Kansas, he outraged every loyal citizen of the state by bringing into it a dive and all who wished an intoxicating drink could get it by tipping the waiter. Let his ministers deny this for him also. He ought to have been arrested as any other dive-keeper.

This President who enjoys the sport of killing innocent animals, this man who costs the people more than any other president, who has so little regard for the people's treasury that he spent a quarter of a million to look at the American fleet and took the treasured relics of the people and sold them to a junk shop, vandalism!

MY VISIT TO YALE UNIVERSITY.

I have been to all the principal universities of the United States. At Cambridge, where Harvard is situated, there are no saloons allowed, but in Ann Arbor the places are thick where manhood is drugged and destroyed. Also Yale, the latter being the worst I have ever seen. I will insert two letters which I got on March 1st, 1904, and have received several more of the kind from the students:

"Dear Mrs. Nation:—As an ardent prohibitionist and an enemy of the liquor traffic, I feel obliged to bring to your notice some of the things that are served to the young men at Yale Dining Hall by the college authorities." (In this letter were several bills of fare.) "You will see how many of the dishes are served with intoxicating liquors as sauces. Yale is supposed to be a christian college, but to give boys these poisons by consent of the college authorities is nothing more or less than starting them on the road to hell! Please give this matter your earnest attention and see if you can not stamp this serpent out."

"Dear Mrs. Nation:—Although it pains me deeply, I feel it my duty to inform you that even after your soul-stirring address of warning and reproof, the Devil still grins at Yale Dining Hall. The enclosed menus tells the story. The hateful practice of serving intoxicating liquors has not ceased. Capt. Smoke holds open wide the gates of hell. Oh, this is terrible! Satan loves to shoot at brightest marks.

"Here are eight hundred shining young souls, the cream of the nation's manhood, on the broad road which leadeth to destruction. God help us. Assist us, Mrs. Nation; aid us; pray for us. Let the world know of this awful condition and rouse the public indignation until it has ceased. Publicity will do it. Let the world know that Yale is being made a training school for Drunkards, and Capt. Smoke will never dare to serve liquors again. A LONE BUT TRUE FRIEND OF THE TEMPERANCE CAUSE."

I spoke to the students at the entrance of their dining hall. They spoke up and told me that "Champagne" was served on their ham three times a week. They gave me the menus, and on them were: "Claret Wine Punch", "Cherry Wine Sauce", "Apple Dumpling and Brandy Sauce," "Roast Ham and Champagne Sauce," and "Wine jelly". While I was talking to the young men, many were smoking cigarettes in the entrance of the dining hall, which was contrary to rules, but Capt. Smoke only laughed at this practice of vice. There should be an investigation and that quick. Students are crying for it. Faculties should demand of students a high standard. At Yale the students are pleading for a moral faculty.

I then went to the Y. M. C. A., and found on the first floor, billiard tables, cigars and cigarettes; they also have a "smoking room." A poor mother wrote to a friend of mine in New Heaven to please use her influence to save the boys. That her boy wrote her that the brandy was so strong on the food that it made his head dizzy. One poor boy said that he did not wish such food but that he had no other to eat. Students are crying out against this outrage. While I was there a "Smoker" was advertised to be held by the law students. A student told me that a beer wagon was engaged by the Seniors of Sheffield School of Yale for their wrestling match procession. These Seniors upon application can get a tin cup and help themselves to this rotten slop that will destroy their willpower and make them slaves of the drink habit. What can be expected of Freshmen if Seniors set such an example? This will show what it leads to:

The demoralization of the students is talked of universally. They have what is called Freshman "Games", which are as follows: Upon appointed evenings they will meet at a select hotel (saloon). They take their places at the table, then, each one at the table, "sets them up" to all the rest. If there are twelve at the table each one gets twelve drinks. You can imagine the "games" after such a debauch. I saw some young men there from Kansas and I asked them: "Why do you come to Yale?" I would never send a boy of mine to Yale. If I had a hundred I would send them to a state, that made such things a crime. Here is a college that has received donations of millions lately, that young men may be prepared and fitted for stations of moral, mental and physical eminence and it is a school of vice to a great extent. The distillers and brewers dominate the republican party and they are the controlling party at Yale and will desolate and enslave our darling boys. I went to see the president of Yale, Professor Hadley, and I asked him about these things. He said he thought the intoxicants were "fruit juices". I spoke of the smoking. He said he used to think it was wrong but when he went to Germany he saw they smoked there. He was taught it was wrong in America but when he saw it in Germany he thought better of the vice and is now teaching it to our boys. People ought to demand another faculty or refuse to patronize such a school.

While I was at Harvard I saw Professors smoking cigarettes. Parents should demand that the teachers in these colleges and schools should be free from the practice of the vices of drinking intoxicating liquors and the use of tobacco. I hope we will have some generous hearted man who will donate to build a college in Kansas with the capacity of Yale. What a shame to have professors in our schools aping the vices of foreigners.

These same professors are the followers of Huxley and Herbert Spencer, who did far more to make the world ignorant than wise. Huxley saw in man only the elements of a weed. Herbert Spencer would have destroyed all family life. Such men as these degrade thought and see only the animal. "For after that in the wisdom of man, the world by wisdom knew not. Yet it pleased God by the foolishness of preaching to confound the wise" (as a fool would determine wisdom).

The great controversy between Yale and Harvard now, is, which shall excel in brute force, and foot-ball seems to be the test. Colleges were founded for the purpose of educating the young, on moral, intellectual, and spiritual lines. The test of these is oratory, debate, intellectual contests. It used to be conceded, that the mind made the man, now the forces of the mule and ox are preferred.

Taft, of the noted 'Taft' Cigar has position of lecturer, and the inference is, there will be more vile cigars smoked than ever, under such patronage.

Oh, mothers and fathers! Rise in protest against these outrages, slaughter, bloody anarchy, and treason.

CHAPTER XVIII.

PROHIBITION OR ABOLITION.—WHAT IT MEANS.—THE FREE METHODISTS AND OTHER MINISTERS ENDORSE THE WORK.—A CATHOLIC PRIEST'S ENDORSEMENT.— MODERN DEBORAH.—JOHN P. ST. JOHN.

God is a politician; so is the devil. God's politics are to protect and defend mankind, bringing to them the highest good and finally heaven. The devil's politics are to deceive, degrade and to make miserable, finally ending in hell. The Bible fully explains this. The two kinds of seed started out from Abel and Cain, then Ishmael and Isaac, Esau and Jacob. There are but these two kinds of people. God's crowd and the Devil's crowd. The first law given and broken in Eden was a prohibition law. God said: "Thou shalt not." The devil tempted and persuaded the first pair to disobey. He did it by deceiving the woman. The fact of redemption now is to bring them back to the law of God. What is law? God says that sin is a transgression of law. Blackstone says: "Law commands that which is right and prohibits that which is wrong." Law is one, as truth is one. It is not possible to make a bad law. If it is bad, it is not a law. We have bad statutes. Law is always right. Nothing is wrong that is legal, and wrong may be licensed, but never legalized. I find lawyers who do not understand this. I often hear the term "legalized saloon". When I was passing the building of the supreme court in New York City, on Madison Avenue, I read an inscription on one of the marble statues representing a judge with a book on either side of the door: "Every law not based on wisdom is a menace to the state." This is a false, misleading sentence for all law is wisdom. It might have read: "All statutes not based on wisdom, are a menace to the state." Then at the base of the statue of a soldier, on the other side of the entrance, was this statement: "We do not use force until good laws are defied." Which ought to read: "We do not use force until laws are defied." Such ideas as these are corrupting courts, and biasing the public mind, and the injury is more than apparent to the observer. If law is not a standard, what standard can we have? We must have one. We repeat again: "Law commands that which is right and prohibits that which is wrong." Any statute that does this is lawful. Any that does not, is anarchy.

God is truly the author of law. The theocratic form of government was perfect and the only perfect government that ever existed, we need no other statutes than those that God gave. He said: "We must not kill a bird sitting on her young; must not see our enemy's beast fall under his burden and not help him rise." And the refinement of mercy was taught in the statute that said: "You must not kill the mother and lamb in one day; must not seethe a kid in its mother's milk; must not muzzle the ox that treadeth out the corn." The use, and the only use, of law is to prevent and punish for sin. All law has a penalty for those who violate it. Governments that are the greatest blessing to its citizens are those who can prohibit, or abolish the most sin or crime. Crime is not prevented by toleration, but by prohibition. Nine of the ten commandments are prohibitive and begin with: "Thou shalt not."

The success of life, the formation of character, is in proportion to the courage one has to say to one's ownself: "Thou shalt not." It is not the man or woman who has no temptation to sin, who has the strong character, but the man or woman who has the desire but will not yield to sin. Some people ask: "Why did God make the Devil?" The Devil is God's fire. Like an alchemist God is purifying souls. The Devil is an agent in salvation. "Every Devil in hell is harnessed up to push every saint into heaven."

Those who are counted worthy to enter into the delights of that heavenly land are those who have had their "fiery trials," tried and made white. Man would have no credit and could not hear: "Good and faithful servant;" if he had no temptations to do otherwise, man would be but a mere machine.

God has never used for his work, any but those who prohibit evil. The pilgrim fathers were forced from the mother country because this principle of prohibition burned in their hearts. When England would oppose the colonies, it was prohibition that smashed the tea, over in Boston harbor. George Washington was put at the head of the colonial armies that prohibited, by much bloodshed and suffering, the oppression from the mother country. Our Civil War was the result of the principle to abolish or prohibit the slavery of the colored race. Now we have a worse slavery than England threatened us with or the poor blacks suffered at the hands of their taskmasters. This slavery of soul and body, is one that leads to eternal death. The forces of God are with the abolition, or prohibition of wrong. The forces of darkness and death are with those who are willing to be led captive by the Devil at his will, and to lead others under this grievous yoke of those who are trying to perpetuate the cause of evil.

There are men who desire to be loyal, who are voting for license or in license parties, because they do not stop to think. The people are generally right on all questions. They go wrong more for lack of thought, than for lack of heart. Edmund Burke, the greatest English stateman, said: "The people have as good government as they deserve." Because the people have always had the power, and in America especially, they are sovereign. The president and all others in office, are but servants of the people. In another chapter I have given what the supreme court says about the impossibility of licensing wrong by law, or according to law.

Hear the language of the Declaration of Independence: "We hold these truths to be self evident, that all men are created free and equal, that they are endowed by their creator, with certain inalienable rights, that among these are life, liberty, and the pursuit of happiness, that to secure these rights, governments are instituted among men deriving their just powers from the consent of the governed." The licensing of intoxicating drink results in suicide and murder, whether or not the saloon- keeper or state be held responsible. Some one is. Who? The man who consents to or aids by his vote is most criminal. It is said that drink kills a man a minute. Suppose that we had a war that killed a man every five minutes. Would there not be howling for an end of bloodshed. This is more than ten times worse, for the soul is more valuable than the body.

Freedom or liberty in animals is following instinct and underlying appetite. Not so with man; to the reverse. It is the freedom of conscience and will, from the bondage of ignorance of the person, the gratification of appetite and passion. The body is a good servant, but a tyrant when it is master. A man must be master or slave. One must first, like Daniel, "purpose in his heart that he will not defile himself". Liberty or freedom is only attained by prohibition of opportunity to do wrong to ourselves or allow any one else to do so. Citizenship not only requires one to obey law but must see that others do so also.

The principles of government are founded on liberty and self-control. Drunkenness is a loss of self-control. Anything that animalizes men, is a menace to the life of the state and prevents the purpose of government. Thus replacing the weapon of destruction in the hands of its foes and the danger is great, because so many citizens are under the domination of their own will and passion. This class is being multiplied by this licensed crime. These willing classes are an integral part of the nation. By licensing rum, we are fostering a power that is increasing the weakness, and preventing the self-control of its citizens. This is conspiracy, treason, black as night. Some plead the revenue of our wealth. Our wealth is in our citizens. The state can not add to its treasury at the expense of its manhood without punishing herself. The state must guard the character of its citizens. It can not make them honest but it must punish dishonesty; can not make them humane, but it must prohibit an act of inhumanity; and should oppose and forbid every license that man would desire or try to obtain that which would allow such gratification of the animal over the moral.

The nation is what its homes are. The family first, then the nation. Nothing can injure an individual or a family that is not an injury to the state. The fight for firesides means a fight for our national life. Our revolutionary sires fought for this. This is the fight that Carry A. Nation is making. It is the heart of love, liberty and peace. Some of these thoughts I have copied from an article I read on a few leaves of a torn pamphlet, no name. But the writer has the true meaning of government. I am a prohibitionist because I am a christian.

I want to get to heaven. None but prohibitionists ever do. Hell is made for those who take license to sin.

HELL'S CONSPIRACY.

England has the same struggle that we have. The government conspiring against the people. This article from the pen of Lady Carlisle tells of the same vile plot the Prime Minister of England sustains, the brewer against the people, just as Roosevelt and his crowd here:

THE PEOPLE'S STRUGGLE AGAINST THE LIQUOR TRADE.
(Spirited appeal by Lady Carlisle.)

Throughout the past year we have been face to face with a grave crisis in the history of our temperance movement, but the present Session of Parliament is the moment of our most imminent peril.

In March, 1903, the Prime Minister, surrendering to the threats of the liquor trade, recklessly attacked the Magistrates because in the public interest they had here and there reduced the number of licensed houses, and he declared to the Brewer's Deputation that in so doing the Magistrates had been guilty of "gross injustice," and that "to such unjust confiscation of property the Government could not remain indifferent." In April the Government supported Mr. Butcher's Compensation Bill, and in August Mr. Balfour gave a pledge in the House of Commons that the Government would introduce legislation "at the earliest possible moment in the following Session," which would put an end to the present "wide- spread feeling of insecurity on the part of English license-holders."

Since the Prime Minister made these pronouncements, our forces have everywhere set themselves in array to fight the impending legislation, by which the 'Trade' is to be endowed at the expense of the nation's welfare, and is to have its privileges and its powers greatly increased. The government, having yielded to the dictation of the Publican interest, indicated that either the Magistrates must be hindered from exercising their ancient power of not renewing annual licenses when in their discretion they deem such renewal to be against the public good; or else that some measure of compensation must be enacted, whereby this wealthy liquor monopoly should have its huge financial profits made permanently secure by the grant from Parliament of a vested interest in their licenses. If after the passing of such a measure the Magistrates should, for the protection of the people, refuse the renewal of a license, the holder of that speculative public-house investment would be by law guaranteed against loss. He would thus no longer need to insure himself against the risk of non-renewal, for the State would have turned this annual license into a freehold property. Then for the first time this dangerous 'Trade' would have obtained that fixity of tenure which it has so long coveted, but which Parliament in its wisdom has always vigorously refused to grant; and the nation, which has already too long suffered under the oppression of the Liquor Traffic with its terrible licensed temptations, would then be permanently crushed under one of the most perilous of all the political tyrannies that ever sapped the strength and the freedom of a great people. For these Liquor Traffickers have proclaimed cynically their anti-social aloofness, from the ideals of good citizenship; "they know no interest but their own," and their defiant boast is heard at all elections, "Our Trade our Politics."

Today the people and the 'Trade' have come to close quarters in their conflict; and all Temperance workers must join with dedicated fervour in unremitting and widespread agitation, till the danger is past. Deep and living must be the zeal and the faith that inspire our work. The campaign of protest and of "active resistance" has started vigorously, and it must never slacken till victory is won. Day by day the pressure of public opinion must increase, till the impression made on Parliament by resolutions and petitions shall be overwhelming. The struggle against the 'Trade' and its Government backers is hard, but we must fight straight on, for the issue is of vital importance and we should be ready to make a determined and triumphant resistance to the Prime Minister's sinister and unashamed attempt to sell our immemorial rights to England's most dangerous foe, that gigantic Drink Trade, which lives and thrives on the sorrow and degradation of our people.

The worth of our temperance party as a fighting force is once more being tested, and I trust that we shall not be found unworthy servants of the great cause which is in our keeping. It rests with the Temperance stalwarts, leading the conscience of the nation, to win the day. They fought and they won the same battle in 1888, and again in 1890, and the achievement of those years can assuredly be repeated today, if we rightly grip the principles that underlie our old Temperance beliefs, holding fast to them without wavering or losing heart, and if we work ever zealously, glowing with the cheerful faith which belongs to those who know that Right will win in the long run, if only reformers are patiently steadfast in their task, even when the ultimate goal is not yet in sight. We must spend ourselves, still marching with our faces set. ROSALIND CARLISLE, President North of England Temperance League. President British Women's Temperance Association.

THIS ARTICLE IS FROM THE TEMPERANCE WITNESS OF NORTH OF ENGLAND.

This explains the danger to honest trade. The reason why we have capital against labor. The concentration of money without compensation to labor. The funds that accumulate corrupt the government and enslaves the people:

THE CAUSE OF BAD TRADE.

"Every shilling invested in the liquor traffic inflicts a distinct injury to the cause of labor, for there is no trade which pays less wages in proportion to its receipts than the traffic in intoxicants. If therefore the capital which is now invested in the manufacture and sale of these liquors could only be turned into other channels there would be no difficulty in finding an honest wage for an honest day's work for every unemployed laborer in the land. Let us illustrate this. In a blue book on wages and production, issued from the Board of Trade in 1891, it was stated that for every L100 received in mining, L55 went in labor; of every L100 in shipbuilding, L37 went in labor; of every L100 in railways, L31 went in labor; of every L100 in cotton manufactures, L29 went in labor; but of every L100 in brewing, L7 only goes into the pocket of the workman. The same result was shown in another way by Mr. W. S. Caine, M. P., when he said: 'He was in Scotland, in the neighborhood of a very large soap factory. He was shown in the locality twelve old cottages and one hundred new ones. A short time ago the soap factory was a distillery, and then the twelve old cottages sufficed for all the men the industry employed; but when it was turned into a soap factory it became necessary to build one hundred cottages to accommodate the extra hands which the manufacture of soap required.'

The shutting up of the distillery and the building of these hundred cottages meant increased trade to all the local shopkeepers, and in turn this benefited the wholesale trade and caused increased employment. The way in which labor is starved by the liquor traffic is further illustrated by the following facts:-

The Publicans' Paper says: "Two breweries in Sheffield turn out 50,000 barrels of beer a year each, but they only employ 660 men. An Edinburgh Distillery with a turnover Of L1,500,000 a year only employs 150 men. An Iron Ore Company in Cumberland, with a turnover of L250,000 a year, employs 1,200 men. Our largest ironworks employ 3,000 men each for the same turnover that the distillery employs 150."

Say She Is Insane. From a minister, Rev. William Ashmore, D. D.— "They say Mrs. Nation in insane. The wonder is that tens of thousands of mothers and widows are not insane along with her. The wonder is that instead of one hatchet slashing away among the decanters there are not ten thousand of them all over the land. To stand by the grave of a husband or son ruined by drink is enough to drive a woman crazy. Instead of criticising Mrs. Nation, let us turn on those heartless saloon- keepers and the negligent and responsible judiciary and that indifferent and callous community. They are the ones who put the edge on Mrs. Nation's hatchet. The Master said: 'If these should hold their peace immediately the stones would cry out.' It is because those pledged to public order hold their peace that Mrs. Nation's hatchet is flying about."

A Catholic Priest. Mendota, Minn.—"Mrs. Carry Nation. Dear Sister:— These days back the season's routine duties of a Catholic priest have prevented me from expressing to you my sympathy and my admiration for your pluck. You are the John Brown of the temperance cause. Your smashing of saloon fixtures has been but a very little thing beside the effect it had, and was bound to have, all over the country, and the world, in building up backbone and courage and holy emulation in hundreds of thousands of those reading of it. You are a credit to womankind and humanity; you are infinitely more deserving of the gratitude of the country than are the men at the head of our armies and fleets in needless and demoralizing war. I want to send you $2.00 but have some fears it may not reach you safely if I enclosed it herein. Praying that the Lord may comfort and sustain you, I am yours very respectfully, MARTIN MAHONY.

Trinadad, Colorado, Feb. 28, 1901.—Dear Carrie Nation:—Go on save all you can. If it had not been for the drink and dance halls I would not be at deaths door at the age of 28. I am thankful to have enough life to repent, MINNIE MAY.

Mrs. Nation a Modern Deborah.. Thus Saluted by the Boston, W. C. T. U., at Memorial Service in Honor of Francis Willard. Boston, Mass.— Mrs. Carry Nation, the strenuous Kansas temperance reformer, was hailed as a "modern Deborah" at a meeting of the local W. C. T. U. yesterday afternoon in the vestry of Park Street Church. Not a dissenting voice was heard from among the gathering of perhaps 200 women, but all over the room there was audible expressions of approval of the Characterization, which was applied by Mrs. Mary H. Hunt, a prominent member of the local branch of the union. Mrs. Hunt said that Mrs. Nation is like Deborah of the Book of Judges, who led an army of 10,000 men to victory against her country's enemies, when not a man could be found to lead the enterprise. She aroused unmistakable evidences of indorsement from her audience when she remarked that the lady with the hatchet can truly say, "Until I arose, there was no man to punish unpunished rebellion against the law." Mrs. Hunt concluded by saying that thoughtful reformers are waiting with much interest to see what will be the result of Mrs. Nation's cyclonic campaign.

A Son Wrecked By Liquor. "Some day the mothers of this country will burn all the saloons and never a man in all the land will dare to check them."— New York Journal.

DEAR MRS. NATION:-I am one of these mothers and would be willing to help you to wreck or burn these saloons. I have a son who is a wreck from the accursed stuff. Oh! 'tis a dark blot on this republic. Even Mohammedans do better than we, a Christian people, for in all Turkey one can not purchase strong drink. But it follows our flag wherever it is planted. Let me know if I can help you. MRS. P. D. OLIVER.

Helen M. Gougar, Lafayette, Ind., writes: "I want to thank the editor of the SMASHER'S MAIL for the good she has done by her unique method of campaigning against the liquor traffic. Her message has gone around the globe for everybody has heard of Carrie Nation and her hatchet. By the way I think the funniest thing on the pages of history is the scare that has caused men (God save the mark!) to bolt and bar their doors and turn pale with fright, because one little, old enthusiastic lady was headed their way!! Oh, ye braves!! You are almost as brave as if you used your opportunities to protect your offspring from the accursed liquor traffic. Let the smashing go on."

Far Away New Jersey. Camden, N. J.—"Mrs. Carry Nation: DEAR SISTER:—When our New Jersey Prohibition Conference was held at Trenton February 14, we sent a telegram to you endorsing your work in Kansas, a prohibition State. It was signed by our former candidate for governor, Rev. Thomas Landon, Rev. James Parker, a former state chairman, and myself, who offered the resolution. Not having received an acknowledgement, I do not know that you received it; if so, will you kindly let me have a word from you to give to our State Convention that will be held May 7? I wish New Jersey had either statutory or constitutional prohibition, there would be some smashing done here, too. Yours for the extermination of the liquor traffic, D. W. GARRIGUES."

What St. John thinks of my work in Kansas: John P. St. John, who was governor of Kansas twice and once headed the National Prohibition ticket as candidate for President of the United States, warmly indorses the acts of Mrs. Nation in her crusade against the liquor traffic. In a letter written to Judge W. J. Groo from Olathe, Kans., he likens her crusade to that of John Brown against slavery. The letter was not written for publication, but Judge Groo secured permission to give it to the World. It says: "My dear Judge: It was almost like grasping the hand of an old friend to receive your letter of the 31st ult. Mrs. Nation is all right. She is engaged in the very laudable business of abating what our statute declares to be a common nuisance. She is not crazy, nor is she a crank, but she is, a sensible Christian woman and has the respect of our best people. Her crusade is much like that of John Brown's, and I hope and pray that it may terminate as disastrously to the liquor traffic as John Brown's did to human slavery. How much more in accord to Christianity it would be if our government would use its soldiers to protect our own homes in our own country, instead of sending them 8,000 miles away to destroy the homes of a people who wanted to be our friends and whose only offense is their love of human liberty, the same that actuated our Revolutionary fathers four generations ago. Yes, the Leavenworth mob was an awful affair and a burning shame and disgrace to Kansas. But it seems that under the reign of William of Canton the burning of negroes at the stake and the killing of Filippinos has become a very popular source of amusement. Very truly your friend, JOHN P. ST. JOHN."

SOME OF THE RESULTS OF THE MRS. NATION TEMPERANCE CRUSADE IN KANSAS.
(By Rev. H. A. Ott, in Lutheran Observer.)

Since sending my last article on the Nation temperance crusade, the writer has received a large number of letters thanking him for the article, many of which asked for a second article giving the results of the movement after it had spread over the State. This is the only apology for my intruding a second time on your columns. From these letters I find that the good people of the East do not and can not understand the situation here, because the laws and public sentiment here are so different from what they are in eastern States. It seems strange to us to find many good people in the East indirectly supporting the saloon by their wholesale condemnation of a woman who has had the courage, nagged on by what she has suffered from the drink devil through a former drunken husband, to go right into the drink dens and smash their bottles and fixtures with a hatchet. The smashing of joints and joint fixtures is at an end without doubt as far as Kansas is concerned, although Mrs. Nation still believes that that method of suppression of a public nuisance is the very best. However, the effect of that smashing has been to marvelously stir up the officers of the law, our legislature, and public sentiment all over the State. Mrs. Nation was let out of jail on the bond signed by Rev. J. B. McAfee, an esteemed member of my congregation here. Her bond now is a bond to keep the peace, and her smashing is at an end.

The times were ripe for just such a movement. The people of Kansas, through the indifference and neglect of her officers of the law, saw the jointists getting bolder every day, having their fines paid by the breweries and distilleries of other States, until they started in to give the State "open" saloons, with all the brazen ways in the East, Then Mrs. Nation came. Everything was ripe for a reaction against all this. The coming of this woman was simply the lighting of the match which set off a temperance pyrotechnic display which has lighted up the temperance horizon all over the Union, and has created an unparalleled degree of temperance sentiment and activity. The writer has had Mrs. Nation at his table; has discussed with her her ideas; has differed with her as to the final utility of the "hatchet" as a cure for the disease; has one of the hundred of hatchets and axes sent her from all over the country, this a fierce broad-axe sent her from Hartsel, Col., and which he keeps as a souvenir; has investigated the charges as to her sanity, finds her entirely sane, though possibly somewhat of a crank because of her ultraradical methods in furthering reform against strong drink, tobacco, and other social evils; yet he feels that the temperance cause, despite all her faults, has much for which to thank Mrs. Nation. It needed just such severe movements to arouse the easy-going masses of our State, and awaken public sentiment along these lines, and Mrs. Nation was the "John Brown" for the movement.

The movement in the city of Topeka, a city of 35,000 population, brought out a meeting of 3,000 men who demanded that liquors no longer be sold contrary to law, and that all joint fixtures be removed or they would be smashed. This was promptly done. It was a grand sight to see a dozen men carry down, from upstairs back rooms, long bars to be stored or sent out of the city. What brought them down? Public sentiment, the education resulting from twenty years of constitutional prohibition. To-day the city of Topeka is absolutely free from joints, as far as the writer can see. Of course, liquor can be bought secretly, and always will be, but our boys do not know where it can be bought. You might as well try to absolutely bind the devil as to absolutely bind the liquor traffic in one State with all the brewers and distillers in a dozen surrounding States seeking with determined and cunning methods to extend their business within its borders.

It is like heaven to live in a city where there are no open saloons. There are thousands of public school children here, now nearly of age, who have never seen here a beer-wagon or a beer-keg! Recently a child who had never been out of the State, on going to Kansas City, Mo., looked out of the car window and saw a sign on a building, and spelled, "S-a-l-o-o-n, saloon," and then exclaimed, "Mamma, what is that?" There is no better city in the world in which to bring up a family of boys than Topeka, and many fine eastern families are coming here for that very reason. It amuses me to see the comments made on Kansas in the East. To some it is truly, "The wild and woolly West." One pastor writes: "Is it safe for the next General Synod to go out there?" Let me tell your readers just two or three things about Kansas. Her educational exhibit at the Chicago World's Fair took the highest prize; her per cent of illiteracy is the lowest of all the States of the Union; her regiment, the 21st of Kansas, was the only regiment of the 65,000 men at Chickamauga Park during the late war with Spain in which every man could write his own name on the muster roll; and this same regiment voted unanimously not to have the infamous "canteen" in their regiment, and they would not have it. This is the result of the influence of twenty years of constitutional prohibition. Topeka has far better paved streets and more of them than most other cities of its size in the United States, its sidewalks are all brick, and this without a dollar coming from bleeding the saloon in the shape of a license! Prosperity without the saloon is seen on every hand. True, some people stay away from Kansas because of its stringent liquor laws. That, however, largely accounts for the general intelligence here. Let them stay away. The West is all right educationally and morally. Your readers may not know it, but the State which has the largest per cent of her population in her colleges is a western State.

The influence of the Nation crusade has spread all over our State, and as a result the joints have been suppressed on all sides. Our legislature, just adjourned, gave us the most drastic legislation against the liquor business in her history, and with tremendous majorities. The result of the movement started by this brave woman, who is roundly condemned in the East, is best summed up in the words of a Kansas wholesale liquor dealer, who said recently, "A few weeks ago we had a very fine trade in Kansas, shipping out many car-loads of liquor, but just now they are coming back as fast as they went out." Our city, Topeka, has had considerable notoriety all over the country as the center of the Nation temperance crusade, and because of the presence of Mrs. Nation. However, we think your readers will quite agree with us when we say their eastern cities could well afford such notoriety if thereby they could be rid of their debauching and terribly corrupting saloons.— Pastor, Topeka, Kansas.

TRIBUTE TO MRS. NATION.—CORRESPONDENT OF THE STATE JOURNAL GROWS

ELOQUENT ABOUT HER.

A correspondent of the State Journal who is evidently an admirer of Mrs. Nation has written the following tribute the famous smasher of joints:

"Carry A. Nation, prophetess of God and prohibition, came suddenly like the furious driving Jehu. Her cyclonic joint smashing shook the rum power of the United States from apex to foundation-stone. The great American god Bacchus turned pale on his throne. Gambrinus and his thirty thousand white-aproned priests of debauchery and licentiousness trembled in every saloon and bagnio throughout the union. No whirlwind, tornado or simoon of the desert ever startled a nation as her volcanic career. From ocean to ocean, from Canada to Texas. she faced a storm of relentless criticism and bitter sarcasm from political curs, clerical hirelings and editorial henchmen of the murderous liquor traffic such as no mortal ever faced before. A star of hope to the one hundred thousand despairing drunkards, already in the death-grasp of this licensed Moloch of perdition; volunteer liberator of the hundreds of thousands of hapless slaves of this greater "curse of curses" and more than "sum of all villainies;" precursor of emancipation of the millions of sad-faced women and children whose lives are blasted and crushed beneath the wheels of this cruel Car of juggernaut; betrayed by false friends, imprisoned by the courts, and manacled; no martyr of old ever ran the gauntlet of hotter persecution, yet like Banquo's Ghost and the Man of Galilee she will not down. Denounce her as you may, she is such an one as heroines and world-wide characters are made of. Every one will want a copy of her "Life," forthcoming publication. The boys and girls will find the Old Kentucky Home plantation scenes, interesting as Uncle Tom's Cabin and well worth the price of the book. The pictures and portraits of the noted Smasher of joints are more than worth the nominal sum. To every citizen, student and philanthropist the legal citations for reference are worth it. No temperance person or prohibitionist can afford to be without a copy.—RAY RAND.

WORDS PROPHETIC.

The liquor traffic will never see another hour of peace in this country. Mrs. Carrie Nation has sounded the alarm. There's a growing hatred of the saloon. The speaker has sworn hostility to an institution that feeds on the bodies and souls of men. I will pay my taxes like an honest man and not saddle by my vote, the burden on the tempted and weak, who will pay them over the bar and throw his wife and children on the charity of the public.

What shall the harvest be?

As a people for years we pressed to our hearts the evil of human slavery. It was profitable, we thought, but every drop of blood let by the slaver's lash, God made us pay back with blood of our own upon the altar. Many fortunes were built up by slave labor, but how many of them were left after the war? "Whatsoever a nation soweth that shall it also reap." What shall the harvest be from the wild sowing of the legalized saloon? Our own country is a partner in the business for the of revenue. I pray God that the liquor traffic may be abolished from America, without bloodshed, and yet who dares prophesy that it shall be so. Much blood has been let in these long years by drunken husbands and fathers. Many fortunes have been built up by the traffic. What shall the end be?

Right shall prevail—

> "For right is right, as God is God;
> And right the day will win.
> To doubt would be disloyalty,
> To falter would be sin."

Listen to the voice of the 20th century prophet as it comes ringing down the grooves of change: "The saloon is going! Perhaps not by your political party or mine, your church or mine; but God reigns and his people will awake. And as it lies dying at last amongst its bags of gold, and we stand over it, as I pray we may, if it shall look up into our faces and whisper: "Another million of revenue for a single breath of life!" You will say, as I will: "NO! Down, down to hell and say I sent thee thither."

CHAPTER XIX.

DR. MCFARLAND'S PROTEST.—KICKED AND KNOCKED DOWN BY CHAPMAN OF BANGOR HOUSE.—MEDDLING WITH THE DEVIL.—TIMELY WARNING TO OUR BOYS AND GIRLS.—BRUBAKER OF PEORIA.—WITCHCRAFT.—LAST TIME IN JAIL.

The determination of that rum anarchy in Topeka, Kansas, was such that three consecutive times I was put in jail because I went into these vile dens. Dr. McFarland, pastor of the First Methodist Episcopal church of Topeka, came down at my last trial to see what the trouble was. The police, when put on the witness stand, swore positive falsehoods and Judge Magaw, the republican police judge, appointed there by the democratic Mayor, Parker, that these two might unite their force of corruption, knew that these police were swearing falsehoods but were winking at the crime. I saw that the Doctor was getting ready to offer his protest when the time came, and it came when I was sentenced to jail for contempt of court, because I insisted on asking what kind of business these dive-keepers were carrying on, which the judge wanted to keep out of the witnesses mouths. Dr. McFarland arose and said: "I suppose you want to fine me judge. I say this is an infernal outrage," repeating it the second time. Judge Magaw said: "Yes I will fine you twenty-five dollars." "You may make it a hundred." "Well, I will make it a hundred," said Judge Magaw. I was taken to jail. Dr. McFarland was not, but walked out and said it was worth a hundred dollars to tell them what he thought of such travesty on justice. Dr. McFarland had plenty of friends who offered to pay the amount but I believe he paid it himself. Then he began some investigation of the corruption at the police station. He preached a sermon telling of this. It was published. I was in jail next door to the room in which the mayor, Parker, and the police gathered to discuss a suit for slander against Dr. McFarland, but it was only a bluff. Before this all night long there was loud talking and swearing in the room under mine as if around a card table. After Dr. McFarland's sermon I heard no more of it. There were several of these poor degraded girls in jail. I knew of actions and words that were not decent between the officers and these girls. This exposure of Dr. McFarland's was very salutary. Before that, officers would come into my room without knocking and address me in a rough manner. After this they knocked at the door and were respectful and even kind. The Reverend Doctor did a great work by that sermon which was to the point and effective.

I went to Bangor, Maine, to lecture once. Stopped at the Bangor House, run by one Chapman. Roosevelt had stopped there just two weeks before. I heard this hotel had one of those traps, called "dives." When I went into the dining-room I asked a young lady waiting on me, if she could get me a bottle of

- 149 -

beer? She said they kept it and that she would ask the head waiter to get it for me. She spoke to him. He left the dining-room and in a few minutes the man Chapman came out of the winding way to his dive; the proprietor rushed up to me in a drunken rage. He threw me against one of the pillars, then literally knocked me out into the hall in the presence of the guests, perhaps a hundred; then he kept knocking me down every time I rose to my feet. He would not allow me to get my things. I was invited to go home with a prohibitionist, Dr. Marshall. This Chapman was a noted dive-keeper, a rummy, and ran a representative rum-soaked republican hotel. He was angry, because I dared to expose him, in his sneaking way of drugging and robbing his guests. It was marvelous what rages these law-breakers used to have when I came around at first. It is not so now. Their bands have been smashed and they are not as bold; and more marvelous that I was not seriously hurt.

Once in Nebraska City, Neb., I was knocked in the temple by a saloon-keeper. I reeled and fell and while I knew he struck me with his clenched fists as hard as he could, so it seemed to me, I did not have a bruise.

I always prayed to God to take care of me, but to lead me into these tumults to rouse the people to think and to talk.

THE BEGINNING OF THE GRAVEYARD ASSOCIATION OF MEDICINE LODGE.

I never saw anything that needed a rebuke, or exhortation, or warning, but that I felt it was my place to meddle with it. I have been called a "meddler". Yes I say: "It is my place to meddle with the devil's business. Jesus meddled with the law-breakers in the temple."

I will give you a few facts to prove what I mean and hope it will inspire my readers to do likewise. What injures one is the interest of all. We are personally responsible for all wrong that we neglect to make right, when it is in our power to do it. If anything injures my neighbor it injures me. If my neighbor is blessed so am I.

I used to ride out north of Medicine Lodge past the graveyard. It was situated on an elevated place, barren of trees, for trees could not well grow where it was so dry. Grave-yards are not pleasant places at best, but to see one barren of trees or flowers, just the graves, the white marble, the sunshine, rain, and prairie grass, in sight of the pleasant yards and homes of the living, I feel a sense of reproach, as if the dead were complaining of this neglect. The only ground Abraham ever bought was a piece of ground to bury his dead and it had trees on it. I wanted to see a better condition of things. I knew this neglect was because no one would make a move. I felt I was not the one, but I wrote an article for the papers, "Index and Crescent", of Medicine Lodge, and I took it to a widow, Mrs. Young, who had recently lost a husband who was very dear to her. I told her she was the one to organize a grave-yard association. That this letter would call the ladies together. After making a few changes in the language she published the letter, and the ladies met, organized, and in a few months all was changed. One will rarely find a more attractive resting place for our beloved dead than in the cemetery of Medicine Lodge. I could not have effected what Mrs. Young did, but there are more ways of doing things than one, and when people say: "I can never carry out any plans", I know they have not tact or perseverance.

MEDDLING WITH THE DEVIL.

A friend who lived a few miles in the country came to my house in Medicine Lodge, threw her arms around my neck and said: "Oh, Sister Nation, Matt has gone to Wichita for a bad purpose. I am almost wild; can't you help me? She is in love with Will, and he does not care for her but he has gotten her into trouble and does not intend to marry her." She told me that Will wrote her a note to go to the Goodyear Hotel. I wrote to Matt and told her if she became the murderer of her child that a fearful judgement was in store for her. I also wrote to Will and told him to marry Matt or I would expose him. Will's father got the letter, as it was directed to Medicine Lodge. His father came down to see me, weeping as if his heart would break; told me of the trouble this boy had given him; said that he was preparing to marry another girl and could not marry Matt; but that he had forwarded the letter to Will, as he had gone to Wichita. Will and Matt got their letters at the same time and were filled with terror. Both came back to Medicine Lodge and in a few months poor Matt was the mother of a little girl. Her mother, sent for me. I stayed until the little angel died. From the time Matt looked on the face of the little one she loved it with all the intensity of a true mother and grieved so when it died. In a few hours I went to the grave-yard With the little coffin. This Will or his father never spoke to me again. He married the other girl. In a few years father and son were both killed. The sister of Will, who also treated me coldly, wrote me a letter and told me to tell Matt it would have been a blessing if he had married her. That he loved her the best and that she felt quite differently towards me.

TIMELY WARNING TO OUR GIRLS AND BOYS.

I was going down to a neighbor's one dark night. I heard voices, as if some parties were sitting by the roadside. I went into the neighbor's house and got a lantern. I came up to these parties, they were a young man of Medicine Lodge and a young lady visiting there. I told them that such actions would lead to mischief. Told the young boy to act towards a girl as he would wish his sister treated. Told the girl that ruin would be her fate and she hid her face and soon both of them ran down the alley. I knew they would think that I would expose them, so I wrote a letter to the young man and told him the injustice to himself and the girl, that would follow such actions, told him that no one would hear it from me. That it was not my desire to expose them only to warn and prevent trouble. That young man is in Medicine Lodge now and is a good friend of mine.

I often see actions, especially with the young, that I know will end in heartaches and woes. I get these parties out of hearing of others and speak to them. So often in traveling I see silly girls being led astray by men who for a vile purpose will fawn and flatter. I never let such a thing pass my eye now without a little wholesome condemnation: "Thou shall not in any wise suffer sin upon thy brother but shall rebuke him."

SOME OF MY TRIALS WITH MR. BRUBAKER OF PEORIA.

When I visited Chicago for the first time after the smashing a Mr. Brubaker called to see me. He was from Peoria and was hired by the Peoria Journal men to get me to edit that paper for one day. The arrangements were satisfactory to both parties. I went to Peoria. Mr. Brubaker met me, took me to a hotel run by a woman who owned one or two saloons, but had none in the hotel she kept. I had not one line of copy for the paper but I got up at four in the morning and wrote continuously that day. I know God helped me. Mr. Brubaker took the copy. I never saw any of the Journal men until after the paper was out. I went to see them, told them that only a small part of my copy that I wrote was in the paper. They said that several times they asked for my copy but Mr. Brubaker gave them his own. So he destroyed a great deal of my copy, supplying only what he wanted put in.

I spoke in the Opera House and this Mr. Brubaker was to give me fifty dollars for my lecture that night. After I had spoken I was asked to go into a noted saloon, Pete Weise's place. Mr. Brubaker said: "If you go I will not give you your fifty dollars," as the contract said I was to speak at no other place in the city. But as I had already spoken for him I did not feel bound. This man was posing as a prohibitionist but he was as loyal to the cause as Judas was to Jesus. I went to Pete Weis' place, one of the most expensive dance halls I was ever in. I spoke for the hundreds of poor, drugged and depraved men and women. There was a large picture or rather statuary of naked women among trees which I said must be smashed, Mr. Weis treated me very kindly and said: "I will have that boarded up," and so next day he did.

This Mr. Brubaker would not pay me a cent for my lecture and tried to garnishe the $100, the Journal was to pay me, and had it not been for a stroke of policy on the part of the Journal he would have taken every cent from me and left me to pay my expenses there and back. Jesus said: "Beware of wolves in sheep's clothing." In a month from this time the saloon keeper sent me $50. The prostitute loved more than Simon.

I saw in Peoria the largest distillery in the world. Not one of the hands are allowed to drink what they make. What would you think of a dry goods concern that would not allow its employes to use what they make? Mr. William McKinley was entertained here by Joe Greenhut, president of the "Whiskey Trust."

I was in Peoria when the prohibitionists held a convention there and was astonished that they would put up at a saloon or a hotel that run one. I never eat or sleep in one. My conscience will not allow me. I never saw so many ragged children or dirty streets, as in Peoria.

WITCHCRAFT.

I heard so much of the "Weltmer treatment" for disease. I sent twenty-five dollars for a "mail course" so I could see for myself. This man Weltmer had a large institution in Nevada, Mo., for humbugging the people. I always like to investigate these things myself, as I did Dowie, who I found out to be a false prophet. This Weltmer's papers were a complete treatise on witchcraft, spiritualism and hypnotism. I exposed this in every way I could. The Bible fully prepares people to expect such "lying wonders and miracles." The "Christian Science" is a witchcraft but very subtile. The most dangerous counterfeit bill is nearest like the genuine.

IN JAIL IN PHILADELPHIA.

The last jail I was in was in Philadelphia. I went down to lecture between the acts of "The Heart of a Hero." There was a very vile saloon kept by a Mr. Donoghue. This man stationed police to arrest me if I went in his place. In going home from the theatre at night I would look in and call to the poor victims not to be drugged and robbed. This man had five or six bartenders handing out this poisonous drink to our boys, our mothers treasures. This man has amassed a fortune at this vile business and tries to pose as respectable, because he has a lot of this blood money. I was passing there on the 14th of January, 1904. I just opened the door when a two legged beer keg in the form of a policeman grabbed me and almost dragged me over the streets to the station. I was locked in and I spent the night in jail. Next morning I was discharged.

The next day when I went to the Pennsylvania railway depot to take the train a little ragged boy came to me and asked for a hatchet, the depot police shook the little fellow and hurled him away. The little boy began to cry and I said to the police: "Let that child alone! he is doing no harm to any one." He told me in a very angry tone to mind my business, and would not let the little boy take the hatchet from me. After this I was sitting on the bench waiting for my train, and a person came to me saying: "Let me see one of your hatchets." I opened my grip to show the little souvenirs, several came up to look at them. This same policeman was watching his chance to arrest me. He came up and said: "You will have to stop that." I said: "I am making no trouble, I have a right to meet people and talk to them and show my souvenirs too. You are the only one, making a disturbance here." Two policemen came up and caught me one by each arm, dragging me through the depot and down the elevator, and I was carried to the police station in a "black maria". This was done for spite and to show his authority. I spent a night in prison, and next morning I was fined ten dollars. I was my own lawyer. The magistrate before whom I was tried would not compel the officer to answer the questions I asked him.

In a few days I returned to Pittsburg and was invited by the Providence Mission to go out on the streets. Quite a crowd gathered and while I was speaking, I was arrested again by an officer who refused to tell me what I was arrested for. I was taken to the police headquarters. The kind hearted matron wanted to give me a pillow and some bedding for I had nothing but a hard board in the cell. The Chief of Police forbade the matron to give me anything to make myself comfortable. He said: "That woman is giving us a great deal of trouble and we want to get rid of her." The matron came to me when no one was looking and advised me to give a bond of thirteen dollars and get out so that I might have a bed. I did this and went to my boarding house. I secured the services of a lawyer, Mr. Buckley. I was fined ten dollars which was afterwards remitted. This republican, rum-soaked police force make it a point to arrest me on every pretext. They have told me that if I win they will lose their jobs. Eighteen months before this I had been put in jail at Pittsburg, making three times all for doing my duty in that city.

CHAPTER XX.

WHY I WENT ON THE STAGE.—THE VICE OF TOBACCO.

I got hundreds of calls to go on the stage before I did. Gradually I got the light.

This is the largest missionary field in the world. No one ever got a call or was ever allowed to go there with a Bible but Carry Nation. That door never was opened to any one but me. The hatchet opened it. God has given it to me. My managers have said: "This is a variety house at, Watsons and the Unique, of Brooklyn, or the Boston on the Bowery. You do not wish to go there." Yes, those need me more than the rest; never refuse a call even from the lowest. If Jesus ate with publicans and sinners I can talk to them. Francis Willard said the pulpit and stage must be taken for God.

Persons often say: "Why do you take the money of such?" I say "I can do more good with the money than they can." After the battle the victor takes the spoils and is entitled to them. I will take all I can get in a good way. Money is a blessing, if used as such. I go on the stage to do good, I take their money for the same reason. The curse of it is when it is desired above the good of humanity. I am fishing. I go where the fish are for they do not come to me. I thank God for this unspeakable gift. I take my Bible before every audience. I show them this hatchet, that destroys or smashes everything bad and builds up everything that is good. I tell them of their loving Deliverer who came to break every yoke and set the Captive free. When I look upon the hundreds of faces before me, I say: "Oh, these poor aching hearts! God give me a loving message." Words can not tell of the love I would like to bestow upon them. I often weep. "Oh, Jerusalem, Jerusalem, how oft would I have gathered you as a hen gathereth her chickens under her wings." Then I say: "There is one that loves more than you. He can make all things right."

There are but a handful comparatively that try to obey the commands of Jesus: "A remnant shall be saved." Caleb and Joshua were only two in six hundred thousand but they alone of this great multitude lived to see and inherit the promised land. Christ said. "Go out into the highways and hedges and compel them to come in that my home may be full." Where are the highways and hedges: They are places where men and women are the most lost. How can they be compelled to come in? Love is the only compelling influence. If no one goes with love, how are these lost ones to know they are loved. Christ brought love down to us; He came down to do it. We must take His love to the low places—"Condescend to men of low estate." I praise my God for opening a door to me never opened to anyone else. I find the theatre stocked with boys of our country. They are not found in churches. I have not sought to get into the so-called "respectable set" but I have told my managers to get me into the worst class. They need me most. They are as brands snatched from the burning.

I am not only a reformer on the line of the licensed or unlicensed saloon, but on other evils. I believe that, on the whole, tobacco has done more harm than intoxicating drinks. The tobacco habit is followed by thirst for drink. The face of the smoker has lost the scintillations of intellect and soul it would have had if not marred by this vice. The odor of his person is vile, his blood is poisoned, his intellect is dulled.

A smoker is never a healthy man, either in body or mind, for nicotine is a poison. Prussic acid is the only poison that is worse. Nicotine poisons the blood, dulls the brain, and is the cause of disease. The lungs of the tobacco user are black from poison, his heart action is weak, and the worst thing to contemplate in the whole matter is that these tobacco users transmit nervous diseases, epilepsy, weakened constitutions, depraved appetites and deformities of all kinds to their offspring.

Deterioration of the race is upon us, and unless there is some reform, idiocy, imbecility and extinction will be the legacy of the future generations.

A man that uses tobacco cannot have the nice moral perceptions on any point that he should have. I find him to be dulled and sluggish. The Bible says: "If thine eye be single, thy whole body is full of light. If thine eye be evil, thy whole body is full of darkness." The use of tobacco is a vice, and to the extent of that one vice, it degrades a mail. It opens the gate for other vices, for it is the gratification for one form of lust. It is a filthy habit, and I care not how often the smoker changes his clothes or washes his person, he is filthy. The stench from his breath indicates that his body repudiates such uncleanliness.

The tobacco user can never be the father of a healthy child. Therefore he is dangerous for a woman to have as a husband. If I were a young woman, I would say to the men who use tobacco and who would wish to converse with me: "Use the telephone; come no closer!" I would as soon kiss a spittoon as to kiss such a mouth. When a man begins to smoke he is taking his first lessons in drink. The two habits travel together.

A man never can attain his majority and use tobacco. He never can realize his full capabilities or his possibilities. He can always attain to a better standard without nicotine.

There is one objection that, from a business standpoint, every business man ought to make to tobacco. When he employs a man that uses tobacco he gets only a certain per cent. of his employee's time and of his brain, because the employee must serve his tobacco master part of his time and when he is not smoking his mind is preoccupied because he is thinking of smoking. Consequently, he cannot concentrate his mind upon his business.

I have heard poor, silly, empty-headed women say that it is manly to smoke. If it is manly to smoke, why isn't it womanly to smoke? The tobacco habit is the reverse of manhood and destroys manhood, for manhood means strength of character, not the gratification of lust.

If tobacco is good for men, it is also good for women. I do not suppose that one could find a man so low and degraded as to walk down the street with a woman who had a cigarette or cigar in her mouth. Women should make the same standard for men that men do for women. Many women would smoke in public if men did not denounce it. MEN WOULD QUIT SMOKING IN PUBLIC IF WOMEN DENOUNCED IT AS MUCH.

I have heard some women say, "I like the smell of a good cigar." I never smelled a good one. It is not made. They are like snakes; they are all bad. I never knew of but one good use that tobacco was put to, and that was to kill lice on cows. My father used it for that purpose on his farm. It does kill that kind of germs.

The evil has become so common that whenever you go abroad you are compelled to breathe the contents of somebody else's month. It would be rude of me to take a piece of fruit out of my mouth and throw it into somebody else's mouth, but anyone may throw his poisonous breath and smoke into my mouth and I have no defense. Spitting is forbidden in the cars. Smoking is a great deal worse, but the reason why it is not denounced is that people can get a revenue from men's smoking, while they have to clean up after spitters, and there is no money in that.

I can prevent a man spitting into my mouth, but I cannot avoid his smoke. A man seems to think that he is free to project his stinking breath in my face on the street, in hotels, in sleeping cars, coaches—indeed, in every public place. Now I would as soon smell a skunk. There is some excuse for a skunk; he can't help being one. But men have become so rank in their persons from this poisonous odor that they almost knock me down as they pass me. And when I say, "Man, don't throw that awful stench in my face," he answers, "You get away." I reply, "If I smelled as badly as you do, I would be the one to get away."

Oh, the vile cigarette! What smell can be worse and more poisonous? I feel outraged at being compelled to smell this poison on the street. I have the right to take cigars and cigarettes from men's mouths in self-defense, and they ought not to be allowed to injure themselves. "Liberty is the largest privilege to do that which is right, and the smallest to do that which is wrong." Governments are organized to take care of the governed. I believe it ought to be a crime to manufacture, barter, sell or give away cigars, cigarettes and tobacco in any form.

Oh, for the success of the Prohibition Party that will bring in reforms along these lines—and this is the only party that will do it! Tobacco degenerates body and mind. Physical and mental culture demand its discontinuance.

Dr. Jay W. Seaver, associated physical director of Yale University, says: "Among college students, the gain of growth, in general, is 12 per cent. greater among those who do not use tobacco than those who smoke. It has also proven by tests in the laboratory that the nicotine in a fairly mild cigar will reduce a man's muscular power from 25 to 40 per cent."

Were it not for the tobacco habit, we would need no smoking car. Suppose women had a vice that required them a separate apartment from the men when they travel. Even in the cars where the women travel there are rooms fixed up in luxuriant style while poor mothers with their babies have to sit upright and smell this rank and poisonous odor. But of course women have no redress, or are made to think they have none. Shame to you men, a decent dog will not bite a female, while men the impulse of protecting their females they are lower than a decent beast.

While I was in New York City last week April the 2nd a Mr. Thomas McGuire, treasurer of the Fourteenth Ave., Theatre had his tongue cut out to prevent tobacco cancer from spreading. This was from smoking cigars. General Grants' tongue rotted from the same cause.

This is one of the best poems on the vice I ever read. Author unknown.

> HE SMOKES.
> "In the office, in the parlor;
> On the sidewalk, on the street;
> In the faces of the passers,
> In the eyes of those he meets,
> In the vestibule, the depot,
> At the theatre or ball;
> E'en at funerals and weddings,
> And at christenings and all.
>
> "Signs may threaten, men may warn him;
> Babies cry and women coax;
> But he cares not one iota,
> For he calmly smokes and smokes.
> Oh, he cares not whom he strangles,
> Vexes, puts to flight, provokes;
> And although they squirm and fidget,
> He just smokes and smokes and smokes.
>
> "Not a place is sacred to him;
> Churchyards, where the flowers bloom;

Gardens, drives, in fact the world is
Just one mighty smoking room,
And when once he quits this mundane sphere,
And takes his outward flight,
From the world he made a hades,
Day he's turned to murky night.

"When he reaches his destination,
Finds 'tis not a dream or hoax,
And the Judge deals out his sentence,

Then I'll wager that he smokes;
Oh, he'll care then whom he has vexed,
And their mercy he'll invoke;
But although he squirms and fidgets,
They'll just let him smoke and smoke and smoke."

CHAPTER XXI.

TRIP ON FALL RIVER STEAMBOAT, FROM BOSTON TO NEW YORK—OFFICERS TRIED TO LOCK ME IN MY STATE ROOM—SEQUEL SATISFACTORY, MADE PLEASANT TRIP AND MANY FRIENDS.

In the summer of 1903 I took a Fall River boat from Boston to New York. These boats are said to be the finest in the world. There was quite a commotion among the several hundred passengers when I went aboard, and the door was blocked in the women's cabin to get a look at the Crazy Smasher from Kansas.

Men were smoking pipes, cigars and cigarettes. I said: "Men, get away from the door with your smoke, you make me sick." They paid no attention to me. I went to the clerk and complained of being compelled to submit to the outrage of being subject to the poisonous fumes, in such a manner as to attract the attention of all to the matter. The Clerk told me to be quiet and sit down. I said, "I will, if I have a decent place to stay, why do you not have these men get away from the door?" But they were men, we were only women and children. Oh, the outrage on poor mothers in delicate condition, to be subject to such treatment by selfish, dirty men. I believe every one who smokes in a public place should be fined. If men will smoke or commit nuisance, let it be where others are not injured. I have no right to bring a skunk into any public place. People should be taught that others have the right to object to anything done that is wrong.

While I was still persisting in my request to the men to leave the door, I was shown my state room; to which there were two doors, one leading from the corridor and the other opening out next the water. The captain, accompanied by the First and Second mate appeared at the former, saying. "Madam, you are to keep your room this evening." I replied, while eating a sandwich, "I do not feel like this, and neither will I." Said he, "I will see that you do" at the same time telling the officers to lock the doors. I said: "You can lock the doors to restrain me of my liberty, but having paid my fare for the service of this company, I will tie up this boat, when we reach New York, and you will learn that I can turn a lock as well as yourself." I saw his countenance change. Mr. Furlong, my manager, who was on the boat, and almost shaking with fear, began to make excuse for me, etc, etc, but I said, "Never mind, Mr. Furlong, I can attend to this little captain and myself too." He said no more. The three men walked out of the corridor, shutting the door after them, but did not lock it, in a few moments, they returned and opened both doors for fear I would think they were locked. This was about supper time. When I finished my lunch, and, having put on a clean tie and fixed my hair, I took from my valise a lot of little hatchets and put them in a little leather case I carry by a strap over my shoulder. Thus equipped I entered the ladies cabin, where there were perhaps fifty people sitting. When I went in, they began to look at one another, some smiled, I knew they had heard of the captain trying to prevent my coming out. Taking my seat on a sofa in the middle of the room, I was listening to the lovely string band when some one came up and opened a conversation with me. After a while I was quite surrounded and the cabin soon becoming crowded some one asked to see a little hatchet, so I opened my satchel to show them. One of the officers who had come to the State Room with the captain, had been standing near the stairway, and when he saw the people begin to press to me to get the hatchets, he came up saying, "Madam, you are not allowed to sell these here." I replied, "You sell wine, beer, whiskey, tobacco, cigarettes and anything that will drug these people. Now these are my own little souvenirs, and they will advertise my cause, help me, and be a little keep sake from the hand that raised the hatchet, so I claim the right to sell them, where you have no right to sell bad things." He went up to see the captain, who said, "I am too busy to fool with that woman." So he came down, and called up Mr. Furlong, asking him to compell me to stop selling hatchets, but he told him he could not prevent Mrs. Nation doing anything she had set her head to. We had a nice time. I repeated poetry on the evils of drink and smoking, all were happy, and at ten o'clock, I bade good-night to many friends who regarded me not as the wild vicious woman, but one who meant well.

Next morning when we went ashore in New York, and were identifying our baggage, a small man was passing, Mr. Furlong remarked in an undertone, "Our captain." He had changed his uniform to go ashore, and I had not recognized him. I extended my hand which he took, and I said, "Captain, I know you were told I was a nuisance," "Yes, they said you would raise the devil, but if anyone thinks you are a fool they are very much mistaken." We parted in a very pleasant humor. Thus it is, my life is a constant contention, but there have been many laughable circumstances and none hurt. I can truly say that there is no ill will in my heart toward a creature God has made, but it is a hatred for the enemy of mankind for I have an intense hatred for the enemies of those I intensely love.

CHAPTER XXII.

TRIP TO CANADA, CORDIAL RECEPTION—RETURN TO CHICAGO TO FILL ENGAGEMENT— SECOND VISIT TO CANADA—TRIP TO MARITIME PROVINCES—VISIT CLUB IN CHARLOTTE TOWN—PREJUDICE AGAINST ME OWING TO MALICIOUS REPORTS—SPOKE IN PARLIAMENT IN FREDERICTON—VISIT TO SIDNEY— SCOTT ACT—MY ARREST AND RELEASE—EPISODE IN JAIL.

Having a spare month in May of 1904 I made a trip to Canada, and never was so cordially received in my life, selling all the hatchets I had in three meetings.

I returned to fill a Chicago engagement of six weeks, which was made by my manager, with Mr. Houseman, one of the Editors of the Chicago Inter-Ocean, who owned a theatre with which a museum was connected. Realizing that this would provide an excuse for the papers to lie about me, I wrote my manager if possible, to cancel the engagement. I was, however, persuaded to stay one week, with the result, that it was published all over the country that Carry A. Nation was in a Museum getting $300 a week just to be looked at, when in fact, I spoke in the theatre, not in the museum. I would not object to going into a museum or any place to bring my cause before the people, but resented the idea of being placed on exhibition.

As I had promised to return to Canada, I did so in the month of June, visiting the Maritime Provinces, where I was very much delighted with the people, finding in Prince Edward's Island the most intelligent and moral people, as a body, that I have ever met.

That Island has a Prohibition Law similar to Kansas, but the primier, Peters, told the former premier, Mr. Farguason, that the Club in Charlotte Town, the Capitol, had to be an exception to the prohibitive amendment or he would vote against and ruin it. This condition is similar in our own government-conspiracy and treason. I visited this club, strange that I should get in, God opened the way. It was fitted up like other drinking clubs, where men congregate together to act in a manner and talk of subjects they would be ashamed for their wives to see and hear. The back room was stacked with empties and imported liquors of different brands. I went up into the parlor about nine o'clock in the morning, where I met one of these beer-swelled outlaws, I asked him, "Will you object to answering some questions about this place." His pompous and indignant reply was, "No, I will do nothing of the kind." I said, "I will tell you some things about it. You are a set of traitors, you pose as being the elite, but you are criminals, shame on such villainy." He held his paper up before his face. I had the satisfaction of telling him the truth in plain language, such men are well dressed, gold fobbed, diamond studded rummies that are more hateful than those behind the prison bars, their bodies a reeking mass of corruption.

Prince Edward's Island is a large farm, one hundred miles long, by forty broad. Can only be reached by boat. A very high grade of cheese, milk, butter, oats and turnips are raised there. Instead of weather-boarding the houses they have the sides shingled. They have the nicest, small, fat horses, fine travelers.

On this, my second visit to Canada, the people did not receive me as cordially as before, owing to a report that I had been in a museum in Chicago on exhibition. In order to counteract this prejudice against me, I offered a reward of $50.00 for any one who had ever seen me in a museum or on exhibition, which had the desired effect. There are rum bought papers in Canada as there are in the States.

I was asked to speak in Parliament in Fredericton. There was a great laugh when I said that governments like fish stink worse at the head.

On my visit to Sydney, Cape Breton, I found that, although they have the Scott Act, which makes it a misdemeanor to sell intoxicants there are dives there just like in Kansas, the officers and political wire pullers defending them just in the same way.

I went into a vile den, the Belmont Hotel. There was a crowd gathered around the place. When I went out in front an officer came to me, saying, "You will have to get off the street, you are collecting a crowd." I said, I am not disturbing anything, if you object to the crowd, disperse them, let me alone. He insisted, and so did I. He said nothing to the crowd no one was doing anything, but standing around when he walked up to me and arrested me in the King's name—Two got on either side of me and carried me to jail—When I was there, I found a young boy of about 14 or 15 years of age. I asked, "Why are you here?" He began to cry bitterly, said, he was put in for calling names. "Oh, if I had a father or mother to help me out, but they are dead, and I have no friends." "What is your fine?" I asked, "Only a dollar." "My dear boy, I will do what mother would do, if she were here, kneel down here and let us pray." He did, weeping so bitterly all the time. I asked God to make this a means of saving that dead mother's precious one. I said to him, "Now my boy, mother would say my darling son, don't use bad language. Be good and love God. Now I will pay your fine just as mother would do." So I called the jailer, who seemed to be a kind man, and paid the dollar. The boy with his face glowing with happiness, fairly flew out. In a few minutes the door was opened, a friend went on my bond, and I left to fill my appointment. There were as many as twenty-five men who volunteered to testify to the unfair arrest. The case was tried the next day and I was acquitted, the judge saying that. "All Carry Nation wanted was advertising. Man's inhumanity to woman." I was glad to open the prison door to the boy, and give him advice at a time when he would take it, for he promised me to be a good boy and serve God. I expect God sent me there for that purpose.

CHAPTER XXIII.

COWARDLY ASSAULT BY SALOON KEEPER, G. R. NEIGHBORS OF ELIZABETHTOWN, KY.—APATHY OF OFFICERS, BUT PEOPLE MUCH MOVED BY OUTRAGE, LECTURED AFTERWARDS, THO' VERY FAINT AND WEAK FROM LOSS OF BLOOD.— CIGARETTE SMOKING IN HIGH PLACES DISCUSSED WITH MISS GASTON, PRESIDENT NATIONAL ANTI-CIGARETTE LEAGUE.

A saloon keeper, G. R. Neighbors, of Elizabethtown, Ky., struck me over the head with a chair, July 23, 1904. In going up to the hall to fill an engagement. I passed this man and walking into his saloon, said, why are you in this business, drugging and robbing the people? "Hush! You get out." I replied, "Yes you want a respectable woman to get out, but you will make any woman's boy a disgrace, you ought to be ashamed." I then passed out going to the hall. After the lecture I passed by his place again. He was sitting in a chair in front of the saloon, and I said, "Are you the man that runs this business?" and in a moment with an oath he picked up the chair and with all his strength, sent it down with a crash on my head. I came near falling, caught myself, and he lifted the chair the second time, striking me over the back, the blood began to cover my face, and run down from a cut on my forehead. I cried out, "He has killed me," An officer caught the chair to prevent a third blow.

There were two officers in the crowd. I cried out, "Is there no one to arrest this man?" No one appeared to do it. He went back in his saloon. I to the hotel. Some one sent for a doctor who came and dressed the wound on my forehead, my left arm was badly bruised, also my back. Had it not been for my bonnet, I should have suffered more. This outragous act roused the people. The women and men came to see me indignant, saying this outrage would not be tolerated. The Methodist minister especially was deeply moved. There were two officers who saw this outrage, but there was no arrest.

Next morning, Mrs. Bettie James, came in two miles from the country, and had a warrant sworn out against Neighbors, but the case was laid over to await the action of the "Grand jury," in November, saloon keepers going on his bond.

I intended to go to Mammoth Cave but remained over on account of trial, and spoke again that night. Elizabethtown is one of those bad rum- towns in Kentucky, but there is a fine prohibition sentiment, and great indignation was felt and expressed that a saloon-keeper even so low and cowardly as to strike a woman, should be tolerated. I was in bed most of the day and nearly fainted during the lecture, but I thanked God that I was counted worthy to suffer, that others might not. I felt some mother might receive fewer blows—that while my head was bruised and bleeding to prevent hearts from being crushed and broken, souls were going to drunkards graves, and drunkards Hells, and this outrage would reveal the enormous brutality of this curse, bringing a speedy remedy.

In the Spring of 1904, I was in the office of Miss Lucy Page Gaston, the National President of the Anti-Cigarette League. I saw on the walls of her room Mr. Roosevelt's picture. I said, "My dear Miss Lucy, why do you have that picture in here? Don't you know, he is a cigarette smoker?" She said, she did not know it. I said, "let me tear that up. Did this man who is at the head of affairs in this nation ever say a word against this vice? Although he is sworn to protect from just such. This brave, good woman, whose heart, soul, and body is dedicated to saving the young men of our land did not seem to recognize the fact that Democrats and Republicans (so-called) were the head and front of all the corruption we have. At last, I said, "If you will write to Mr. Roosevelt and get his statement that he does not, nor ever did smoke cigarettes I will give You $50 for your work, she said she would. She wrote to the President, got no response from him, but Mr. Loeb, his secretary wrote that the President, did not nor ever had used tobacco in any form. She sent this to me, of course I was not to be caught with such chaff. I wrote her so, telling her of the time when Mr. McKinley wished to deny the fact, that he rented his property in Canton, Ohio, for saloon purposes, his minister denied this, but the 'Chicago Voice' proved that he did. I suppose Mr. Roosevelt got his minister to write what he dared not. I wrote her that old birds were not easily fooled with chaff, also stating, that if she would get a statement that Mr. Roosevelt was not a beer drinker, I would give her another $50.00. Of course she could not do this, but the Republican Press published all over the country that Miss Gaston got the evidence and I paid the $50.00, but not one word of this was true.

CHAPTER XXIV.

SISTER LUCY WILHOITE'S VISION.—WRITES TO ME FOR
CO-OPERATION IN MAKING RAID ON MAHAN'S
WHOLESALE LIQUOR HOUSE.—HESITATE ON ACCOUNT
PRESSING ENGAGEMENTS AHEAD.—ANSWER THE CALL.—
RAID SET FOR 29TH.—W. C. T. U. CONVENTION IN
SESSION.—FOUR SISTERS AND MYSELF START FROM M. E.
CHURCH.—A CALL FOR THE POLICE BEFORE WE COULD
EFFECT AN ENTRANCE.—TAKEN TO JAIL IN HOODLUM
WAGON.— UNHEALTHY CONDITION OF CELL.—IN JAIL
FROM FRIDAY TO MONDAY.— GOOD OLD PENTECOSTAL
TIME ON SUNDAY—COUNTY JAIL MONDAY—TRIAL
WEDNESDAY—JAIL SENTENCE AND FINES—APPEAL TO
DISTRICT COURT.

In the Fall of 1904, I received a letter from Sister Lucy Wilhoite of Wichita, telling me of a vision, which I will relate here in her own words: "During a severe illness, last July, the Lord appeared unto me and revealed many wonderful things concerning our work in which I have been engaged for seven years. Temperance and Prohibition.

My life was despaired of by my friends and I knew I was very near the borderland, and as I lay on my bed of suffering in the still hour of midnight, God showed me the awful desolation which our thirty eight saloons and five wholesale houses were making in the homes of Wichita and surrounding country, The sight so overwhelmed me, I cried unto the Lord and said, "Oh my God! Have I done all I could during this life of mine to dam up this fearful tide? Then I said, show me Lord, what this means. Immediately a great cloud of human souls came rolling down a steep decline and as my eyes followed them, saw them rolling on and on until they finally fell into a pit from whence fire and smoke were ascending. Then my eyes were turned again up the ascent from whence the souls were coming. When, Lo! I saw the National Capitol, with her Senate and Congressmen. I saw the Legislative Halls, and our Educational Institutions. I saw our churches with her educated ministry, and her secret societies, our public libraries and reading rooms, our National State and Local W. C. T U's, all of them right in the track of this awful tide of human souls, yet they still rolled on and on until they reached the pit. Then I cried again unto the Lord and said, "Oh, Why do you show me these horrible things, when I am on the brink of the grave? And still the picture or vision remained before me, growing more and more vivid every moment until I struggled to my knees, and said, 'O God, if I can do anything to dam up this fearful tide, just heal this body, and let the healing be the seal that I can do something to help, and I shall do it if it costs my life. Then a deep calm and soul rest settled over me and I sank into a deep sleep, when I awoke I realized the pain was gone and also the fever. I lay there, looking up to God and I said, "Now, Lord, show me what you want me to do. Immediately, like a great scroll reaching across the sky, these words appeared, written in letters of gold. "Spill it out!" Then he showed me the very place I was to attack Mahan's Wholesale Liquor House.

"For many weeks I pondered upon this vision and prayed about it most earnestly, that I might not be mistaken and know of a truth that it was God's will. I never found any soul rest until I wrote to Mrs. Nation, and told her the time was ripe for God and that we must attack Mahan's Wholesale Liquor House, that was helping to degrade so many women and debase so many men. This resulted in an attempt to carry out God's purpose on Sept. 30, 1904.

I was true to the "Heavenly Vision," which is only the beginning of the fulfillment, for there are yet many things to be spilled out, not only the liquor, but also the hypocrites in the church, and the false prophets with sin of every kind, and our lives also.

The Wichita Eagle Reporter, uttered a profound truth, whether he intended to or not, when he said, we walked into the Court Room like a poem, a sort of a 'Lead Kindly Light' poem, for we were lead of God, who is the Light of the world. And we intend to follow on until this vision is fully realized."

Yours for God's love for Him and suffering humanity,
MRS. LUCY WILHOITE.

I had dates ahead that I disliked to cancel, because of disappointing the people and entailing a great financial sacrifice. Sister Lydia Muntz, also wrote me to come to Wichita immediately. I knew it meant smashing and imprisonment, possibly, loss of life, for I wrote Sister Wilhoite, "I am coming to do all I can to destroy the works of the devil, and if need be to die." At first, I told her to keep things quiet. Then I thought it best to give all an opportunity to have a part in this great work of saving life here and hereafter, so I wrote a letter to the Topeka Journal making a call for helpers setting Sept. 28 as the day. When I arrived in Topeka I learned that the W. C. T. U would be in convention session on that day in Wichita, and also that there was a carnival going on in the place, and thought it providential to have a crowd. I arrived in Wichita the 28th, the raid was postponed until the 29th. I took hatchets with me and we also supplied ourselves with rocks, meeting at the M. E. church, where the W. C. T. U. Convention was being held. I announced to them what we intended doing and asked them to join us. Sister Lucy Wilhoite, Myra McHenry, Miss Lydia Muntz, and Miss Blanch Boies, started for Mahan's wholesale liquor store. Three men were on the watch for us, we asked to go in to hold gospel services as was our intention before destroying this den of vice, for we wanted God to save their souls, and to give us ability and opportunity to destroy this soul damning business. They refused to let us come near the door. I said, "Women, we will have to use our hatchets," with this I threw a rock through the front, then we were all seized, and a call for the police was made. There was of course, a big crowd. Mrs. Myra McHenry was in the hands of a ruffian who shook her almost to pieces. One raised a piece of gas pipe to strike her, but was prevented from doing so. We were hustled into the hoodlum wagon, and driven through the streets amid the yells, execrations and grimaces of the liquor element. I watched their faces and could see that Satan was roused in them beyond their control, making the most diabolical faces sticking out their tongues! at what? Just five women, who were doing with their might what their hands found to do, Just five living hearts that dared to give their lives to save them. Just gray-haired women, mothers, and grandmothers, who, for love they could not contain, rushed in to save their loved ones, from ruin.

There never was such a sight. Angels wept and devils yelled with diabolical glee. We were taken to Police Headquarters, that is, four of us, the Police had not taken Blanch, who dodged them, and with her axe smashed out two windows, after which she went to Sister Wilhoite's home, and would not have been arrested had she not called to see us next day, and giving her name was immediately arrested and shut in with us. Water was standing in the low places in the cell we occupied, caused by a leakage in the pipes, I don't think this neglect was intentional, but it was none the less dangerous as it was below ground. The beds were shelves in the wall, very hard of course, but we might have had some degree of comfort if it had not been for the dirt and rats which seemed to delight in having some one to run around and over. It was so ordered that there was a bible in the crowd, and as we were not in stocks we had far more to rejoice over than Paul and Silas, holding a continuous praise and prayer service, reading and repeating the word of God. We were kept there from Friday till Monday morning without a charge against us. Sunday morning we squeezed the juice out of some grapes, some kind friends had sent us, and reading for our lesson where Jesus washed the disciples feet and partook of the sacrament, sister McHenry sprang to her feet after partaking of the emblems, said she saw the most beautiful cross on the wall, surrounded by a divine halo, exclaiming, "Now I know what it is to have a vision, I thought it might be imagination." We had quite a time one way and another. Our friends were not permitted to come into the jail or even to the door, so many of them came to the railing on the outside, where some of the officials threw water on them from the upper windows to keep them away. We were taken to the county jail on Monday and had a trial for malicious mischief on Wednesday. We plead our own cases, and never in the history of the world did a nation or people see mothers tried for trying to save their loved ones from the slaughter of a government whose business is to protect women and their children. Tears were in the eyes of many when sister Lucy Wilhoite and sister McHenry told of their boys being led into vice by the officials of Wichita. Poor degraded Wichita with her corrupt officials and that vile "Wichita Eagle," and its Murdocks. But God has a people there and they will be victors in this fight. We were convicted of course, I got thirty days in jail and $150, the rest $150, except sister Muntz who only got $50. We employed Judge Ray to take our cases to the District Court. At the present writing I am out on bail and so far as the jail is concerned, I do not dread it. God will liberate some when I am in bonds. Poor women, Poor Mothers. God who "tempers the wind to the shorn lamb" will come to her relief from a degradation worse than death.

AFTER TRIAL IN THE DISTRICT COURT.

I am out on parole under a jail sentence of four months and a fine of $250.00. This man Wilson who is in the place of a judge knows that it is a lawless outrage, but true to his party or trust he stands by the combine for as long as the Republican Liquor Power controls office motherhood is sacrificed to the greed of this boa constrictor that coils its huge body crushing out the life and soul of man, woman and child.

If Roosevelt had a sincere interest in increasing the population by urging women to bear children he would say something about what makes it a terror to do so.

CHAPTER XXV.

CLOSING REMARKS WITH PLANS FOR THE FUTURE— PROHIBITION CLEARLY DEFINED.

At the close of writing this book, I am in Oklahoma organizing Prohibition Federations. I am now nearly 60 years of age, I find it necessary to reserve my strength as much as possible in order to put to the best use my remaining years of service. I expect to remain in Oklahoma until the constitution is made, the field is ripe for action, we want the constitution to be an ideal one.

The Federation will not have as a member, any one voting in a license party— Anhauser Busch will effect prohibition as soon—We will not waste time and money in fighting Brewers and Distillers but the cause of them. We want to prohibit the tyranny and unlawfulness in preventing woman from a voice in the Government, Compulsory education, no games on Lord's Day, no profanity on the highways.

There are good, loyal prohibitionists in the Anti-Saloon League, but those who control it are generally there for the salary. Being usually Republicans who by their ballot prove themselves to be the strongest advocates for license, they are hindering the true principle of prohibition. Their votes combine to perpetuate the saloon.

The great thing to be accomplished is to elect a Prohibition President, as long as we have one in favor of license it is useless to expect prohibition by the government. The Anti-Saloon League tacitly effects the perpetuation of a license government and in that they have been traitors, we warn the people against them. If anyone is a real prohibitionist they will vote it. The Prohibition Party is really the only party that is loyal to Republican principles, protecting and saving the home from this onslaught. There is not a saloon vote in our party, which can be said of no other. 'Tis the only deliverance from this bloody slaughter. This "covenant with death, and agreement with Hell and refuge of lies." I took on a Republican voter as a man with bloody hands as Benedict Arnold carried in his boot the paper of treachery, so is a licensed vote in the hand of a voter.

We will so far as possible perfect this organization in all the States. I am owner and Editor of the 'Hachet' of Guthrie. A paper on straight lines. The paper is only 25c a year. I ask all my friends to subscribe for this paper, by sending to 'Hatchet', or office of Prohibition Federation, Guthrie, Oklahoma. I will publish full instructions in the Hatchet so that any prohibitionist so desiring, can perfect an organization in any vicinity. This is in perfect harmony with all efforts for annihilation of the manufacture or sale of intoxicating liquors for any purpose. The constitution gives all the largest liberty to do that which is right and none at all or the smallest to do that which is wrong. I feel much relieved to. get into more definite work, rather than going hither and thither completing nothing substantial.

Almighty God and His people help this breaking heart. "Give us Oklahoma or we die," or are willing to die to save this land of the beautiful. Oklahoma will be a leader. We want a strait path to the election of a Prohibition President. If we can make our efforts a success, in the territories, then this will be the greatest impetus all over. We will not hinder any prohibition movement, we only go to the bottom, laying the ax (or hatchet) at the root of the tree, for we can not succeed by prohibiting intoxicants as a beverage alone, which is what the prohibition party up to this time propose to do. ANNIHILATION is the only principle or true definition of prohibition. 'Tis dangerous to let any of it survive. The advantages of being a resident of Oklahoma will be so great, that, like the promised land to the children of Israel, there will be an exodus from the Egyptain bondage. The degraded and vicious will then leave the place where their facility of engaging in all villainy and corruption is gone, Mothers and Fathers often say, "O for a place where I can raise my children where there is no saloons!" Oklahoma will answer the cry. What an outrage is perpetrated by this Rum-soaked government in not allowing us to have statehood! There is a cause and the people will find it out Republicans know, that, when we do get statehood their allies the Trusts will not be allowed to rob us and that we will not be at their mercy and their appointees. I beg the financial aid of all, with plenty of money we can publish literature showing up the horrors of a rum president. Roosevelt's strong hold is his duplicity and schemes. He has signed the bill licensing the curse on the poor Alaskan. This wholesale murder with the awful lie that it is to build schools and roads. Oh, this gigantic murder Nero was not worse.

I went to Medicine Lodge Feb. 15th, to see my friends, and lecture. No one knew I was coming, got there between twelve and one at night, train late. I got in the buss saw no one, was the only passenger, the chimneys were off the lamps from the jolting and there was danger. I tried to fix them. The driver had not made his appearance up to this time. A man rushed in at the door, cursing, took my head in his two hands, threw me out of the door, using profane and indecent language. He was reeking with the smell of liquor. I was surprised and terrified, not knowing any reason for this. The conductor, Mr. Knight, took me in his carriage up to Mrs. Martin's. My friends said the outrage was such that I ought to make complaint, which was done. Sam Griffith, that was my old enemy, was still prosecuting attorney. He refused to prosecute Bill Hall, the buss driver, one of the most disreputable infidel vulgar character in the town, if not the worst, a tool of Jim Gano the one who was republican sheriff when I was smashing in the county, and the manager of the buss line. Bill Hall's lawyer was Poly Tincher, the son-in-law of Southworth, the drug-store jointist here, who at this time had an injunction served against him for selling liquor. There were six jurymen called, mostly of the caliber, that suited this lawless, rum- defending class of Medicine Lodge. They said Bill Hall was right, because I snatched a cigar out of his mouth. I did not even see one. This reminds me of a case where one would bring suit for injury in hell where the devil was the judge, and expect to get a verdict for the defiance. The indignation of the people at this insult has resulted in the election of other officers. Jesus went to Nazareth and they tried to throw him over the brow of the hill, still he had followers from Galilee.

This Republican rum God defying set of Medicine Lodge, were glad to resent my exposure of them in my book and they would inflict any outrage on me or my cause. I was glad to see that this was opening the eyes and mouths of the best element. I can suffer if the people wake up. I am appointed for this. "The world hateth me because I testify of it that the works thereof are evil. Marvel not that the world hates you ye know that it hated me before it hated you."

FINALE.

I again ask that as you read my book you will often pray for me and this great cause of humanity. We are organizing Prohibition Federations and I here give the Constitution and By-Laws of this movement. Annihilation is the only method of dealing with intoxicating drinks and never will this question be settled except by prohibiting it for any purpose. Any one can send to our office in Shawnee and get the necessary literature to organize. This is not to cause any friction in the prohibition party for we are in hearty cooperation with all thorough workers.

CONSTITUTION AND BY-LAWS OF THE PROHIBITION FEDERATION.

PREAMBLE.

Trusting in Almighty God and our Savior Jesus Christ as the source of all true government, and seeing the necessity of an organization that will materialize votes and secure the election of officers who will pledge themselves to the utter annihilation of the liquor traffic, we call on all men, women and children to join this organization, which shall be known as the "Prohibition Federation." We exclude from our organization any person who will not vote for the total annihilation of intoxicating liquors for any purpose. We co-operate with the Prohibition Party, but go a step further, making it a crime to manufacture or sell intoxicating liquors for any purpose.

ARTICLE 1.—OBJECT. The objects of the organization shall be: To oppose in every way the use of intoxicating liquors, making it a crime to manufacture, barter, sell, give away, export or import the same into the United States for any purpose. To take charge of the local elections, seeing that only those who will oppose the liquor traffic in such manner as stated above, shall be nominated. To demand constitutional prohibition and woman suffrage, and to secure the election of a prohibition President. To recommend compulsory education. To see to the strict enforcement of all laws relating to Sabbath observance, making it a misdemeanor to play any public games on the Lord's Day. That the use of blasphemous language in any public place be considered a misdemeanor, punishable by fine and imprisonment. To make it a misdemeanor, punishable by fine and imprisonment, to manufacture, sell, or use cigarettes. To examine the petitions of all saloon keepers as to their compliance with the statutes, seeking to revoke those that have not complied, and in every way seeking to prevent them from obtaining license.

ART. 2.—MEMBERSHIP. Any person may become a member by pledging their loyalty to this constitution.

ART. 3.—OFFICERS. The officers shall consist of a President, four Vice-Presidents, Secretary and Treasurer. They shall be elected at the first regular business meeting in January and serve until their successors are duly elected and qualified.

SEC. 2. The officers shall constitute the Executive Committee, which shall have oversight of all the work of the Federation. The Executive Committee shall have power to fill all vacancies occuring between the annual elections.

ART. 4.—DUTIES OF OFFICERS. The President shall perform the duties usually assigned to his office. He shall be a member ex-officio of all committees.

SEC. 2. The first Vice-President shall be chairman of the Membership Committee. This committee shall devise ways and means of securing members and pledges for the support of the Federation.

Sec. 3. The second Vice-President shall be chairman of the Program Committee. This committee shall arrange for all social and literary meetings.

Sec. 4. The third Vice-President shall be chairman of the Press and Literature Committee. This committee shall see that all meetings are duly announced by the local press and otherwise and report such meetings to the local papers and also to the national organ. It shall secure and distribute literature for the aggressive work of the Federation.

Sec. 5. The fourth Vice-President shall be chairman of the Law Enforcement Committee. This committee shall report to the Federation the non-enforcement of all statutes, suggesting means to secure the enforcement of such statutes. It shall also investigate all lines of law enforcement, instructing the Federation in statutory law.

Sec. 6. The Vice-Presidents, by and with the advice of the President, shall select the persons to assist them in their several departments.

Sec. 7. The Secretary shall keep an accurate record of all business meetings and a complete register of all members. The Secretary shall be the authorized collector for the local Federation and shall be entitled to a commission of ten per cent of all collections.

Sec. 8. The Treasurer shall be chairman of the Finance Committee. This committee shall devise ways and means of securing pledges, and raising money in any other way deemed advisable to further the interests of the Federation. He shall report to the Secretary all pledges that have been paid by members and others, so that the Secretary's book shall show correctly all money received and paid out.

Sec 9. It shall be the duty of the Membership and Finance Committees to take pledges from the members of the Federation, and any others, to further its work. These pledges shall be for the month and payable quarterly. One-third of such money secured shall be retained by the local organization and the remaining two-thirds shall be sent to the Treasurer at the home office in Guthrie, Oklahoma.

ART. 5.—REPORTS OF OFFICERS. At the annual meeting, each of the officers shall present a full written report of the year's work.

ART. 6.—SPECIAL COMMITTEES. At the regular monthly business meeting preceding the annual meeting, the President shall appoint from the membership the following special committees: An Auditing Committee of three. This committee shall examine all accounts and render a report at the annual business meeting, a record of such report to appear upon the Secretary's book. A Nominating Committee of five. This committee shall report at the annual meeting the name of one candidate for each office.

ART. 7.—MEETINGS. Two meetings a month shall be held. One to transact the business of the Federation, the other for literary and social purposes, conducted under the direction of the Program Committee. This second meeting shall consist of oratorical contests, debates, recitations, songs, or any other educational features.

The regular business meeting in January shall be the annual meeting.

ART. 8.—PAYMENT OF BILLS. No money shall be paid except upon an order signed by the President and Secretary.

ART. 9.—OFFICIAL ORGAN. The official organ of the Federation shall be "The Hatchet," published in Guthrie, Okla., (16-page monthly, 25 cents a year.) The Press and-Literature Committee shall solicit subscriptions to the official organ.

ART. 10.—ORDER OF BUSINESS. The following order of business shall be observed at all regular business meetings:
>Devotional exercises.
>Reading of previous minutes.
>Report of Treasurer.
>Report of Vice-Presidents.
>Unfinished business.
>New business.
>Adjournment with prayer.

ART. 11.—AMENDMENTS. This constitution may be amended by a two-thirds vote of the members present at any regular business meeting (ten being a quorum), provided such amendment shall have been proposed in writing at the previous regular business meeting.

CHAPTER XXVI.

CARRY NATION CLOSES CRUSADE IN DAYTON, OHIO—HOLDS THREE LARGELY ATTENDED MEETINGS—SPEAKS TO LARGE AUDIENCE IN ARMORY—HAD ENGAGED NATIONAL THEATRE, BUT INSPECTION OF AUDITORIUM INTERFERED— REVIEW WEEK'S WORK.

Mrs. Carry Nation closed her crusade in this city, Dayton, Ohio, yesterday by holding three remarkable meetings.

In the morning she filled the pulpit of the Home Avenue U. B. church and as usual the church was not large enough to hold the crowd and many had to stand outside.

Mrs. Nation was afterwards entertained at dinner by Rev. H. A. Thompson at his residence, opposite the U. B. seminary.

The National theatre had been engaged for Mrs. Nation's Sunday afternoon meeting, though Broadway M. E. church wanted her, but Mrs. Nation desired to hold that meeting in as large a place as possible, as she anticipated that there would be a large attendance. At the last moment the National theatre management decided they could not permit the house to be used Sunday, as they expected an inspection of the auditorium, so Mrs. Nation's committee secured the big Armory around the corner from the theatre at Sixth and the canal. Mrs. Nation had especially invited the saloonkeepers, sports and unmarried young men and ladies. The meeting was announced for 2:30, but at 1 o'clock the crowds began to assemble. The large choir from McKinley M. E. church, under direction of Rev. C. T. Lewis and his wife, arrived about 1:30 and rendered a fine lot of selections until Mrs. Nation opened the meeting at 2:30. There were only seats for about 3,000, but Captain Hooven estimated the crowd as about 3,800 people. The galleries were crowded and nearly the entire auditorium. All sorts of people were present—business and professional men, saloonkeepers, and preachers, while W. C. T. U. ladies were in evidence by their white ribbons. Representatives from probably every church in Dayton were present and it is safe to say that it was the greatest gathering of its kind ever held in this city. A collection box was at the door and a splendid offering was obtained as everybody contributed—many liberally, among whom was Dr. L. T. Cooper, who handed in a silver dollar, stating: "I don't agree with her in all things, but she means well."

Mrs. Nation made a characteristic talk of over an hour, giving much advice in a kindly way and, as usual, backing up all her arguments with Scripture.

Mrs. Nation held her last meeting at 7 o'clock at Summit Street U. B. church, and a thousand or more people stood around the outside of the church unable to get in.

Mrs. Nation answered many questions put to her at this meeting and from the view of the radical temperance advocates this was probably the strongest talk she made. In every respect the meeting was a success.

Mrs. Nation left for Chicago on the Panhandle at 9:30 last night.

Saturday was also a busy day with Mrs. Nation. In the morning she was a visitor at the U. B. Publishing house, and after dinner she held a meeting at Christ's mission, Soldiers' Home. At 5 o'clock, accompanied by some of her committee, she went to Salem, O., where she was entertained by Rev. Baker, of the U. B. church, and afterwards held the usual crowded meeting in his church, leaving there at 8 o'clock for Brookville, O., where she held another big meeting at the U. B. church.

Mrs. Nation has certainly worked hard here and proven herself in possession of wonderful energy and capacity for work. The following is a list of appointments here in ten days, every one of which she filled and not once could she fully accommodate the crowd: Friday night, October 21, street meeting corner Main and Fourth streets; afterwards to wedding anniversary of Mr. and Mrs. E. C. Bennett, where many congenial spirits were present. This took on the nature of an entertainment to Mrs. Nation. Saturday night, October 22, U. B. church, Miamisburg; Sunday, October 23, the Dunkard church, Dayton; Sunday, October 23, afternoon at Bellbrook, O., mass meeting of the three churches at town hall; Sunday night, October 23, St. Paul's M. E., Dayton; Monday night, October 24, Riverdale U. B.; Tuesday night, First United Presbyterian; Wednesday night, Trinity M. E.; Thursday afternoon, Free Methodist; Thursday night, mass meeting of colored churches at McKinley M. E.; Friday afternoon, 2 o'clock, U. 13. seminary; 4 o'clock, W. C. T. U. meeting, Broadway M: E.; Friday night, Second United Presbyterian, and balance appointments as given above.

The committees of the various churches, the Citizens' League and Prohibition party are much pleased with the work Mrs. Nation did here and predict great results from it.—Dayton Daily.

CHAPTER XXVII.

(Sketch by WILL CARLETON, in his Magazine EVERYWHERE.)

Some years ago, the American public—always longing for "something new," was treated to an absolutely unique sensation. A woman armed with a hatchet had gone into a Kansas liquor saloon and smashed up its appurtenances, in a very thorough and unconventional manner. After this, she went into and through another, and another: and it began to took as if all the bibulous paraphernalia of Kansas were about to be sent into the twilight.

When the smoke had somewhat cleared away, and time elapsed sufficient to garner these circumstances into authentic news, it transpired that the woman who had done this was Mrs. Carry A. Nation—utterly obscure and unknown until that week.

This raid among decanters was a very singular and startling act, for a woman: but, somehow, people found it refreshing. It represented precisely what many had imagined in their minds, what thousands of women had wished they themselves could or dared do, what myraids of confirmed drinkers, even, had wished might be done. News of Mrs. Nation's swift and decided action went all over the country, like a stiff, healthy gale. She was sharply criticised—but there lurked very often a "dry grin" behind the criticism. This smashing was all very direct and unique and Americans are in general fond of directness and uniqueness. It was, technically, illegal; but, even so, it was remarked that the saloons which Mrs. Nation wrecked, were themselves in brazen defiance of the laws of the state of Kansas—unenforced on account of the fear or venality of public officers.

The work of this determined woman went on with a thoroughness and promptness that made it ultra-interesting. She was imprisoned again and again, and became an inmate, at one time and another, of some nineteen different jails. She had trial after trial—in which was developed the fact that her tongue was as sharp as her hatchet; she often addressing even the judge presiding, as "Your Dishonor," while prosecuting attorneys she treated with supreme scorn. Not much mercy was shown her in the county bastiles: she was often bestowed in cells next to insane people—in the hope, she thinks, that she might become really crazy, as well as reputedly so. One sheriff, finding that the fumes of cigarette- smoking made her ill, treated all her follow-inmates to the little white cylinders, and set them at work puffing vigorously. Chivalry and humanity seemed, for the time being, to have faded from men's minds.

In these different immurments, she had time to write her friends and even published a paper, called, "The Smasher's Mail." She told how she came to do this work: it was, she claimed, by the direct command of God. She had promised Him that if He would forgive her many sins, she would work for Him in ways no one else would; and He took her at her word—ordering her to go and smash saloons. This, of course, provokes a smile, among most people, but Mrs. Nation is not the first one that has worked under God's command—whether real or supposed.

At last, so many fines were heaped up against her, which must be paid before she could be liberated, that it seemed to her as if she would never get free; but in this dark hour, a lecture agent appeared, and said he would pay the amount if she would give him some "dates." She laughingly says now, that she did not know what she meant: and actually wondered if he thought she was a fruit dealer. But when he explained what he meant by "dates," a chance to go on the platform and give the people a reason for the hatchet that was in her hand, she saw the gates were opened; and enthusiastically went from jail to the lecture platform.

She became immediately a drawing card—in assembly halls in some churches, and even at county fairs. She often made "big money" by selling miniature hatchets as souvenirs. She worked, tirelessly and industriously, to pay back the lecture agent for the sums he had advanced; and after a time found surplus amounts on hand.

She did not hesitate very long as to the purposes for which they were to be applied. Her personal expenses were very small; she dresses plainly; and believes that God is entitled to her financial gains.

"A home for drunkards' wives," was her first thought, after paying the fine money, and she set about it, and is working for it now.

After her platform work had proceeded for a time, it was decided that she should star in the play, "Ten Nights in a Bar-room." As all know, who have witnessed this simple but powerful drama, every act of it is a prohibition lecture, and Mrs. Nation's part, that of the mother of the murdered boy, was a lecture of itself. In one scene, she was represented as smashing a saloon, most thoroughly; and this business was the most popular of anything in the play—even at theatres that drew most of their patronage from habitues of saloons.

Mrs. Nation's reasons for stepping from the churches to the footlights, is not without its logic, in these days. "People go to the theatres more than they do the churches," she says, "and I want to go where there are plenty of people to hear me, and where they need me."

From the regular theatre she passed, and for the same reasons, to the vaudeville, and did her regular "stunts" along with the singers, the dancers, the harlequin's, acrobats, and the burnt cork humorists. The writer of this has seen her in one of these performances, and considers it entirely unique and unmistakably commendable.

It was in one of the most "free and easy" vaudeville shows in Greater New York, and the audience, composed of men and boys, was a hilarious one, and could have even become a turbulent one, if anything had occured that did not please them. Many were half drunk, or nearly so. "Smoke, if you want to," was lettered on a conspicuous sign, and most of this audience wanted to. In the midst of the exercises, an interlude occurred, in which the audience was invited to a saloon down stairs, where they could proceed still farther in the liquid burning out of their bodies. On the same stage of this same vaudeville theatre, John L. Sullivan, the retired prize fighter, had, only a week before, appeared "in monologue," and had sometimes been so drunk that he could not go through with his part.

In the midst of all this, Carry Nation was announced, and she stepped upon the stage, unattended by any glare of colored lights or fanfare of music. A quiet, motherly looking woman, plainly dressed, with a Bible in her hand, she commanded almost immediately the respect of that large crowd—from the men in the orchestra stalls to the gallery gods. One half intoxicated fellow began to scoff at her, but was almost immediately hushed by the scarcely less drunken ones around him. It was a sight that hushed them all into respectful silence, for a respectable, earnest woman, with the Holy Book in her hand, will have a subduing effect upon almost any company of people.

Mrs. Nation announced her text, and preached a sermon, and delivered a temperance lecture, both within the half-hour. (The latter she calls a "prohibition lecture"—hating the word temperance, as applied to drink.)

She said words, such as had probably not been heard by most of those there, for a great many years. She told them what sots they were making of themselves, and made her points so emphatic that they cheered her —almost in spite of themselves. She commenced her speech as an experiment, so far as that day's audience was concerned; she closed a heroine. She did not remain idle during the time between her appearances on the stage, but cultivated the acquaintances of the actors and actresses, and, it is said, to their good.

That is what Mrs. Nation is doing now, on what is called the eastern vaudeville circuit; and it would be hard to see how one woman could do more good in half an hour, than she does; and that among those that need it most.

Mrs. Nation's whole name is Carrie Amelia Nation, but having noticed from old records that her father wrote the first name "Carry," she now does the same, and considers the name portentous as concerns what she is trying and means to do. She believes, she says, that it is her mission to "carry a nation" from the darkness of drunken bestiality into the light of purity and sobriety; and if she can do this, or in any great measure contribute to it, there are millions of people in the world, that will bid her Good speed.

CHAPTER XXVIII.

A scientific article on the effects of alcohol on the human system. If any doctor should try to deceive you here is the proof of his malicious intent to drug you.

LIQUOR DRINKING IN HEALTH AND DISEASE.

REPORT OF THE COMMITTEE UPON THE PROGRESS MADE IN MEDICAL SCIENCE IN FAVOR OF TEMPERANCE DURING THE YEAR ENDING JUNE 1, 1902—A. W. GUTRIDGE, CHAIRMAN. READ AT THE THIRTY-FIRST ANNUAL CONVENTION OF THE CATHOLIC TOTAL ABSTINENCE UNION OF THE ARCHDIOCESE OF ST. PAUL, AND ORDERED PUBLISHED BY THE CONVENTION.

In order to understand what progress has been made during the year, it is necessary to note the condition of affairs at the commencement of the period.

Long before this committee began work the leading physicians of every enlightened country, the men to whom the entire profession looks for guidance, had declared against the use of alcohol both in health and in disease.

IS ALCOHOL A DRINK!

One reason why all the greatest physicians believed it harmful was because it had been found that alcohol was not a drink. The most abundant substance found in the human body, is water. About 130 pounds of the weight of a 160-pound person is water, "Quite enough if rightly arranged to drown him." Man has been irreverently described as "about 30 pounds of solids set up in 13 gallons of water." So it is quite natural for us to hunger for water; "death by thirst is more rapid and distressing than by starvation." "It is through the medium of the water contained in the animal body that all its vital functions are carried on." Dr. W. B. Richardson of England has pointed out more than fifty characteristics of the action of a natural drink upon the system. The action of alcohol is the opposite of these in every particular, and therefore it is not a real or natural drink. Of course the water which is found in mixture in all alcoholic liquors serves to quench thirst, even though it is often foul water.

IS IT A FOOD!

We also found, upon taking up the work imposed upon us, that alcohol had been demonstrated not to be a food. Many classifications of foods have been made, but about the best is that which divides them broadly into two classes:

to use homely language, flesh formers and body warmers; those which build up or repair the bodily waste, and those which sustain the animal warmth. The slow fire within us being necessary to life we hunger for that only which will replace the substance destroyed by the burning. "To the child of nature all hurtful things are repulsive, all beautiful things attractive," As to flesh formers, it had been noted that all foods useful in repairing bodily waste contain the element nitrogen. Alcohol contains no nitrogen, and so could not be classed among body builders. The chief body warmer is sugar. Alcohol being a product of sugar, people were all misled for years into thinking that it does in some kind and degree feed the system. The mistake was easy, since after taking alcohol there is a temporary increase in vivacity of mind and manner and in surface temperature, and a lessened requirement for regular foods. These opinions had been tested in the light of truth and proved erroneous. Axel Gustafson, in his Foundation of Death, considers this subject at length. As early as 1840 French physicians discovered that alcohol actually reduced the temperature of the body. Prominent German and English medical men soon confirmed the statement, and in 1850, Dr. N. S. Davis of Chicago, the founder of the American Medical Association, in speaking of a number of observations during the active period of digestion after ordinary food, whether nitrogenous or carbonaceous, the temperature of the body is always increased, but after taking alcohol, in either the form of the fermented or the distilled drinks, it begins to fall within half an hour and continues to decrease for from two to three hours. The extent and duration of the reduction was in direct proportion to the amount of alcohol taken." The most prominent physicians in Austria, Italy, Switzerland, Scandinavia and Russia reached similar conclusions shortly after this. In explorations in the Arctic regions where the cold is intense, no alcoholic drinks are permitted. Dr. Nansen, the great Norwegian, attributes the fatalities of the Greely expedition to the use of liquor, and this is the only expedition of recent years which permitted the use of alcoholic drinks. As a matter of fact it was long ago proved that "Alcohol does not warm nor cool a person, but only destroys the sensation and decreases the vitality." Superficial observers, however, have upheld the use of alcohol as a food, saying, "See how fleshy it makes people." Well, healthy fat is not always an advantage, but beer drinkers' fat is not the genuine article. Healthy fat represents a stock of body warming food laid up for a time of need and is formed only in health. The "fat" usually exhibited by beer drinkers is not a fat at all; oil is not its chief factor. It consists of particles of partly digested flesh forming food which the system required, but which it was unable to assimilate owing to the presence in the body of the alcohol which the beer contained. This sort of fat instead of indicating health points to disease. This general teaching as to the worthlessness of alcohol as a food had been set forth by the leaders in medical profession, and accepted largely by the rank and file of practitioners for about twenty-five years. An occasional cry came from the other side, however, and late in 1899 Dr. W. O. Atwater, professor in Wesleyan University, announced that he had, by an extended series of experiments, proved the truth of the claims of those experimentors who believed alcohol to have value as a food. Dr. Atwater's reports were widely published by the whiskey press, and a state of some unrest amongst thinking physicians followed, which had not been wholly quieted when this committee began work.

IS IT A MEDICINE?

At the time we began work, however, it had been demonstrated that alcohol is not a medicine. Many years ago Dr. Nottinghham, a great English physician, said: "Alcohol is neither food nor physic." Dr. Nicols, editor Boston Journal of Chemistry, long ago wrote, "The banishment of alcohol would not deprive us of a single one of the indispensable agents which modern civilization demands. In no instance of disease in any form, is it a medicine which might not be dispensed with." Dr. Bunge, professor of physical chemistry in the University of Basle, Switzerland, said: "In general let it be understood that all the workings of alcohol in the system which usually are considered as excitement or stimulation are only indications of paralysis. It is a deep-rooted error sense of fatigue is the safety value of the human organism. Whoever dulls this sense in order to work harder or longer may be likened to an engineer who sits down on his safety valve in order to make better speed with his engine." Dr. F. H. Hammond of the U. S. army said: "Alcohol strengthens no one. It only deadens the feeling of fatigue." Dr. Sims Woodhead, professor in Cambridge University, England, had given the following list of conditions in which alcohol should not be used: In those (1) who have any family history of drunkenness, insanity or nervous disease. (2) Who have used alcohol to excess in childhood or youth. (3) Who are nervous, irritable or badly nourished. (4) Who suffer from injuries to the head, gross disease of the brain and sunstroke. (5) Who suffer from great bodily weakness, particularly during convalescence from exhausting disease. (6) Who are engaged in exciting or exhausting employment, in bad air and surroundings, in work shops and mines. (7) Who are solitary or lonely or require amusement. (8) Who have little self-control either hereditary or acquired. (9) Who suffer from weakness, the result of senile degeneration. (10) Who suffer from organic or functional diseases of the stomach, liver, kidney or heart. (11) Who are young.

Much has been said concerning the stimulating effect of alcohol upon the heart, and this had been treated at length. There is an increased action of about four thousand beats in twenty-four hours for every ounce of alcohol used. This fact still misleads some physicians into prescribing it to strengthen the weak heart, but the increase is not due to new force. The heart action normally is the result of arterial pressure and nervous action, two forces mutually balancing each other. The nervous action is diminished by the introduction of the alcohol; this destroys the balance and deranges the arterial pressure. Dr. James Edmunds, a great English physician, years ago said: "When we see a man breathing with great vigor, does it occur to us that he must be in good health? Is it an indication that he gets more air? We all know better. It simply shows that he has asthma or some such disease, and that his breathing is strained and imperfect. He is making use of less air than the person who breathes quietly. This is the case with the blood, work, so it plunges and struggles in the effort. And the cause of both cases is the same. There is more carbonic acid in the blood than either the heart or the lungs can handle. If for example I were suffering from general debility and milk were the food best suited to my needs, and if I should discover a tramp in my apartments drinking of my already too limited supply, would it be reasonable to assert that the exhibition of strength which I made in forcing him to desist is an indication that the entrance of the vagrant bettered my enfeebled condition? The greater activity of the heart is not due to the added strength resulting from recruits of friends but to a desperate struggle to beat back a reinforced enemy."

That alcohol does not allay pain had been established when this committee was organized. The only proper method of allaying pain is to remedy the disorder which produced it. It is no remedy to deaden the nerves so that we cannot feel it. This reasoning had been found good in the case of alcohol as a remedy in "colds." Whiskey does not relieve the uneasiness and oppression we experience when ailing from a cold, it only benumbs the nerves so we do not feel the trouble. The cure is not hastened but delayed in this way.

IS IT THE CAUSE OF DISEASE?

Besides the fact that alcohol had, before this committee's existence, been proved to be neither a drink nor a food nor a medicine, it had also been shown to be the cause of disease. Over five thousand of the most prominent physicians in this country had so stated it, and the proportion was equally great in all the enlightened countries of Europe. The most pronounced in this way, perhaps, have been the great leaders in medical science in Austria, Germany and France. Some of the points made against the use of alcohol were that it interferes with digestion by rendering insoluble the active principle of the gastric juice, and especially by preventing the solution of body-building foods. The natural action of various organs of the body is more or less arrested by alcohol, thus reducing the temperature. This from Dr. Edmunds already quoted: "The blood carries certain earthy matters in it in a soluble state, these earthy matters being necessary for the nutrition of the bones and other parts of the body. You all know that when wine is fermented and turned from a weak sweet wine into a strong alcoholic wine, you get what is called a 'crust' formed on the inside of the bottle. What is that crust? That crust consists of saline or earthy matters which were soluble in the saccharine grape juice, but which are insoluble in the alcoholic fluids. We find in drunkards that the blood vessels get into the same state as the wine bottles from the deposit of earthy matter which has no business to be deposited, and forms the 'beeswing' or crust in the blood vessels of the drunkard, in his eye and in all of the tissues of the body." Alcohol had been found to prevent the elimination of waste, thus the body is loaded with worn and decaying tissues, leaving the system an inviting field for all sorts of diseases. Life insurance companies, influenced by business interests wholly, make a distinction between liquor users and non-users. Nelson, a distinguished actuary of England, employed as an expert by life insurance companies, found after investigating over 7,000 cases, none of which were drunkards, that between the ages of 15 and 20 the proportion of deaths in total abstainers to those in moderate drinkers is as 10 to 18; between the ages of 25 and 30, as 10 to 31; between 30 and 40 as 10 is to 40.

With reference to the effect on the offspring of drinking parents, the medical profession had accepted the teaching of the French specialist, Dr. Jaccound, that "of the children of drinkers some of them become imbeciles and idiots; others are feeble in mind, exhibit moral perversion, and sink by degrees into complete degeneration; still others are epileptics, deaf and dumb, scrofulous, etc.," and of the English teacher, Dr. Kerr, that "long continued habitual indulgence in intoxicating drink to an extent far short of intoxication is not only sufficient to originate and hand down a morbid tendency, but is much more likely to do so than even repeated drunken outbreaks with intervals of sobriety between."

Thus the men who have been of the greatest honor to the profession in every land were a unit in opposing the use of alcohol in health or disease and in holding that if people are determined to use it there is less danger in health, as then the system is in better condition to throw off its evil effects.

PROGRESS DURING THE PAST YEAR.

Now as to the progress made during the past year. In June, 1901, the American Medical Association met in St. Paul. The branch of it giving special study to the temperance question held several sessions, about one hundred of the most distinguished physicians in the country attending. Much time was given to considering Dr. Atwater's teaching to the effect that he had proved alcohol to be a food. During the previous year he had published the details of his experiments, and at the convention it was shown that his own experiments upset his conclusions. It had been held that except in rare instances alcohol taken into the system passed away from it as alcohol without change. Dr. Atwater's experiments strengthened somewhat the position of those who held that change is not infrequent, but he concluded that the portion broken up while in the body served as a food. A closer examination of his own experiments showed that the portion oxidized had gone to form other compounds in the system which were possibly more harmful than if it had all passed off unchanged. Dr. Max Kassowitz, professor in the University of Vienna, said, after Dr. Atwater's statement had been published: "For the animal and human organism, alcohol is not both a food and a poison, but a poison only, which like other poisons is an irritant when taken in small doses while in larger ones it produces paralysis." In connection with the fact that alcohol is simply a poison, it may be worth stating, that the original meaning of the word "intoxicated" was "poisoned." After reading Dr. Atwater, the Russian Commission for the study of alcoholism, after two years' work, said: "The claim that alcohol is a food in any proper sense of the term is not sufficiently proved." In the St. Paul convention spoken of, politics obtained a foothold, and some weak resolutions in favor of the army canteen were adopted but not even the champions of the canteen were willing to subscribe to the statement that alcohol is ever a real food.

Just previous to our last convention much noise was made through the daily press concerning a finding of some English scientist to the effect that an acquired tendency cannot be transmitted to offspring. We were told that this would upset the theory that children inherit a craving for intoxicants from intemperate parents, and "the moralists and reformers would have to readjust this logic on these points." In the annual report of the president of the Union a year ago, attention was drawn to the fact that those who indulge in this sort of sophistry have not read what the teachings of temperance workers have been on the subject. Such was not the opinion of the scientists making the report, for it says "Children of drunkards are liable to be mentally and physically weak and tend to become paupers, criminals, epileptics and drunkards." It will be seen from what has been said that this is the position we have held all along. Dr. Davis, the dean of American physicians opposing the use of alcohol, has published during the year a number of articles showing the impossibility of alcohol's being of service as a medicine, and has dwelt especially upon its harmful effects in fevers, diseases in which it is still much prescribed. The two influential temperance societies composed of American physicians have, during the past year, kept up the agitation against alcohol as a medicine, and good is coming from it, as gradually medical journals are giving more and more space to the question. The following international manifesto has been issued by the leading physicians of the world:

INTERNATIONAL MEDICAL MANIFESTO.

"The following statement has been agreed upon by the Council of the British Medical Temperance Association, the American Medical Temperance Association, the Society of Medical Abstainers in Germany, the leading physicians in England and on the continent. The purpose of this is to have a general agreement of opinions of all prominent physicians in civilized countries concerning the dangers from alcohol, and in this way give support to the efforts made to check and prevent the evils from this source.

In view of the terrible evils which have resulted from the consumption of alcohol, evils which in many parts of the world are rapidly increasing, we, members of the medical profession, feel it to be our duty, as being in some sense the guardians of the public health, to speak plainly of the nature of alcohol, and of the injury to the individual and the danger to the community which arise from the prevalent use of intoxicating liquors as beverages.

We think that it ought to be known that:

1. Experiments have demonstrated that even a small quantity of alcoholic liquor, either immediately or after a short time, prevents perfect mental action, and interferes with the functions of the cells and tissues of the body, impairing self-control by producing other markedly injurious effects. Hence alcohol must be regarded as a poison, and ought not to be classed among foods.

2. Observation establishes the fact that a moderate use of alcoholic liquors, continued over a number of years, produces a gradual deterioriation of the tissues of the body, and hastens the changes which old age brings, thus increasing the average liability to disease (especially to infectious disease,) and shortening the duration of life.

3. Total abstainers, other conditions being similar, can perform more work, possess greater powers of endurance, have on the average less sickness, and recover more quickly than non-abstainers, especially from infectious diseases, while altogether escape diseases specially caused by alcohol.

4. All the bodily functions of a man, as of every other animal, are best performed in the absence of alcohol, and any supposed experience to the contrary is founded on delusion, a result of the action of alcohol on the nerve centers.

5. Further, alcohol tends to produce in the offspring of drinkers an unstable nervous system, lowering them mentally, morally and physically. Thus deterioration of the race threatens us, and this is likely to be greatly accelerated by the alarming increase of drinking among women, who have hitherto been little addicted to this vice. Since the mothers of the coming generation are thus involved the importance and danger of this increase cannot be exaggerated.

Seeing, then, that the common use of alcoholic beverages is always and everywhere followed, sooner or later, by moral, physical and social results of a most serious and threatening character, and that it is the cause, direct or indirect, of a very large proportion of the poverty, suffering, vice, crime, lunacy, disease and death, not only in the case of those who take such beverages, but in the case of others who are unavoidably associated with them, we feel warranted, nay, compelled to urge the general adoption of total abstinence from all intoxicating liquors as beverages, as the surest, simplest, and quickest method of removing the evils which necessarily result from their use. Such a course is not only universally safe, but it is also natural.

We believe that such an era of health, happiness and prosperity would be inaugerated thereby that many of the social problems of the present age would be solved."

The year has been marked by more detailed examination of the effects of alcohol upon the human system, with the result that progress towards its eventual overthrow as a medicine has been distinctly made. The greatest reforms are brought about quietly, but truth is mighty and does prevail. It will take time but gradually all will come to feel the suggestive power in the fact that "The table of nature is spread, and bountifully spread, for all its millions upon millions of guests, but wine and strong drink are not on the table."

SCIENTIFIC TESTIMONY ON BEER
(From speech by SENATOR J. H. GALLINGER, M. D., January 9, 1901.)
OPINIONS OF LEADING PHYSICIANS.

The alarming growth of the use of beer among our people, and the spreading delusion among many who consider themselves temperate and sober, that the encouragement of beer drinking is an effective way of promoting the cause of temperance and of aiding to stamp out the demon rum, impelled the Toledo Blade to send a representative to a number of the leading physicians of Toledo to obtain their opinions as to the real damage which indulgence in malt liquors does the victim of that form of intemperance.

Every one is not only a gentleman of the highest personal character, but is a physician whose professional abilities have been severely tested, and received the stamp of the highest indorsement by the public and their professional brethren. More skilful physicians are not to be found anywhere. We have not selected those of known temperance principles. What they say of beer is not colored by any feeling for or against temperance, but is the cold, bare experience of men of science who know whereof they speak.

A BEER DRINKING CITY.

Toledo is essentially a beer drinking city. The German population is very large. Five of the largest breweries in the country are here. Probably more beer is drank, in proportion to the population, than in any other city in the United States. The practice of these physicians is, therefore, largely among beer drinkers, and they have had abundant opportunities to know exactly its bearings on health and disease.

Every one bears testimony that no man can drink beer safely, that it is an injury to any one who uses it in any quantity, and that its effect on the general health of the country has been even worse than that of whiskey. The indictment they with one accord present against beer drinking is simply terrible.

The devilfish crushing a man in his long, winding arms, and sucking his blood from his mangled body, is not so frightful an assailant as this deadly but insidious enemy, which fastens itself upon its victim, and daily becomes more and more the wretched man's master, and finally dragging him to his grave at a time when other men are in their prime of mental and bodily vigor.

BEER KILLS QUICKER THAN OTHER LIQUORS.

Dr. S. H. Burgen, a practitioner 35 years, 28 in Toledo, says: "I think beer kills quicker than any other liquor. My attention was first called to its insidious effects, when I began examining for life insurance. I passed as unusually good risks five Germans—young business men—who seemed in the best health, and to have superb constitutions. In a few years I was amazed to see the whole five drop off, one after another, with what ought to have been mild and easily curable diseases. On comparing my experience with that of other physicians I found they were all having similar luck with confirmed beer drinkers, and my practice since has heaped confirmation on confirmation.

"The first organ to be attacked is the kidneys; the liver soon sympathizes, and then comes, most frequently, dropsy or Bright's disease, both certain to end fatally. Any physician, who cares to take the time, will tell you that among the dreadful results of beer drinking are lockjaw and erysipelas, and that the beer drinker seems incapable of recovering from mild disorders and injuries not usually regarded of a grave character. Pneumonia, pleurisy, fevers, etc., seem to have a first mortgage on him, which they foreclose remorselessly at an early opportunity.

BEER WORSE THAN WHISKEY.

"The beer drinker is much worse off than the whiskey drinker, who seems to have more elasticity and reserve power. He will even have delirium tremens; but after the fit is gone you will sometimes find good material to work upon. Good management may bring him around all right. But when a beer drinker gets into trouble it seems almost as if you have to recreate the man before you can do anything for him. I have talked this for years, and have had abundance of living and dead instances around me to support my opinions."

WRONGS WE CAN NEVER UNDO.

(By Delle M. Mason.)

I have come home to you, mother. Father, your wayward son
Has come to himself at last, and knows the harm he has done.
I have bleached your hair out, father, more than the frosts of years;
I have dimmed your kind eyes, mother, by many tears.

Since I left you, father, to work the farm alone,
And bought a stock of liquors with what I called my own,
I've been ashamed to see you; I knew it broke you down,
To think you had brought up a boy to harm his native town.

I've given it all up, mother; I'll never sell it more.
I've smashed the casks and barrels, I've shut and locked the door.
I've signed the temperance pledge—the women stood and sang,
The clergymen gave three hearty cheers, and all the church bells rang.

But one thing seemed to haunt me, as I came home to you;
Of all the wrongs that I have done not one can I undo.
There's old Judge White, just dropping into a drunkard's grave;
I've pushed him down with every drop of brandy that I gave.

And there's young Tom Eliot—was such a trusty lad,
I made him drink the first hot glass of rum he ever had.
Since then, he drinks night after night, and acts a ruffian's part,
He has maimed his little sister, and broke his mother's heart.

And there is Harry Warner, who married Bessie Hyde,
He struck and killed their baby when it was sick, and cried,

And I poured out the poison, that made him strike the blow,
And Bessie raved and cursed me, she is crazy now, you know.

I tried to act indifferent, when I saw the women come,
There was Ryan's wife, whose children shivered and starved at home,
He'd paid me, that same morning, his last ten cents for drink,
And when I saw her poor, pale face, it made me start and shrink.

There was Tom Eliot's mother, wrapped in her widow's veil,
And the wife of Brown, the merchant, my whiskey made him fail;
And my old playmate, Mary, she stood amid the band,
Her white cheek bore a livid mark, made by her husband's hand.

It all just overcome me; I yielded then and there,
And Elder Sharpe, he raised his hand, and offered up a prayer.
I know that he forgave me, I couldn't help but think
Of his own boy, his only son, whom I had taught to drink.

So I have come back, father, to the home that gave me birth,
And I will plow and sow and reap the gifts of mother earth.
Yet, if I prove a good son now, and worthy of you two,
My heart is heavy with the wrongs I never can undo.

SHE'S COMING ON THE FREIGHT.

Or, The joint Keeper's Dilemma.

Say, Billy, git ten two-by-four
   'Nd twenty six-by-eight,
'Nd order from the hardware store
   Ten sheets of boiler plate,
'Nd 'phone the carpenter to come
   Most mighty quick—don't wait,
For there's a story on the streets
   She's coming on the freight.

O, many years I've carried on
   My business in this town;
I've helped elect its officers
   From mayor Dram clear down;
I've let policemen, fer a wink,
   Get jags here every day;
Say, Billy, get a move on, fer
   She's headed right this way.

I don't mind temp'rance meetin's
   When they simply resolute,
Fer after all their efforts bring

But mighty little fruit;
But when crowbars and hatchets
   'Nd hand axes fill the air—
Say, Billy, git that boiler iron
   Across the window there!

It beats the nation—no, I think
   The Nation's beatin' me,
When I can pay a license here
   And still not sell it free;
Fer I must keep my customers
   Outside 'nd make 'em wait,
Because the story's got around
   She's comin' on the freight.

There, Billy, now we've got her—
   Six-eights across the door,
'Nd solid half-inch boiler iron
   Where plate glass showed before;
But, Bill, before that freight arrives
   Ye'd better take a pick
'Nd pry that cellar window loose,
   So we can git out quick. ED. BLAIR.

A. WOMAN.

(Dedicated to Mrs. Carry Nation.)

When Kansas joints are open wide
To ruin men on every side,
What power can stem their lawless tide?
      A woman.

When many mother's hearts have bled
And floods of sorrow's tears are shed,
Who strikes the serpent on the head?
      A woman.

When boys are ruined every day
And older ones are led astray,
Who boldly strikes and wins the fray?
      A. woman.

When drunkenness broods o'er the home,
Forbidding pleasure there to come,
Whose hatchet spills the jointist's rum?
      A woman.

When rum's slain victims fall around,
And vice and poverty abound,
Who cuts this up as to the ground?
　　　A woman.

When those who should enforce the law
Are useless as are men of straw,
What force can make saloons withdraw?
　　　A woman.

When public sentiment runs low,
And no one dares to make them go,
Whose hatchet lays their fixtures low?
　　　A woman.

Who sways this mighty rising tide
That daily grows more deep and wide,
Until no rum shall it outride?
　　　A woman.

Who then can raise her fearless band
And say 'twas "Home Defender's" band
Who drove this monster from the land!
　　　A woman.
　　　—DR. T. J. MERRYMAN.

THAT LITTLE HATCHET.

The world reveres brave Joan of Arc,
Whose faith inspired her fellowman
To crush invading columns dark.
So, modern woman's firmer will
To conquer crime's unholy clan,
Crowns her man's moral leader still.

A century was fading fast,
When o'er its closing decade passed
A matron's figure, chaste, yet bold,
Who held within her girdle's fold
　　　A bran' new hatchet.

The jointists smiled within their bars,
'Mid bottles, mirrors and cigars—
The woman passed behind each screen,
And soon ocurred a "literal" scene—
　　　Rum, ruin, racket!

At first she "moral suasion" tried,
But lawless men mere "talk" deride:—
'Twas then she seized her household ax
And for enforcing law by acts,
Found nought to match it.

The work thus wrought with zeal discreet,
Has saved that town from rum complete;
Proving that woman's moral force
Like man's, is held, as last resource,
By sword or hatchet.

And following up that dauntless raid,
The nation welcomes her crusade;
All o'er the land, pure women charmed,
Are eager forming, each one armed
With glittering hatchets.

Talk of "defenders of the nation!"
Woman's slight arm sends consternation
'Mong its worst foes, on social fields,
Worse than the "Mauser," when she wields
The "smashing" hatchet.

Mahommed sought by arts refined,
To raise his standard o'er mankind;
But found success for aye denied,
Until at length he boldly tried
The battle-hatchet.

When soon his power imperial, shone
O'er countless tribes, in widening zone;
And wine was banished from the board
Of Moslem millions, by the sword
And victor's hatchet.

So may it be with this great nation,
When woman tests her high vocation;
Persuasion proves a futile power
To quell the joints, but quick they cower
At the whirling hatchets.

True chivalry must come again,
And men, more noble, but less vain,
Responding to its modern sense,
Guard woman, while in self-defense
She plies her hatchet.

When honor bright appeals to men
"The weak confounds the mighty," then
Side doors and slot-machines must close
And such games hide, when women pose
      With sharpened hatchets.

'Else are men brutes, and all their pride
And gallant valor, they must hide
In coward shirking. This shameful end
They must accept, or else defend
      The "home-guard" hatchet.

'Tis woman's crucial, fateful hour,
Her fine soul's test, 'gainst man's coarse power.
In war, she can not be man's peer,
But for home's weal, all men sincere
      Bow to her hatchet.

Man's "Vigilance" is oft condoned,
When Vice and Crime has been enthroned.
Shall women then, be more to blame,
When she In Virtue's sacred name
      Raises her hatchet?

'Tis she must grasp the nation's prize—
A pure, proud home, earth's paradise.
The joints must go, but, never till
Woman exerts her potent will
      And holy hatchet.

As men, once slaves, their freedom gained
By force, and power at length attained;
So, cultured brains and force combined,
Shall mark the sphere of womankind
      And surely reach it.

In valor, more Joan d'Arc's are needed,
Woman's high social power's conceded,
But she herself, must blaze the path
To public morals, by her own worth
And "Little Hatchet."
      —C. BUTLER-ANDREWS.

Dr. Howard Russell told in his address at Kokomo, Sunday, March 24, how when Mrs. Nation was on her way from Topeka to Peoria recently, a passenger on the same train came into the car where she was and sang a song of his own composition. He was evidently a farmer with a large stock of mother-wit. He was lame, and limped into the car, and hopped up and down while he sang. A great deal of merry enthusiasm was aroused, and the car, packed full of people, expressed their appreciation by round after round of applause. It is evident that Mrs. Nation is quite popular in that part of the country.

The song is as follows:

Hurrah, Samantha, Mrs. Nation is in town!
So get on your bonnet and your Sunday-meeting gown.
Oh, I am so blamed excited I am hopping up and down,
Hurrah, Samantha, Carrie Nation is in town!

Get you ready, we are going to the city,
    Where the "Home Defenders" are all feeling gay,
And the mothers all exclaiming, "Its a pity
    That Carrie Nation does not come here every day."

I want to hear that mirror-smashing music,
And to look in Mrs. Nation's blessed face,
And to see the saloon men all cavorting
    With that hatchet bringing sadness to their face.

Hurrah, Samantha, Mrs. Nation is in town!
So wear your brightest bonnet and your alapaca gown.
Oh, I am so jubilated I'm a-hopping up and down,
Hurrah! hurrah! Samantha, Mrs. Nation is in town.

OUTCAST.

(Found in manuscript among the personal effects of a prostitute, 22 years of age, who died in the Commercial Hospital, Cincinnati, O.)

Once I was pure as the snow, but I fell,
    Fell like the snowflakes from heaven to hell;
Fell to be trampled as filth on the street
Fell to be scoffed, to be spit on and beat;
    Pleading—cursing—dreading to die,
Selling my soul to whoever would buy,
    Dealing in shame for a morsel of bread,
Hating the living and fearing the dead.
    Merciful God, have I fallen so low?
And yet I was once like the beautiful snow.

Once I was fair as the beautiful snow,
    With an eye like a crystal, a heart like its glow,
Once I was loved for my innocent grace—
    Flattered and sought for the charms of my face!

Fathers,—mothers,—sisters,—all,
God and myself have I lost by my fall;
    The veriest wretch that goes shivering by,
Will make a wide sweep lest I wander too nigh;
For all that in on or above me I know,
There is nothing so pure as the beautiful snow.

How strange it should be that this beautiful snow
    Should fall on a sinner with nowhere to go!
How strange it should be when the night comes again,
    If the snow and the ice struck my desperate brain.
    Fainting,—freezing,—dying alone,
Too wicked for prayer, too weak for a moan,
    To be heard in the streets of the crazy town,
Gone mad in the joy of the snow coming down;
    To be and to die in my terrible woe,
With a bed and shroud of the beautiful snow.

Helpless and foul as the trampled snow
    Sinner, despair not! Christ stoopeth low
To rescue the soul that is lost in sin,
    And raise it to life and enjoyment again.
    Groaning—bleeding—dying for thee
The crucified hung on the cursed tree,
    His accent of mercy fell soft on thine ear,
"Is there mercy for me? Will He heed my weak prayer?"
    O, God! in the stream that for sinners did flow,
Wash me and I shall be whiter than snow.

THE LIPS THAT TOUCH LIQUOR MUST NEVER TOUCH MINE.

You are coming to woo me, but not as of yore,
For I hastened to welcome your ring at the door,
For I trusted that he, who stood waiting for me then,
Was the brightest, the noblest, the truest of men.

Your lips on my own when they printed "Farewell,"
Had never been soiled by the "Beverage of Hell,"
But they come to me now with the bacchanal sign,
And the lips that touch liquor must never touch mine.

I think of that night, in the garden alone,
When whispering you told me your heart was my own,
That your love in the future should faithfully be,
Unshared by another, kept only for me.

Oh sweet to my soul is the memory still,
Of the lips that met mine when they murmured "I will,"
But now to their pleasure no more I incline,
For the lips that touch liquor must never touch mine.

O, John! How it crushed me when first in your face,
The pen of the "Rum Fiend" had written "Disgrace,"
And turned me in silence and tears from that breath,
All poisoned and foul from the chalice of death.

It shattered the hopes I had cherished to last,
It darkened the future and clouded the past,
It shattered my Idol and ruined the shrine,
For the lips that touch liquor must never touch mine.

I loved you, O! dearer than language can tell,
And you saw it, you proved it, you knew it too well;
But the man of my love was far other than he
Who now from the "tap room" came reeling to me.

In manhood and honor, so noble and right,
His heart was so true and his genius so bright,
And his Soul was unstained, unpolluted by wine,
But the lips that touch liquor must never touch mine.

You promised reform; but I trusted in vain;
Your pledge was but made to be broken again,
And the lover so false to his promises now,
Will not as a husband be true to his vow.

The word must be spoken that bids you depart,
Though the effort to speak it would shatter my heart,
Though in silence with blighted affections I pine,
Yet the lips that touch liquor must never touch mine.

If one spark in your bosom of virtue remain,
Go fan it with prayer, till it kindle again,
Resolved, "God helping," in future to be
From wine and its follies unshackled and free.

And when you have conquered this foe of your Soul,
In manhood and honor beyond its control,
This heart will again beat responsive to thine,
And the lips that touch liquor must never touch mine.
                    —Unknown.

WAR AMONG THE POETS.

From the Royal Arch News, the warhorse of the booze hoodlums, the snapdragon of the jungle, the siren of Hades.

"The Lips that Touch Liquor Shall Never Touch Mine," so sings— Miss Cora Vere, who writes jingle for the Anti-Saloon press, and this is the reply that the R. A. News would make:

The lips that touch liquor don't hanker to touch
The lips of a maiden like you—not much!
If a man—not a milksop—should happened to wed
A creature like you, he had better be dead;
For never a moment of peace would he see
Unless he would bow to your every decree,
If he smoked a cigar, or drank beer, you would make
A hell of his home, and perhaps you would break
Into court and denounce him, in search of divorce,
And fools would uphold you, as matter of course.
Perhaps, like the Nation, a hatchet you'd take
And his bottles of beer and cigar-boxes break,
And get your name blazoned in all of the papers,
By your rowdydow talk and unwomanly capers,
No! the lips that touch liquor don't hanker to touch
The lips of a female like you are—not much!

I am not a poet myself but I am fortunate in having a friend that is, so I called on him to meet this antagonist with a nobler steel, and behold the defeat of this champion of a dying cause:

AN AMERICAN COUNTESS, OR LADY VERE.
"The lips that touch liquor, shall never touch mine;"
The meaning is clear, the sense is divine,
Bespeaks a clear head, an unsullied heart—
A fortune from which no sane man would part.
O, God! give us more of such women, we pray,
Then slop-pots of whisky we'd urge to the fray.
The hatchets of "Carrie," and Cora Vere,
Would knock out the spigots and bungs of whisky.

An army like those would drive them pell-mell;
For safety they'd Hazen, and think they did well
To escape from the jury of women turned loose
Who have drank to its dregs the damnation of booze.

The idea that women would "hanker" to touch,
The lips of a demijohn; I guess not—"not much;"

A forty-rod pole should line up between,
No nearer than that a fair lady be seen.

So now, "Indiana, of Royal Arch News,"
You've taken great pains to give us your views;
I take up the gauntlet, and venture reply;
I stop not to argue, but simply defy.

You say in one case one had better be dead
Than with a good woman in wedlock be wed:
But somewhere I've read your kind do not die;
But passing from earth, 'are hung up to dry."

Besotted with whiskey,—unfitting to tell,
Even Satan himself avoiding the "smell;"
Before then we part, I would bid you adieu,
Reform while you may—begin life anew.

If you have a surplus—like Lady Vere,
Please pass them around, turn them over to me;
"A la Hobson"—I'd venture to sample the store,
And look o'er the field—yes! and "hanker" for more.
Sparta, Mo. D. E. GRAYSTON.

"GOD BLESS OUR CARRIE NATION."

May she live to see the day,
When the liquor traffic will be no more,
When the traffic of the devil
Will all be swept away
And God's peace remain supreme from shore to shore.

God bless the hatchet wielder,
May it never cease to strike,
Till it drives the cursed intemperance from our land
Let us stand for God and duty,
Till we gain the Eden of beauty
And be what God designed for us,
A happy union band.

God bless our Carrie Nation,
Give her courage, strength, and might,
To go forth in former battlements arrayed.
Till this cursed intemperance,
Will be driven from our shore,
From every village, hamlet and the glade.

O, God raise up a million,
Of our Carrie Nation minds,
That they may fight for freedom, from the thrall.
Let's join our hands with Carrie
And do not let us tarry,
Oh, let us toil for Jesus one and all.

AMERICA'S HISTORIC HATCHET.

Ere Yankee Doodle came to town,
    And routed king and tory,
Three words sublime were writ by time
    To live in song and story;
"George Washington"—immortal name
    There's few or none can match it;
His father's favorite cherry tree,
    And "George's little hatchet."

In Boston's harbor next we trace
    The little hatchet's story;
In smashing up the Crown's tea-chests,
    It won a crown of glory.
And every time Wrong shows his head,
    That weapon "bald doth snatch it,
For patriot hands are ever found
    To wield the "Yankee hatchet."

A century and more has passed,
    With blooms and blizzards blowing
O'er Kansas' plains—where corn and grains,
    'Round happy homes are growing;
Where statutes pure close each "joint" door,
    Forbidding to unlatch it,
There, in the fight, defending Right,
    We find our "loyal hatchet."

The boy who 'could not tell a lie,"
    The flag of freedom planted,
He shelled "Corn"—wallis to the "cob"
    On Yorktown's field undaunted.
Since then, our tea is duty free
    No Briton dare attach it;
While the new woman in the case,
    Now poses with the hatchet.

She dares to fight a gorgon fight!
  A cruel monster hell-born,
Whose hungry maw, ignoring law,
  Mocks misery's tears to scorn.
She may not slay the beast, but aye
  Her blows will badly scratch it;
All praise is due the woman true,
  Who wields the "home-guard" hatchet.

When time shall build the marble guild,
  That marks man's reformation,
Its arch of fame shall bear the name
  Of dauntless Carrie Nation.
Her righteous scorn of rum and wrong—
  May all creation catch it,
And join the "Woman's World Crusade,"
  Armed with "our nation's" hatchet.

—Minna Irving, in Leslie's Weekly. Revised and
second stanza added by C. Butler Andrews.

THE HATCHET CRUSADE.

(Dedicated to Mrs. Carry Nation.)

Oh, woman, armed with one little hatchet.
  Fighting for justice and right,
And with your brave mother courage
  Knowing your cause was right,

You've done more to hasten God's kingdom,
  And to crush satan's power o'er men,
Than countless numbers of creation's lords,
  With the power of the ballot thrown in.

You've awakened the mothers to action
  Whose powers have long dormant been,
While the minions of satan have strained every nerve
  To ruin our boys and our men.

Rouse, mothers, too long we've been sleeping,
  Shall one of us let it be said
That we calmly stood by while those who are dear
  Were down to destruction led.

American mothers, hear me,
  If you think God will not send the warning

In hieroglyphics upon the wall?
 God is not mocked, He is just the same,

 And has given the power to you.
If you're weighed and found wanting our nation will fall
 Because you did not your duty do.
Then let us unfurl our broad banners,
 Fling their folds to the breezes high,
Let this still be our motto,
 "We'll trust in God, and keep our powder dry."
    —CARRIE CHEW SNEDDON.